Create Your School
Library Writing Center

Praise for *Create Your School Library Writing Center*

"Virginia Woolf famously said that all writers need a 'room of one's own.' But young writers need more than that. They need a safe, collaborative space where they can develop ideas and get feedback and guidance. Timothy Horan's book provides a blueprint—and inspiring success stories—on how educators can turn the library into just such an encouraging, yet rigorous, environment. Writing, as a solitary experience, can be scary. Tim Horan shows you how to transform it into an engaging, enjoyable, and satisfying collaborative experience."
—Patricia McCormick, author of *Sold, Cut, I am Malala: How One Girl Stood Up for Education and Changed the World*, and other novels

"Dr. Horan has used his unique expertise to create a High School Library Writing Center that supports students in understanding the art of written expression by leveraging the power of peer tutors. In economically challenging times, library writing centers support students in developing their ability to write for a variety of audiences, and do so in the hub of an exemplary school . . . the library!"
—Patricia Sullivan-Kriss, Superintendent of the West Hempstead Union Free School District, and President of the New York State Council of School Superintendents

"I have visited schools all over the world, and I can tell you from firsthand experience that most kids need guidance and inspiration to learn how to write. The School Library Writing Center created by Dr. Timothy Horan gives them just that, with their peers acting as aspirational guides. A truly unique resource in today's educational environment. However, this book is not just for school librarians. It's for teachers of writing everywhere, and for anyone who wants to master the gentle art of writing."
—Denis Belliveau, author of the Emmy-nominated documentary film and book *In the Footsteps of Marco Polo*

"School librarians: Take note. This is a helpful and inspiring guide."
—Susan Isaacs, author of numerous bestselling novels.

CREATE YOUR SCHOOL LIBRARY WRITING CENTER

Grades 7–12

Timothy Horan

 LIBRARIES
UNLIMITED™

An Imprint of ABC-CLIO, LLC
Santa Barbara, California • Denver, Colorado

Library of Congress Cataloging-in-Publication Data

Names: Horan, Timothy, author.
Title: Create your school library writing center : grades 7-12 / Timothy Horan.
Description: Santa Barbara, CA : Libraries Unlimited, [2016] | Includes
    bibliographical references and index.
Identifiers: LCCN 2016013113 (print) | LCCN 2016032853 (ebook) |
    ISBN 9781440835780 (paperback) | ISBN 9781440835797 (eBook)
Subjects: LCSH: School libraries. | Writing centers. | School librarian
    participation in curriculum planning. | Report writing—Study and teaching
    (Secondary) | Report writing—Study and teaching (Middle school) | English
    language—Composition and exercises—Study and teaching (Middle school) |
    English language—Composition and exercises—Study and teaching (Secondary)
Classification: LCC Z675.S3 H667 2016 (print) | LCC Z675.S3 (ebook) |
    DDC 027.8—dc23
LC record available at https://lccn.loc.gov/2016013113

ISBN: 978-1-4408-3578-0
EISBN: 978-1-4408-3579-7

20 19 18 17 16   1 2 3 4 5

This book is also available as an eBook.

Libraries Unlimited
An Imprint of ABC-CLIO, LLC

ABC-CLIO, LLC
130 Cremona Drive, P.O. Box 1911
Santa Barbara, California 93116-1911
www.abc-clio.com

This book is printed on acid-free paper ∞

Manufactured in the United States of America

To my parents, who read me bedtime stories.
And to Michelle, who still believes in fairy tales.

CONTENTS

ACKNOWLEDGMENTS

So many people have been good to me over the course of my life, and I want to thank them all for contributing (in some way) to the creation of this book. Immense gratitude to the entire crew at St. John's University (Queens, NY): the fantastic English Department there, for teaching me about literature and writing; Dr. Patrick Maguire (now at LIU Post), for recommending me "highly"; Dr. Angela Belli, for hiring me as a graduate assistant; Dr. Anne Paolucci (in memoriam), for inviting me into the doctoral program; Dr. Derek Owens, for choosing me first for the new writing center; Department Chair Dr. Stephen Sicari, for helping me every time I asked; Dr. Leonora Brodwin (in memoriam), for giving me the gift of Shakespeare.

I wish to thank Long Island University (CW Post campus): the terrific Education Department, for teaching me about teaching; Dr. Roberta Levitt for being so generous and supportive; the wonderful Palmer School of Library and Information Science, for teaching me about libraries; Dr. Bea Baaden, for being so kind and helpful. I also want to thank Mr. Kenneth Graham, for giving me my first school library job; and deep appreciation to all my writing center tutors, past, present, and future: I couldn't do this without you! Enormous thanks to Dr. Deborah Levitov (now at *Teacher Librarian*) for publishing my series of articles on school library writing centers (in *School Library Monthly*); and profound gratitude to Mrs. Sharon Coatney (of Libraries Unlimited), for helping me turn those articles into this book. A special thanks to noted author Patricia McCormick, who told me that, one day, I too would be an author.

An enormous thanks to my parents, who bought me books, every time I asked for them; to beloved friends Tycho and Oscar (now departed), for their love and loyalty; and profound gratitude to my beloved Michelle, who—once upon a time—looked at an acorn, and saw an oak tree. I love you all. If I missed anyone, please forgive me; the omission was unintentional.

PLEASE DON'T SKIP THIS INTRODUCTION! THERE'S GREAT INFORMATION HERE, AND YOU'LL LIKE IT

I'm delighted you have decided to start your own school library writing center! You'll find the process a wonderful complement to your day-to-day duties, and, when you retire, you will look back with great fondness on your time as creator and director of a school library writing center. You'll be rightfully proud, you'll feel a great sense of accomplishment, and you'll know for certain that you helped lots of students and, in a tangible way, changed and improved the world. Count on it.

Creating and running your writing center will be a grand adventure, no question about it. It will be challenging, but also lots of fun. As you go through the process of creating and running your writing center, I encourage you to *believe* in it, and believe in yourself. Believe that your writing center is greatly needed in the world and that *you* are the right one to run it, because you *are* (that will become clearer as you read this book). Realize also that you (and the tutors you train) are helping students immeasurably by giving them individualized help that they can get nowhere else. There is nothing else, anywhere in the world, quite like the school library writing center model that I developed.

When I tutor a student, I never engage in abstract concepts or ivory tower rhetoric; I explain things clearly, directly, and simply. Recently, after a tutorial, I had a student say to me, "I never had someone teach me so much before." It's a compliment that I treasure, and, as you develop your writing center, you'll hear such compliments also. They're great for your soul and wonderful for your motivation. And speaking of motivation, I hope you're highly motivated to create a writing center, and to be its director. Speaking for myself, I find that I'm most motivated when I'm really excited about something, and I love how that feels. Don't you? I'm excited about this book, and I'm excited about my writing center and the students I'm helping. And I'm excited about life in general. I hope you are too.

Quick story. A couple of years ago, I had just finished my third master's degree (this one was in education), and I had gained a few pounds from all the studying.

But I was blissfully free and had the summer off (except for working part-time at my public library). I felt great, and it was time to start exercising again and drop a few pounds. The hardest part was starting. I decided to base my program on the symbiotic siblings diet and exercise, and I immediately joined a local gym, started eating better, began walking in my neighborhood, and read up a bit on fitness and nutrition. The lifestyle change was a little difficult at first (aren't they always?), and it was hard plodding along before seeing results. But I stuck with it, and, after a few quick weeks, wonderful things began to happen. And I also decided to do something crazy. I've always been drawn to things that are challenging and interesting, and I saw that my gym was sponsoring a "mud run" in my area, and it was taking place in exactly six weeks. Bingo! I signed up immediately. I was so excited, I can't tell you.

Do you know what a mud run is? It's a cross-country run with obstacles along the way. Rope climbing, vaulting over wooden beams, crawling through mud pits, and being submerged in icy water. I couldn't wait. I knew it would be challenging, interesting, and lots of fun, and I jumped on it. I now had a *tangible goal*, and this is very important for intrinsic motivation. And in preparing for the mud run, I set other related goals. I decided that, before the day of the mud run, I would drop 20 pounds, and run 3 miles without stopping. I worked toward this *every single day*, and I achieved both goals, and actually lost 28 pounds in six weeks. Was it difficult? Well, yes and no. I was so excited about everything that the entire process was joyful and fun, so it seemed challenging, but not really difficult. It was a fantastic experience, and one of my best summers ever. I did two more mud runs that summer and ended up losing 40 pounds in two months. (But what I did was extreme, so please don't follow my example. Remember, I'm a librarian, not a personal trainer.) When I went back to school in the fall, my coworkers didn't recognize me. It was lots of fun and really gratifying to see all my hard work pay off.

Now, think about my experience there, and notice how the motivation was related to the task. Maybe you can draw some lessons from it as you develop your writing center and increase your motivation and sense of enthusiasm and being excited about things. I suggest setting clear and concrete "interim" goals for yourself. Work toward them consciously and continuously. Whenever I have a large and daunting project in front of me, I tend to get overwhelmed easily. I envision the product not in steps, but in its entirety, and, in that gigantic state, the task looks impossible. And when this happens, I tend to procrastinate. I'm a master at putting things off; just ask anyone I know. So how do I get things done? I sit down with a calendar, break the project into components, and then give each component a due date. And then I meet the due date *no matter what*. This works very well for me. You may have another way of doing things, but this is the only way that I accomplish things, and this incremental approach keeps me from being overwhelmed and shutting down.

As you develop your writing center, I encourage you to do something similar. Try not to focus obsessively on the finished product, and take things one step at a time. When something is valuable and complex, it's not just *worth* waiting for it, it's usually *necessary* to wait for it. For example, if someone earned a black belt in judo in a single year, I would be very suspect about that person's skills and how much he or she learned. Complex projects, culture changes, and education (which produces actual changes in the brain) all take time and can't be rushed if those changes are to be long-lasting ones. Keep this in mind as you create your writing center.

My advice to you is to give it a *minimum* of one year to be "set up" and functioning—longer, if necessary. And then comes the process of your writing center becoming "established" in the fabric and culture of your learning community to the extent that everyone knows about it and understands what it does and how it helps students. Give that process several years, and allow it to happen slowly and deeply, like a tree producing roots as it prepares to stand for centuries.

I encourage you to take things one step at a time, to do that step correctly and thoroughly, and then to move on to the next one. And this is how I structured this book, chapter by chapter. I encourage you to read the chapters in order and to complete the actions of each chapter before moving on to the next one. But remember, your writing center is a work in progress. There is no time limit; every case will be different, and nothing about your writing center will be perfect. Great. So be it. Go easy on yourself and your tutors, and be forgiving of mistakes—especially the ones that *you* make. As one of my favorite graduate professors once said, "If you make a mistake, *get over yourself*!" This is great advice, and over the years, I have followed it more than once. Stick with your writing center no matter what, believe in it, and be proud of it. Celebrate small victories along the way, and, every time you complete a step, be proud of what you have accomplished. And you might do well to remember something they used to tell us in the Marines: *if you're not having fun, you're doing something wrong.*

As you proceed with the creation of your writing center, I want you to keep in mind a concept that may seem strange and abstract at first; nevertheless, here it is: creating your writing center—or creating anything else, for that matter—is a bit like writing a paper. You don't know exactly how a paper (or a writing center) will turn out until it's finished. When I tutor writing, I always illustrate this concept to my students with the metaphor of planting tomatoes. If you plant tomatoes, you have a pretty good idea what the plant will look like when it's grown. However, no one in the world—*no one*—can say *exactly* what it will look like. Plant them, water them, watch them, and let them grow. When they're red and ripe and beautiful, you can stand back and look at them and say "So that's how they turned out!" And that's when you pick your tomatoes; or hand in your paper; or truly begin to understand your writing center. (As usual, Shakespeare was right: *ripeness is all.*)

As you direct your writing center, keep in mind that you will be its leader. However, also be cognizant that it will take on its own distinct and autonomous personality. So you should guide it, but you also need to let it breathe and grow and find itself; that's healthy for any organism. It's a delicate balance for sure and will require a bit of wisdom and perceptive leadership on your part. Years ago, I was heavily involved with lifting weights, and I belonged to an independently owned gym. I was chatting with the owner one day (he was an amateur bodybuilder and a competitive karate fighter) about his gym, and he told me this: "Tim, when I started this thing, I had no idea how it would turn out. Sometimes a gym is a casual place for people to work out a little. Sometimes it's like more of a social scene. Know what I'm sayin'? But this place is hardcore bodybuilding, which is pretty cool. But I had no idea it would turn out this way." Do you see? This fellow (slightly rough around the edges) understood well the nebulous nature of new ventures. When you dump a bucket of water, what will the spill pattern look like? The only way to know is to dump the bucket and then see. Same with your writing center.

The experience of writing or creating (and maintaining) your own writing center is (or should be) a deeply human one, and, in this book, I want to embrace and enhance this humanity with all of its fun and flaws. In this book, I'll be returning to this concept of "humanity" over and over. What else do we have? We're all human, so let's not pretend otherwise. A student in my library (who is also a wonderful human being) recently asked me if I could "teach him to write." Of course, I gave him an enthusiastic *yes! I would love to.* We chatted awhile about writing, and he asked me an interesting question: "Dr. Horan, if you could describe your writing in one word, what would you say?" I thought a moment and said "human." I think it was a good answer, and an accurate one. I'm a human being writing for other human beings, and I don't want to pretend otherwise. How can we escape our own humanity? We can't, and we should all be constantly falling in love with it, and with life. The act of original writing is not (or should not be) grim; it's an exhilarating mix of the maddening and the joyous, it's full of challenge and discovery and unwritten possibility, and it is, above all, a deeply *human* act. What could be more human than expressing to another (or to ourselves) "*This is how I see the world!*"?

Shakespeare knew this and imbued his writing with deep humanity, and this is one of his eternal charms, and it's one of the reasons why we keep going back to him after four hundred years. Writing is life, and life is writing. And both things are (or should be) deeply human. Too often, high-level scholarship sounds as if it were written by (and for) beings unlike us. I've read lots of it. Why does it have to be so dry and clinical? Learning should be fun and filled with humanity. I've always been in love with books, and I approach them with great reverence, but I also try to remember there's a real human being standing behind each one. And this is a comforting thought. In a sense, a book *is* a human being, and, make no mistake, this book is me, in a genuine, unadulterated format.

Now, I want to talk about this book you're reading. I want to talk about its construction, its philosophy, its composition. I'm giving you a peek behind the curtains, a backstage tour, and a revealing of all secrets. I will hold nothing back. And I'm doing this for several reasons. First, I want to shed light on the writing process (at least as it concerns this book), because the more you learn about writing, the better. But also I want you to understand this book very deeply and to use it well. I'm very excited about this book. I've been waiting my whole life to write it and to share it with you.

First, my intention is to write a book that is very different and very original. Just as the school library writing center is a revolutionary concept, I wanted this book to be new, fresh, bold, and different. I wanted it to come from my mind, from my memories and experience and learning, so I didn't want to rely too heavily on things that others said. I wanted this book to be vastly different from the things that are being published today, especially in the fields of academia and education. But I wanted it to be different, not just in subject matter, but in construction and authorial technique. And I really want you to understand this. This book is "different" on purpose. When it comes to writing, I know what I'm doing. I deeply understand the art of writing, as well as anybody in the world. And there are no accidents in this book. Everything you see is intentional.

And how exactly is this book different? Well, first, I wanted it to be enjoyable. This was very important to me. I want my readers to enjoy this book, to look forward to picking it up, and to read and reread it with pleasure. I thought a great deal about the "voice" I would use when writing this book. I can write academese (I've certainly done it enough), but I didn't want to do it here. Who wants to read three hundred pages of dry rhetoric? Not I. And I didn't want to *write* it, either. I'm bored much too easily. And I don't want you (or anyone) to associate the school library writing center with plodding instruction and eye-closing dullness. The writing center is (and should be) a place full of fun and energy and people interested in life and writing, so I tried to make this book mirror its subject. I also wanted to write a book that interested me, one that I looked forward to writing.

After a great deal of thinking and planning and writing, I finally settled upon the casual, conversational, guy-next-door voice you're reading right now. But don't be fooled. This voice you're reading—this voice that seems so clear and readable and effortless—is the product of years of work and study and practice. When someone makes something seem easy, you can be sure that years of monomaniacal dedication and self-denial are behind that image of effortless grace.

And I want to mention something else about the voice I'm using here. I hope you'll forgive me for saying this, but the book you're reading right now—this book in your hands—is very good writing. I worked extremely hard to make sure this book was very well written. Here's the way I figured it: if I'm writing a book about writing, then it better be well written. That makes pretty good sense to me. Form equals function, right? Also, a big part of writing well is having others understand your work, and enjoy it. When you're writing, keep your audience in mind, because you're writing for them, not for yourself.

To make my work more enjoyable, I incorporated fiction-writing techniques and storytelling methods into this book. I have written a good deal of fiction, so I know about things like character development, description, dialogue, reflection, and insight. And I brought all of these into this book. As you read, you'll notice that certain passages read like excerpts from a novel. This is intentional. I describe characters and (re)produce dialogue for the purpose of exposition. And I tell stories. I love telling stories. But all of the stories I tell here are true, drawn from my own life and my own experience. I hope you like them. I use these stories to illustrate certain points, but I also wanted you to get to know me a little. As you read this book, we're going to be spending some time together, you and me, so I wanted you to get to know me a little.

But then I took things one step further. This is an "educational" book, but I wanted the language to be somewhat poetic. I wondered: *could I turn an educational "how-to" book into a literary work?* It seemed like a really good goal to pursue, and I think I did pretty well. I was very careful about phrasing and shaped my prose to have a gentle, human, poetic quality to it. That's pretty uncommon in books about education, which is one of the reasons why I did it.

But trying to write well was not an act of ego, or even pure aesthetics. It had a pragmatic edge to it. Because this book is about learning to write and teaching others to write, I wanted to deliver a "stealth" writing lesson to my audience as they read this book. So please understand, as you read this book, you're encountering and experiencing good writing. This works for our purposes here, because one way to become a good writer is to read good writing. And I want you to know that even when writing is "unorthodox" (as I believe mine is), it can still be good writing. (Think of Mark Twain and the amazing things he did with language.) Give me a rule, and I'll break it. As you read this book, you might notice that I break rules quite a bit. But I do this for rhetorical effect. And I'm not above inventing words when the language doesn't say what I want it to say.

And then comes the matter of gender pronouns. Unfortunately, the English language doesn't have gender-neutral singular pronouns. (Well, it does, but they're new, and they never really caught on. If you do an Internet search, you'll find them. I think they're sort of weird, and I don't use them.) We have gender-neutral *plural* pronouns, which are "they" and "them." These words can be used for a group of women *or* men, or a group of women *and* men, or a group of unknown gender. But what if we don't know the gender of an individual? Much too often, people use the word "they" as a form of a gender-neutral singular pronoun, and it drives me crazy. It just sounds awful. For example, take this ghastly construction: "Someone left a cellphone; I hope *they* come back and get it." See how silly that is? We don't know the gender of the person, so we use the word "they" or "them." It really bugs me. Technically, the sentence should be "Someone left a cellphone; I hope *he or she* comes back and gets it." It's better (and technically "correct"), but it's clumsy and unpretty. I don't mind using the phrase "he or she" every once in a while, but if you're using it in every sentence, it robs language of beauty and spontaneity and the musicality of spoken, natural language. And after a while, it looks terrible on the page. Some writers like to use "s/he," and I suppose this is okay. But it's not how we talk, and it comes across as clinical and unnatural. How exactly do we pronounce "s/he"?

Others like to alternate "he" and "she," and this is what I did here. In this book, when I describe a person (usually a hypothetical student or tutor), sometimes I describe this person as "he," and sometimes as "she." It's not perfect, but I like it well enough. I think it sounds prettier and more natural. I just wanted you to know why I made this choice. As I said above, I don't mind breaking linguistic rules, but I'm highly allergic to using the word "they" in place of a gender-neutral pronoun. I just don't like it.

And now, let's talk about writing. What exactly is good writing? I find that very few people can identify truly good writing. *Very* few. And I find that much of what is published today as "popular" fiction is absolutely awful. Not in terms of story and characters; they tend to be passable, if a bit overwrought. No, the writing itself is usually very bad. I recently tried to read a certain fiction bestseller (I won't say which), and I was actually laughing out loud at the awful writing and at the poor insights into human nature.

So what is good writing? Well, let's start by saying that writing itself is composed of two basic parts: *content* and *style*. Content is what the story is about; style is how the writer puts words together. Here, when I refer to "good writing," I am most concerned with *style*. How a writer writes, the way he or she uses words. Print on a page like paint on a palette. When I read a book, I want to be entertained, but (more important) I also want an encounter with *beauty*. That's very important to me. However (and I hate to say it), very few writers can create beauty with words. Many people have gotten the idea that good writing requires "big words." No. That's deleterious and egregious. Some believe that good writing requires excessively "flowery" descriptions. A tapestry of a thousand roses, each freshly embroidered with a baroque "No." Excessive ornamentation usually equates to "overwritten." Some believe that good writing requires fast-paced action and exclamation points. No! Good writing is interested in people and meaning. I find that the best writing is clear and restrained, and as descriptive as it needs to be. I know that's a little abstract, so I'm going to give you some examples of great writing. And by the way, this is the best writing you'll ever see in your life.

First, let's take the opening paragraph of *Out of Africa* by Isak Dinesen. She writes:

> I had a farm in Africa, at the foot of the Ngong Hills. The Equator runs across these highlands, a hundred miles to the North, and the farm lay at an altitude of over six thousand feet. In the day-time you felt that you had got high up, near to the sun, but the early mornings and evenings were limpid and restful, and the nights were cold. (Dinesen, 1989, p. 3)

What can I say? It's a masterpiece of restraint, clarity, musicality, and gracefulness. And it's got one of the best first sentences ever penned. Read the first sentence over and over, and try to see its greatness and subtle beauty. It's perfect. That first sentence is a self-contained lesson in writing beautifully.

This is from Hemingway's remarkable novel *A Farewell to Arms*:

> That night at the hotel, in our room with the long empty hall outside and our shoes outside the door, a thick carpet on the floor of the room, outside the windows the rain falling and in the room light and pleasant and cheerful, then the light out and it exciting with smooth sheets and the bed comfortable, feeling that we had come home, feeling no longer alone, waking in the night to find the other one there, and not gone away; all other things were unreal. (Hemingway, 2003, p. 249)

Incredible. The distinctive Hemingway style: sparse, repetitive, and gorgeous. His sentences, very often short, traded in for one long, lovely sentence, warm poetry made of short, brisk syllables, and who wouldn't trade everything there is to be one of them, there, that night, to be Frederic or Catherine, to have that experience and that memory to take with you into old age? Who?

This is from *The Great Gatsby*, by F. Scott Fitzgerald (he and Hemingway were good friends):

> Already it was deep summer on roadhouse roofs and in front of wayside garages, where new red gas-pumps sat out in pools of light, and when I reached my estate at West Egg I ran the car under its shed and sat for a while on an abandoned grass roller in the yard. The wind had blown off, leaving a loud, bright night, with wings beating in the trees and a persistent organ sound as the full bellows of the earth blew the frogs full of life. (Fitzgerald, 1995, p. 25)

That man could *write*. Much more ornate than Hemingway, but containing utterly unique descriptions embedded in flawless beauty. *Gatsby* is a poetic high point in the world's literature.

My vote for the greatest *living* writer goes to Cormac McCarthy. Here is an otherworldly passage from his Pulitzer Prize–winning novel *The Road*:

> In the morning they came up out of the ravine and took to the road again. He'd carved the boy a flute from a piece of roadside cane and he took it from his coat and gave it to him. The boy took it wordlessly. After a while he fell back and after a while the man could hear him playing. A formless music for the age to come. Or perhaps the last music on earth called up from out of the ashes of its ruin. The man turned and looked back at him. He was lost in concentration. The man thought he seemed some sad and solitary changeling child announcing the arrival of a traveling spectacle in shire and village who does not know that behind him the players have all been carried off by wolves. (McCarthy, 2006, p. 66)

It's unforgettable, just like the book it came from. More hard edges than Hemingway and Fitzgerald, but it's a shocking burst of brilliance and an ice water splash of jarring beauty. If you haven't read it yet, read it.

And then we have an Irish genius named James Joyce. His collection of short stories *Dubliners* contains a masterwork called "The Dead." For some, this is the greatest short story in the English language. And the writing is certainly among the greatest ever produced by any human being, anywhere. Here is a short passage from it:

> Gabriel, leaning on his elbow, looked for a few moments unresentfully on her tangled hair and half-open mouth, listening to her deep-drawn breath. So she had had that romance in her life: a man had died for her sake. It hardly pained him now to think how poor a part he, her husband, had played in her life. He watched her while she slept, as though he and she had never lived together as man and wife. His curious eyes rested long upon her face and on her hair: and, as he thought of what she must have been then, in that time of her first girlish beauty, a strange, friendly pity for her entered his soul. He did not like to say even to himself that her face was no longer beautiful, but he knew that it was no longer the face for which Michael Furey had braved death. (Joyce, 1990, p. 181)

I'm still shocked every time I read this story. How did Joyce do it? Wonderful descriptions; beautiful, poetic language; prose that sounds the depth of human existence, and the fabric of meaning itself. Read the passage over. Read it carefully. If it makes you cry—even a little—you are starting to understand the power of great writing.

Now, I want to talk a little about two very important elements: *audience* and *purpose*. Remember above, when I said that creating a school library writing center is a bit like writing a paper? Well, that's true. It's a highly complex and open-ended creative venture. But it's also analogous to writing a paper because (like any discourse) it has an intended *audience*, and it's being composed for a specific *purpose*.

A skilled writer (or writing center director) always keeps in mind audience and the specific purpose for creating something. For example, the writer's voice you use for a graduate paper will likely be different from the voice you use when writing for your seventh grade students. And the purposes will be different too. Don't be confused by this; it's very simple. We all use these principles, every day, as we navigate our daily lives. For example, the "voice" you use with your colleagues is very different from the one you use with your dog (or it certainly should be). If you go run an errand, and the *purpose* is to get your dog groomed, your destination should not be a hotdog truck. Do you see? As you write (or create), keep in mind the audience for whom you're creating and your purposes for creating something.

To help with this, always ask yourself two questions as you compose: *Who am I writing for?* and *What is the purpose of this composition?* This will keep you focused and on a direct path to your goal. Likewise, as you create your writing center, always keep in mind—*strongly*—your intended audience (students in your school) and your major purpose (teaching them to write). These are powerful guidelines and reliable navigators as you direct the formation of your writing center. And by all means, explain these concepts to your tutors and the students you (and they) will be teaching, because they will need them. As I created my writing center, I always kept in mind the load-bearing pillars of audience and purpose. And I keep them in mind as I write, which means that I kept them in mind as I wrote this book. I wrote this book for an intended audience and with a specific purpose in mind. And now I want to tell you exactly what these are.

As you can see from the title, the primary intended audience for this book is the school librarian, grades seven through twelve. However, if your school library serves kindergarten through sixth grade, you too will find this book extremely useful. This book will be a great help to learn the art of *writing*, and many of the principles I describe here will transfer well into your school library writing center, no matter what level it's on.

But this book is also intended for other audiences. It's for anyone (regardless of profession) who wants to learn about writing and then give this gift to others. This book is for you too. So if this describes you, you'll find this book very helpful, so please embark on the lovely journey of creating a writing center somewhere new and novel. And by all means, be bold and daring, take magnificent risks, challenge yourself to fail, and then do things that others have told you can't be done. I've done this many times, and it's always wonderful to achieve the "impossible." So challenge yourself to achieve spectacular results, and along the way make spectacular mistakes. Little mistakes aren't worth your time. You don't learn half as much, and they're not nearly as much fun.

And finally, this book is for lifelong learners, students of the world, and anyone who is in love with life and feels a certain surge of joy and wants to write about it. In fact, this book is a love letter to everyone in this beautiful world of ours who realizes what it's like to be alive in the unmapped universe, and that life is a vast unwritten page, and that we're all the struggling authors of our own life stories. And that's why I use the "second person" throughout. I am writing to *you*. You may not often see the second person point of view in "serious" publications, but, when the writing calls for it, I love it. I think it's very personal, and intimate, and human.

And now, on to purpose. The main *purpose* of this book is to urge you (the school librarian) to create your own school library writing center and to show you, step by step, exactly how to do it. And this brings us to the ultimate (and highest) purpose of this book: *it is my utmost hope to see a school library writing center created in every school library in the nation.*

This is an ambitious notion, but I believe it can be done, and it's certainly necessary for the good of our students. You can do it. We can do it. The time is ripe for writing centers, and the feedback I've received from the articles I've written on this subject and the presentations I've done at conferences has been tremendous. Library media specialists everywhere are excited about creating school library writing centers, and the time to do it is *now*. They exist in virtually every college and university. Why aren't they in schools as well? And here, I'm going to make a very clear prediction and stand behind it: *someday every school in the United States will have a school library writing center.* They are needed more than ever, and it is definitely going to happen. It's just a matter of time.

But here you may be wondering if you have the expertise to create and run a writing center and to tutor students in writing. Don't worry; you're going to be a star. I'll show you how to do everything. As an experienced writer, I'm showing you how to create a writing center and how to write. In my hopes to teach you about writing, I hope I don't seem pedantic. I'm simply being practical. I was a writer (and English teacher) before I became a librarian. You are likely a librarian who is becoming a writer (or, at least, a teacher of writing). And, based on the conversations I've had with other librarians, you might feel that your library skills exceed your writing skills and that you're somehow not "qualified" to run a writing center or to teach others how to write. I can certainly understand how you feel, but please don't worry about this. You can do it. I promise. As you work your way through this book, you'll see that the art of writing well is not as impossible (or nebulous) as you might think it is.

Throughout my education, I have had a few professors concoct hippy-dippy personae and bring this into their teaching style, abrogating concrete teaching in favor of kooky ambiguities such as "All our journeys are unique, so you must find your own way." Bah. Abstract self-aggrandizing nonsense which will only confuse students and leave them feeling lost and frustrated. When taught correctly, writing is clear, direct, and accessible. It's not a fuzzy groping in the dark hoping for some ethereal inspiration, the tortured, brilliant artist wrestling with life's existential truths. No. That's cute, but it's not like that at all. Writing well can (and should) be taught clearly and simply. It's a concrete, highly defined task, like building a birdhouse out of pine boards and nails. Trust me on that one. I'm a writer and a carpenter, and I understand both modes of composition very well.

And if you're nervous about "resources," banish the thought. We have the resources to create writing centers. It doesn't matter if (or how) a school is lacking in materials or funding. In its barest form, a writing center requires very little: a willing tutor, a student, and a pencil and paper. And that's it (I will explain this in greater detail in Chapter One). All we need now is the knowledge and the will to make it happen. And I'm hoping that this book will be the catalyst and that it will supply the information and the motivation to make this happen. So let's be the ones to do it. We'll do it together. *Now*. Why wait? Your career won't last forever (nor will mine), so let's get in on the ground floor of this exciting initiative and do something really innovative. I want to see school library writing centers created in school libraries in the United States, and (later) throughout the world. And you've already taken your first step, and that's reading this book.

In addition to the creation of writing centers, this book has another purpose (which supports the main purpose). And this is to improve your writing skills, to demystify the act of writing, and to teach you how to teach others how to write. Learning to write is long, lonely, difficult, complex, and deeply personal. Most people shy away from this lifelong task, possibly because they haven't had any good teachers of writing. I have had many *well-meaning* teachers of writing, but much of their instruction was a fuzzy and abstract system of trial and error, a bit like *it's not working, try again*. It was as if they could spot what wasn't working, but they couldn't tell me what to do next. So they broke out the red pen. *Slash and burn*. And this was always painful and confusing.

Looking back, I suspect that most of them didn't have a deep understanding of the dynamics of writing. None of them explained clearly to me the basics of writing, limpid and concrete, *here's what you do*. And I really could have used that. The process of learning to write, for me, was one of trial and error, and developing slowly, and, I suppose, organically, in pain and solitude. But I think that (somehow) this worked for me. I was destined to be a writer (I knew it in kindergarten), so this was me growing into my best and truest self.

And now I want to talk about how to use this book. I designed it to be an actual, pragmatic, how-to book on how to start a school library writing center. It is not theoretical. It is practical application and tells you how to create and run a school library writing center from start to finish. And it does so in very clear language. And, if you look closely, you'll even find some fun wordplay, along with a sense of humor. These are all good things and are intended to make it very different from other books in the field. My goal was to tell you exactly how to create a school library writing center. I'm with you, I'm next to you, I'm helping you every step of the way.

I suggest you start by reading this book straight through, to get a "global" understanding of school library writing centers. Then I suggest rereading it and performing the actions of each chapter, on a chapter-by-chapter basis. And don't go on to the next chapter until you have completed the actions of the current chapter. I designed this book very carefully. The chapters proceed sequentially, in the order of creating, establishing, and maintaining a writing center. This made good sense to me. And when your writing center is up and running, please read this book again. Read it over and over. Mark it up. Underline it, highlight it. Wear it out.

And now, I have something really important to tell you. I want to invite you to something special. *All* of you. Remember above, when I said that I tell personal stories because "I wanted you to get to know me a little"? Remember that? Well, I really meant it. But here's the thing: I want to get to know you, too. So I created an online forum called "School Library Writing Centers." Here is the web address: http://slwc.freeforums.net/. I want you to go there and join. Go join now. It's free, and it's easy. The "slwc" in the web address stands for "school library writing centers." That's easy to remember, I think.

I wanted this book to be different, and, as far as I know, creating a forum which grows out of a *book* is an unprecedented move. And it will allow you direct access to *me*, the author, so this book doesn't have to end after the last page. You can ask questions on the forum and share the joys, triumphs, and difficulties with me and the other members. I will respond to you directly, and you can also converse with others. That's how it works. It's sort of like being at a party. Conversation, laughter, chit-chat. *Here's my card. Call me.* So join today! I look forward to meeting you there.

And now, turn the page, and learn why your school library really is the perfect place for a writing center. The adventure begins!

Chapter 1

A LITTLE ABOUT ME, AND WHY YOUR SCHOOL LIBRARY IS THE PERFECT PLACE FOR A WRITING CENTER

When I was in kindergarten, I opened a book and said "I'm going to be a writer." My dream and my life's purpose were given to me, full and complete, just like that. I had absolutely no choice in the matter. This began my love affair with books, and I began a ritual of reading two books each week. I gobbled them up; I couldn't get enough of reading. In the third grade, my parents took me to the public library, and I worked my way through the gorgeous novels of Jules Verne.

Of course, English became my favorite subject.

In high school, I was spotted as having "talent" in English, so they asked me if I wanted to be put in their "Talented and Gifted" English program. And before I could answer, they put me in. I loved the reading and the writing, the high-level discussions, and the laissez-faire trust of the teacher. It was a wonderful experience.

But don't ask how I did in math. Let's just say my aptitudes were not evenly distributed.

In college I majored in English and minored in Classical Civilizations. Loved it, loved it. I graduated, went into the Marines as an officer, and eventually managed a bookstore. After a few years, I returned to my alma mater, where they were kind enough to pay me to study English literature. Yes, you read that right: I got *paid* to study English. This was through fancy scholarships called Graduate Assistantships and Fellowships. They involved working for the English department, but for me, it was like winning the lottery.

I worked extraordinarily hard in my new position. I wore a tie every day, showed up an hour early, left an hour late, studied 12 hours a day—sometimes 14—and tried to be perfect in everything. I earned a master's degree and was invited personally into the doctoral program. Once again, I was spotted as having "talent" and was asked to teach courses in literature and writing. I loved the work, and I loved being called "Professor." Everything was working out for me, and each day brought me closer to some unspecified dream.

But there was a crisis looming.

It was getting close to the end of the semester, and I was concluding my coursework, wrapping up the class I was teaching, preparing for a series of intimidating comprehensive exams, and getting ready to start writing a doctoral thesis (it was on Shakespeare, if you're curious). It was all overwhelming, but my biggest problem was this: my fellowship was about to end. This meant no more tuition remission and no more stipend (these fellowships are awarded only to full-time students). I was effectively out of a job, and I would have to start paying for my dissertation tuition, which was six credits per year in a private university. This was very expensive, and I had no idea what I was going to do. I wasn't qualified to teach in a high school, I lacked the credentials to teach full-time in a university, and I was starting to feel a little panicky.

And just then a miracle happened.

Dr. Daniel Ahrens (this is not his real name) asked me a simple question in a university basement, and, just like that, my life changed.

I had known Dr. Ahrens for a few years (he insisted I call him "Dan"), and we got along very well. He was hired while I was in the program. He was young and sharp and just a few years older than I was, and the book he wrote on Writing presaged a terrific career in academia. He was hired as a Composition specialist—his area of expertise was writing, which was "Composition" with a capital "C"—and came to us from Harvard University, where he had been a writing instructor. We both loved writing, and we hit it off immediately.

I worked closely with him right from the start. My program required me to complete a teaching internship at the university, so for a year I worked alongside Dan as he taught (and I cotaught) courses in Composition and Rhetoric. He had a really unique approach, and connected well with the students, and I learned a lot from him about writing and teaching. Later, I took his advanced course in Composition Theory, where I read a great deal, wrote a great deal, and learned a great deal more about composition and writing and the teaching of writing.

But included in the readings and discussions was a curious subject: the one-on-one writing tutorial. This was a particular type of writing instruction in the form of a personal tutorial about a specific piece of writing. I liked this personal format and developed a good feel for it pretty quickly. It's highly effective and seemed a logical component in a course on writing taught to budding teachers. But there was a reason Dr. Ahrens included this new type of instruction in his course. I would learn this later.

One day, toward the end of my last semester, panicked, overworked, and unsure of my future, I encountered him as I emerged from a men's room in a university basement. Not a very glamorous place for a life-changing event, but sometimes we take what we can get.

"Hey Tim," he said, and seemed happy to see me.

"Hey Dan," I said. "How's it going?" I was on my way out, so my arms were full of books and other survival equipment, and I hugged it all to my chest.

"Good," he said, and grinned at me. And then he said "I want to ask you something."

"Okay," I nodded, and shifted the bundle in my arms.

"I'm starting a writing center. Want to be its first Assistant Director?"

I froze. *Wow.* Flush of excitement; my burden seemed suddenly lighter. I knew something really good was about to happen.

At the time I had never heard the term "writing center" before, but I was young and in search of new knowledge and experience and, of course, the all-important funding, so I said to him "Yes, I would love to! When do we start?" He grinned again and told me to think about it, but I told him "No, I don't have to think about it—I *definitely* want to be the Assistant Director of the Writing Center" (whatever that was). I just had a feeling this would be a terrific experience and that I would be in for an adventure. And I was.

As it turns out, this was one of the best things that ever happened to me.

Writing centers, I found out, are some of the most wonderful and necessary places in the world. Today, you can count on pretty much every college and university having a writing center. In fact, I can't think of a single college that doesn't have one. But this wasn't always the case, and, speaking personally, I really could have used one as an undergrad. And my writing was better than most. Writing centers are indispensable, and students need them, perhaps more so than you (and they) think.

If you're reading this, you're likely an adult, a writer, a teacher, or a librarian (or some combination of the three). You may have earned a bachelor's degree and a master's degree, and your reading is very good, and your writing skills are strong. (They would have to be, for you to get where you are today.) However, think back to when you were entering college for the first time. You may have been 18 or 19, but regardless of age, you were probably unprepared for the rigors of college-level writing. And, to be honest, when it came to writing, your professors probably engaged in a "hands-off" brand of teaching. They assigned a paper, and, in academic sink-or-swim fashion, you were expected to do a good job on it. And if you didn't, then the unspoken sentiment was *Oh well. Try harder next time. It's your tuition money, and if you want to "waste" it by not working harder, then that's your problem.* It's not a "nice" system, and although there were exceptions to this, I found it pretty common in higher education. And if you were in college before the proliferation of writing centers, what did you do? How did you approach the writing of a paper? How did you learn to write?

That was you. Now, think about today's students entering college for the first time. I don't want to glorify or mythologize the past too much, but things are a little different today. Many contemporary students have coasted through primary, middle, and secondary school, spending (in my opinion) too much time staring at cell phones and computer screens, and not enough time reading books and writing original compositions. When I was in middle and high school (which really wasn't that long ago), we didn't have cell phones, and we didn't have the Internet. And while plagiarism was still fairly common, it was nowhere near as prevalent as it is today in the cut-and-paste environment of cyber-academia.

The Internet enables our students to easily *assemble* papers, most of which lack original thought and writing. These papers help them to pass their courses and graduate from high school, but—and I'm being uncomfortably honest here—many of them don't learn too much about "authentic" writing, and most are not prepared to write on a college level. And we send them along and they get to college, and when it comes to writing a complex paper, they just don't know what to do. And in many cases, they'll resort to their old ways: copy-and-paste plagiarism. And when they're "caught" plagiarizing in college, the repercussions are often much greater than those in high school. Colleges take plagiarism very seriously, and the "real world" takes it even more seriously. Many fine careers of prominent people have been ruined by discoveries of plagiarism. So what can our modern university students do? When students have unlimited access to a vast Internet, how can they learn to write a real, college-level paper? How?

Thankfully, today there will almost certainly be a university writing center to assist with this. I mean, think about it. What else would you do? If you were in college today, how else would you learn to write? These questions are not merely rhetorical, they're logistical. Remember when I said earlier that I was put into a "Talented and Gifted" English program in high school? Well, on that basis, I was funneled into an "Advanced Composition" course when I started college. I felt like this was where I belonged, but it wasn't that simple.

My English skills were pretty good, and I entered the course a little cocky, so imagine my shock and horror when I received a D+ on my first university writing assignment. That actually happened, and I'll never forget it. It really stung. There was no writing center back then, but with my love for the printed word and my aptitude for writing I was able to compensate, and eventually I began writing competent college-level papers. But what about the students who lack knowledge, experience, ability, and love for the subject? What can they do? Honestly, a well-equipped and properly run writing center is the best choice here. And I don't want to sound overly dramatic, but it's really the *only* choice for these students. And I say this based on my own experience. My English skills were pretty good, but a writing center would have been a golden apple for the undergrad-me. And now, 15 years later, I was being asked to help start the writing center in the same university—in the same *building*—where I once received a D+. Sometimes, the world is a strange and wonderful place.

After I agreed to be the assistant director of the new writing center, I saw all the prior work Dr. Ahrens had done to make the writing center a reality. He had obviously been at this for some time, and I still don't know all the work he did "behind the scenes" to make this happen. It couldn't have been easy; there were probably proposals, meetings, discussions, and tons of persuasion and politicking with the powers that be. But somehow he pulled it off. I got a tour of the new space, and I loved it. It was a classroom that had been fully renovated: spackle, paint, new inner walls, a small room resembling a lounge, couches, armchairs. It even had its own restroom. The university had clearly put a good deal of time, money, and energy into the new writing center, so it needed to succeed.

I began meeting with Dan, and he explained to me his vision of the writing center, some of our goals, and the parameters of my role. Yes, I would be the assistant director, but I would also be a tutor (I liked tutoring writing, so I was happy to hear this). As a professor of Composition and Rhetoric, he was in a perfect position to encounter and choose the most talented student-writers to become tutors in the writing center. And he wanted me to help train them and get to know them a bit. Remember the one-on-one writing tutorial we discussed in the course? That would be the basis for the instruction occurring in the writing center. I worked closely with Dan, observed, asked questions, and soaked up everything I could about how writing centers work. The whole thing was very exciting, and I was thrilled to be a part of it. Looking back, I now realize that this was a very unique and precious experience. I was witnessing, and taking part in, the creation of a writing center, from its inception, through opening day, to many days of writing tutorials that left me exhausted and happy and feeling good about things in general. It was a fantastic experience.

In my new position, I helped train tutors, helped publicize the writing center, and, in general, helped get it ready for opening day. And for the next few years, I supervised its daily operations and tutored hundreds of college students in the art and science of writing. During this time, I developed a "feel" for writing centers and mastered the intricacies of the writing tutorial (which is often called the "one-on-one writer's conference"). I also developed a deep understanding of writing centers and how they can help students. I discovered that writing centers, in fact, address a very important need in the world.

Over and over and over, students came to the writing center, and nearly all of them had similar concerns. They needed help with beginning the paper, defining a thesis, developing ideas, editing a draft. And writing centers certainly help with all of these things. They provide students with individualized instruction in writing, tailor-made to their needs as developing writers, as well as to the requirements of a particular assignment. All instruction is conducted by peer tutors who have been culled from the student body (based on their superior writing skills) and then trained in the format of the one-on-one writer's conference. It works. It works spectacularly well.

Along the way, I learned quickly an extremely important point which is one of the foundations of writing centers: the purpose of writing centers is not to "fix" individual papers, but to create fully independent *writers* who are capable of creating authentic and original discourse. Although the student's individual paper or project almost always dictates the focus of a tutorial, the ultimate goal of the conference (at its core) is to teach students how to compose academic (and other forms of) writing or, to put it more simply, to teach them *how to write*. And here, we get to the true purpose of writing centers: *they exist to teach students how to write*. This is their raison d'être; this is their sine qua non.

If you're an educator or a librarian (and if you're reading this, you probably are), you are undoubtedly aware of several basic overarching truths when it comes to writing: it is an extremely important skill in school, the workplace, and life in general; it is highly complex and difficult to teach and to learn; and many students—in both the high school and college levels—simply don't know how to write. But how, exactly, do writing centers assist students with learning how to write? And what, exactly, do they do? Allow me to illustrate with a hypothetical student (and situation) that is based on countless examples drawn from my direct experience supervising the operations of a university writing center.

Let's take an "average" college student, and let's name him Bob. Although Bob did passably well in high school (receiving Bs and Cs on most of his writing assignments), he arrived at college unprepared for the rigors of college-level writing, a conundrum which is, of course, very common. His first writing assignment is for his "Composition and Rhetoric" class and requires him to read Jonathan Swift's essay "A Modest Proposal" and to write an original essay analyzing the text. Have you read "A Modest Proposal"? It's a terrific essay and has been enriching (and maddening) students for nearly 300 years. As the language is elegant, complex, and somewhat archaic, it is certainly challenging to contemporary students. In case you haven't read it, here's the gist: in this essay, Swift describes a situation of awful poverty and starvation in Ireland, and then describes a solution: *the Irish should sell their babies as a food source.* This, he tells us, will accomplish three important and noble goals: it will cut down on the surplus population, it will feed the hungry, and it will improve the economy. A brilliant solution, no? And a brilliant essay. It is written with deadpan earnestness, and (as you can imagine) caused quite a stir when it came out. Swift was making a political statement, of course; the essay was an impassioned call to help the Irish, who were being slowly "consumed" by the forces of imperialism. This essay remains one of the world's greatest satires—perhaps even the best. And now, this masterpiece is being given to a reluctant student whom we have named Bob. He is in for a treat, but a challenging one.

According to the assignment description handed out by the professor, Bob must read and annotate the essay carefully, and then generate an original thesis statement regarding its purpose and its effectiveness as an independent text. Next, Bob must argue his thesis clearly and carefully by doing a close reading and by analyzing the text carefully and thoughtfully. Bob may not consult outside research for this assignment and, above all, he must not plagiarize. His argument must be exclusively text-based and completely original. The professor is most concerned with her students' abilities as independent readers, thinkers, and writers. The assignment is due next week, Bob is panicking, and he has not slept for the past three nights. However, Bob has just been given a glimmer of hope: while studying in the university library, he saw a sign for the university "Writing Center." The writing center (whatever that is) promises to "assist students with all phases of the writing process." Although a bit skeptical of these grandiose claims, Bob is willing to try anything that might help, so he heads for this mysterious place called the Writing Center.

When Bob walks into the writing center (it seems to be a refurbished classroom), he looks around and sees a place of casual academia and pulsating activity. It has a nice feel to it; it has a nice energy. It is filled with tables and chairs, a row of computers, a rack of books, and a station where various scholastic materials are available: printer paper, lined paper, pens, pencils, highlighters, and staplers. All the basic materials for writing in one place. Cool. More important, however, there are *people* in the writing center. There is a murmur of human activity, ticking rhythms on computer keyboards, the hum of a printer, conversation and laughter, delicate scents of popcorn and coffee hanging in the air like distant memories. There is a feeling of energy in the atmosphere; something good is happening here. Bob notices the people: some are working independently, some are on computers, some are reading, some are writing longhand. The people at the tables are working in pairs. Each pair is speaking together, some are taking notes, and the subject being discussed at each table is a text that is (obviously) a work in progress. Bob can see that tutoring is taking place, but in some cases (and this is surprising to him), he is not sure who is the "tutor" and who the "student." A young woman approaches Bob and smiles at him.

"Hi, I'm Brianne," she says, "but everyone calls me Bree. Can I help you with anything?"

"Hi, I'm Bob. I could use some help with a writing assignment."

Bree smiles and says, "Okay Bob, you've come to the right place; we can definitely help you." Bree walks to a desk and flips through an appointment book. "Did you want to come in today? You're in luck, because we have an opening in"—she looks at the clock—"about fifteen minutes. Interested?"

"Maybe," Bob says. "How does it work?"

"Well, that depends," Bree says. "Have you written a draft yet?"

"No," Bob confessed, and then grew a bit bolder. "Honestly, I have this assignment, and I really have no idea what to do."

"No problem," Bree said. "In a way, it's good that you haven't written anything. We'll get you off to a good start. Here's the way it works: you make an appointment here, or you can call us. Next, we pair you with a tutor. You'll be working with Kevin today. He's terrific. You'll do all your sessions with him."

"*All* my sessions?" Bob asked. "You mean, this is not just a one-time thing?"

"No," Bree said, and laughed. "Multiple sessions work best. Maybe . . . five? Four or five sessions? It depends. Usually, the more the better. Your project and your writing skills will develop nicely through multiple revisions and drafts and lots of editing. Good writing is not 'one and done,' you know. Writing is difficult, no question about it. Even the pros have to work at it." Bree smiled at this. "Today, you'll work with Kevin on starting your essay. You two will probably brainstorm some topics for potential thesis statements, and maybe create a tentative outline for your essay. Sound good?"

"Sounds good," Bob said. "And then . . . what comes next?"

"Kevin will go over that with you. Most likely he'll give you some specific directions to do some writing on your own and then set you up with another appointment. But remember to always bring your draft with you so Kevin can look at it and make suggestions for improvement. You'll be surprised at how quickly your essay will start to take shape. What we do in the writing center really works. You're gonna love this place," she said, and smiled again, and then said, "Hey, here's Kevin! Kevin, meet Bob. I think you two are all set."

And that's how a student's journey in the writing center starts.

You've noticed, no doubt, that the above hypothetical encounter took place in a *college* writing center, while this book is about the creation of writing centers in middle and high school libraries. (On this point, I want to mention that writing centers can also be set up in libraries that serve kindergarten through sixth grade. This is the subject of my book *Create Your School Library Writing Center, Grades K-6*.)

My reasons for describing a college-level writing center are simple and pragmatic: college writing centers have been around for a while (most commonly in the last several decades) and have been undeniably effective in helping students learn to write as they navigate their way through the academic demands of college and even (I discovered) graduate school. To put it bluntly, they work amazingly well. In fact, they have been so successful that most colleges and universities now have fully functioning writing centers that constitute an integral academic resource for their students. Honestly, I'd be shocked if a college *didn't* have a writing center.

And they work so well that I believe strongly that middle and high school writing centers should emulate the college model in their form and function. That's what I did, and that's what I urge you to do. This is a very important component in the school library writing center model that I created, so I want to emphasize this point: as you read this book and follow my directions, you will be creating a writing center that (in its functioning) is based on the university writing center model. But don't worry; I adapted it to the differing environments and developmental levels of the students we tutor.

At present, some high schools do indeed have writing centers, but these constitute a very small percentage. And the high school writing centers which I have encountered personally are not run like their (highly successful) college counterparts. These are usually set up in a classroom and structured in a rather traditional "extra help" format in which teachers function as tutors. They may call themselves "writing centers," but really they're not. I'm sure they're helping students, but in all likelihood their potential as an educational resource can be improved greatly by emulating the university model. As I stated in the Introduction, my goals in writing this book are twofold. First, I want to help other educators create school library writing centers so that they can help students learn to write. My larger (and related) goal is this: I want to bring writing centers into every school library in the nation (and perhaps even the world) and to have them function like college-level writing centers. It is a grandiose goal to be sure, but is one that I believe strongly to be possible and perhaps not as difficult as you think. Let me explain.

After I finished my tenure as assistant director of the writing center at St. John's University, I became a teacher of high school English. In this position, I now saw students *before* they got to college and was not surprised to see that most couldn't write well. This is a systemic problem, I thought. Wouldn't it be wonderful if we could teach them to write *before* they left for college? That would be a good thing and would really help them out. I thought about it some more and could not come up with any magical panaceas. So I kept teaching writing and literature, had a great time, and prepared them for college the best I could.

After teaching English for a number of years, I felt called by libraries (you know the feeling), and I enrolled in library school. Being a lifelong bibliophile and lover of libraries, this was the right place for me. After completing my master's degree in Library Science, I landed a position as Library Media Specialist in a large public high school on Long Island (New York). There, I once again observed students struggle with writing. As I made the transition from English teacher to school librarian, I learned the intricacies of the job and began to wonder how I might improve an already-good library. What were the library's deficiencies? Where could it be improved? What was it missing? Where could it be updated? How could it better benefit the students? As a new "teacher-librarian," I wondered how I could expand my role as *teacher*, while also being a librarian. One day I was walking through my library and silently reminiscing about my time in graduate school, and the things I encountered there: the wonderful professors, the fabulous courses I took, the courses I taught, my dissertation, Shakespeare, my lovely days in the writing center. Yes, the writing center. The writing center. Something occurred to me, and I stopped walking and stood still, right there in my library, and thought.

And thought.

And thought some more.

It occurred to me quite suddenly that my high school didn't have a writing center, and maybe I could create one. And, based on my background, I thought I would be the best person to do this. I pondered this idea, and, for perhaps a year, I considered it from all angles. And I became convinced that it could actually work.

The fulfillment of projects like this is always difficult, especially in an environment where space is rare, budgets are tight, and people are busy. How could I create a writing center in a busy building with no space to spare and no budget allocated? How could I do this? Where would I put it? Who would staff it? I thought about all of these things. I thought about them a great deal, and one day, I had a blissful epiphany. I'll never forget it. Remember the university writing center which I described above? It was fictional, but based quite closely on the one where I served as assistant director. Think about it, and how it was set up. The layout, the atmosphere, the ingredients. It was a space which contained the following materials: *books, computers, printers, tables, chairs, and scholastic materials.*

Think about those materials that I just mentioned. What does that sound like?

You got it: a school library.

There, standing in my school library, I suddenly realized that *I was standing in the writing center.* The library was it, and this is where it would be. It was all suddenly very clear and simple: the school library contains all the physical and material infrastructure of a fabulously furnished writing center, all in one place. The tutors—students who are highly accomplished writers—are already present in the building. From my time as an English teacher, I knew the school would have a population of gifted writers who could be trained to serve as effective tutors. And I, the librarian, would be (and should be) the director of the writing center. I thought about it some more. It seemed like a beautiful idea, and I thought it could work. I was very excited.

Although this was the basic plan, I knew that setting up a fully functioning writing center (structured along the lines of the university model) would be long and complicated. As time passed, however, I became increasingly sure that it could be done. As I proceeded over the next year and the project took shape, I began to develop a highly effective model that is completely unique. And it has become a vital resource available to all students.

As the months passed and I devoted myself to this exciting project, I watched a new and unique type of writing center begin to emerge. I eventually named this the "School Library Writing Center." Although structured conceptually like the college writing center paradigm which preceded it, I instituted pedagogical and logistical modifications in accordance with the school setting and the developmental levels of the students and their tutors. The result is a highly innovative educational resource that is available to all students, regardless of grade level or writing ability. It is an entirely new species of writing center, and we are claiming undeveloped real estate in the educational landscape of America.

At this point, I want to articulate and summarize the five mainstays of the School Library Writing Center model which I created:

1. It is located in the school library
2. It is open during the day and after school
3. The majority of instruction is performed by students (peer tutors)
4. It is modeled closely on the university writing center paradigm
5. The school librarian is the sole director and is also a tutor

Your school library really is the perfect place for a writing center. I realize that I have been a bit sketchy here with regard to precise details of what I did to make things happen and how things work. Not to worry; I did this for a reason. I want this book to unfold slowly and logically, just as your writing center will. In forthcoming chapters, I will explain very clearly all aspects of how to create and maintain your own school library writing center. And there will be lots of benefits to this, I promise. You will increase your library's educational offerings, you will elevate its visibility as a vital (and irreplaceable) place of learning, and you will be helping your students immeasurably.

However, along with these professional perks, there are some "personal" ones as well. Not only will you visibly underscore your role as a multifaceted educational leader (thereby looking good to students, parents, teachers, and administrators), you will be having a heck of a good time developing and running your own writing center. Think about it: every year, you'll get to know, and work with, a team of true all-stars, and indeed, this is my perennial nickname for my team of tutors. Most of my group emails start off by greeting them "Hello, All-Stars!" It's an accurate moniker, and they like being recognized and appreciated.

I tend to imagine things visually and symbolically, and sometimes I picture myself looking over an undeveloped continent: lush valleys, cool blue mountain tops, wind-swept plains. A silent plea for good things to happen. There are writing centers in virtually every college, but very few in middle and secondary schools.

Why not? Where are they? Do you see my point? There is a conspicuous vacuum in the educational landscape of America and the rest of the world. Let's fill it in! I challenge *you* to be the school librarian who creates a proper writing center in your school. Be the first person in your district to do this. You'll love what happens. Make no mistake, this is a new field of vast potential, and if we as librarians embrace this challenge, we can be pioneering agents of change who can collectively transform education in America and eventually (I hope) in the rest of the world.

Now, turn to the next chapter, and see how to get started!

Chapter 2

GETTING STARTED:
AN IMMODEST PROPOSAL

As an officer in the Marines, I was repeatedly told that "first impressions are last-ing ones." I've discovered this to be true, so as you create your writing center, make sure you get off to a good start. At all costs, you must avoid getting the dreaded "no" from your administration. In the world of education, beginnings are the time when major decisions are made (ones that often become policy), and they are the time when those in charge can reject an enterprise that is new, different, and untested.

As I move through the world, I have found that most people live in the land of "no." I live very happily in the bold land of "yes," so I find this very frustrating. But I understand it. "No" is safe. "No" is cozy. "No" stops new things from happening. When presented with something new (and therefore perceived as risky), the word "no" is much less stressful than the word "yes." So it's vitally important that you prepare, proceed cautiously and well, and make all the right moves. And a little luck doesn't hurt either.

Before I took the first step in creating my writing center, I thought about it for over a year. Exactly how would it work? What did I need? How would I run things? Etc. Over and over I asked myself questions about the writing center, devised prob-lematic scenarios, anticipated hurdles, and devised solutions. And over and over I saw that the writing center could work. I could not come up with a definitive reason why it couldn't succeed (and I tried). And when the writing center was fully constructed and complete in my mind, I approached my immediate supervisor and told him that I wanted to speak with him.

My original supervisor—the guy who hired me—was an assistant superinten-dent who loved libraries and librarians, and I always got the impression that he asked to be put in charge of all the district libraries. His management style was aggressive, he was an innovator, and he loved charging into situations and shaking things up. It was fun working with him, and I loved meeting with him and discussing ways to improve the school library. But alas, he retired. *Darn it*. The district began searching for a replacement and quickly hired an interim chairperson (for a year) until they could find a permanent replacement.

My new supervisor liked to be called "Doc," so that's what I'll call him here. I was lucky. He was a very nice guy, and I got along well with him. Doc was a retired high school principal who had become an adjunct university professor at a local college. And although he was temporary on the district landscape—and the writing center would be permanent—I decided to approach him first about this new venture. Chain of command, and all that.

When I was ready to make my pitch about the writing center, I emailed Doc and asked if he could swing by the library for a few minutes (I thought meeting him in the library would be more effective than meeting him in his office). Later that day, he walked in, shook my hand, looked at me expectantly, and smiled a little. He had a gentle spirit and a kindness about him. I had only known him for a few months, but I really liked him. We stood in the middle of the library and made small talk. I was a little nervous, and it was busy in the library, and I thought this was probably a good thing. A busy place would be a good place for the writing center. It would suggest that we'll do a vigorous business and really be a "happening" part of the school. Our conversation went something like this:

"Hi Tim," he said, looking around. "Wow, library's busy."

"Hey Doc," I said, "yep, we're doing well. No problem getting kids in here." I paused a moment. "So, Doc, I wanted to ask you a question. There's something I'd like to do here that will really help the students, and will be great for the school."

"Okay," he said, and looked at me expectantly. I started making my case.

"Well, I did a doctorate in English at St. John's University. And while I was there, I helped start their writing center. I don't know if you knew that."

"No," he said, and I could tell he was a little surprised.

"Yes," I said, and nodded. "I was the writing center's first assistant director. And after that I became a high school English teacher."

"Really?" he said. I could see he was starting to get a little interested in what I was saying, and probably also wondering where I was going with all this.

But let me interrupt myself here. I have a very unusual background, and I was giving myself shameless plugs, no doubt about that. But I really, *really* wanted the writing center to happen, so I took every possible advantage, even if that meant reading my full résumé to Doc. I wanted to convey not just that I was "able" to start and run a writing center, but that I was literally *the best person* for the job. And later, I would pitch the library as the best place for the writing center.

"Yes," I said. "I'm very passionate about writing, and I have good background in it. Here's what I'm thinking. I helped start a very good university writing center, and helped it grow during its first few years. This taught me a lot about writing centers, so"—*here we go*—"I want to start a writing center here in the high school. It would be great for students, and a great way to support the curriculum. What do you think?" There it was. This was the moment. How would he react? I looked at him and waited.

Doc looked off into the distance, and his eyes grew narrow and thoughtful, and then he came back to me. And he smiled again, just a little.

"You have a very interesting background," he said. "And I have an interesting background too."

"Okay," I nodded. "You do?" *Where was he going with this? Would it be yea or nay?*

"Yes," he said. "I used to be a high school principal. Did you know that?"

I nodded again. "Yes, I heard that."

"And I do a bit of creative writing also. I'm sort of a playwright. Even had some plays produced onstage. You didn't know *that*, did you," he said, more of a statement than a question. And he grinned at me.

"No, I didn't," I said. It was my turn to be surprised. And I'm always impressed by talent.

"Yeah," he said, "a high school principal who writes plays." He smiled, leaned into me, and whispered, "You know, a knowledge of acting really helps in this crazy profession of ours," and we both laughed. And then he said something really interesting: "And the last school I was at, before I retired, I helped start their writing center." And he looked at me and smiled, and nodded his head.

I blinked. *Wait—did he just say . . .?* Was this really happening? What a stroke of luck!

"You started a writing center?" I asked him. "I didn't know that!"

"Yeah," he said. "Aren't they great? So helpful to kids. Most people don't really understand them." He grew thoughtful for a moment. "But since I left, I heard it sort of fell apart."

I nodded, and the word "leadership" crossed my mind.

He looked around the library. "Where did you want to put it?" he asked.

Fellow librarians, this is a question you will definitely have to field. This question is born of a fear of carpenters and electricians, new walls and windows and paint, and budgets that are already strained. It's also the result of an ingrained belief that any sort of "club" with a formal name must also have a designated place. But that's not the case at all. The writing center isn't a place, it's a *process*. This is a very important guiding principle to keep in mind as you set up your own writing center, so please internalize it deeply: the writing center is not a place, it's not a thing, it's a *process*. It's two people sitting and talking about interesting things, enjoying themselves, and improving themselves and their writing. It's two people struggling over the best way to write an essay. It's two people wondering if a certain simile is the "right one" for a poem about a lost love who is missed dearly by the writer. Do you see? It could be happening in the coffee shop down the street, or on a park bench, or on a beach, or in a basement, or at a party, or in a car, or on a train, or in the booth of an evening bistro as you lean forward and look into someone's beautiful eyes as candlelight dances warm and golden over your little world and makes you feel as if you're living in a timeless fairy tale, and everything will be happily ever after. It could be like that. It could happen anywhere. It could even happen in a school library.

People have trouble with this concept; they really do. In the time since my first articles on school library writing centers appeared, I have assisted several school librarians with creating their own writing centers (and it was certainly a privilege to do so). And many of them (and their administrators) simply don't understand that, according to the model I created, the writing center happens in the library. *In the library.* Why set it apart, like it's some sort of shrine? The truth is that librarians can set up their writing centers anywhere they want to, and I'll be happy to help them. If you have a spare room, and you finally want to assign it a use (besides a place to store boxes, hang your coat, and eat your lunch), then go for it. It might be a nice, quiet place for writing tutorials to take place, and it might work well for some of your students' learning styles. However, this is contrary to the model I created. In my exquisitely informed opinion, to separate the writing center from the library is a mistake. And this is for two reasons.

First, if you don't have an extra space to put the writing center (and I suspect this is the case for most school librarians), then I strongly advise that you don't ask for one. This will be the end of your writing center. Space in schools tends to be extremely limited, and most administrations simply won't approve (or create) a space to be designated solely for a new and untried program.

But there's also a pedagogical psychology involved: a separate space will simply be unappealing to many students. For one thing, students don't like being separated from the herd. It makes them feel uncomfortable. Also, a separate space may feel too much like "extra help," might feel "remedial," and might even feel like a punishment. This will discourage voluntary attendance in the writing center (which we definitely want) and will likely create resentment in students who have been "directed" to go to the writing center. And these scenarios are most decidedly *not* what we're going for. We might get kids in there for one self-conscious session, but this probably won't create repeat customers. And repeat sessions are where we do our best work. The writing center isn't "extra help," it's not remedial, and it certainly shouldn't be perceived as some sort of punishment. It's a place to learn and to grow. It's a place to talk and think about authentic human expression and things that really matter to us. It's a place where writers are born. For all of these reasons, I strongly advise you to simply place your writing center *in the library* as a part of your library offerings, where it will be simultaneously invisible and on display. I explained this to Doc.

I swept my arm across the library in my best dramatic fashion and said, "It will happen here. In the library." I let that sink in. "All writing tutorials will take place *in the library.* The students will just sit at tables. Wherever they want. Wherever there's a spot. The writing center is the library. And the library is the writing center. It's a seamless integration."

Doc looked around and nodded again. He was beginning to see that this could work. "Okay," he said. "Who's doing the tutoring?"

I was prepared for this question. "I'm modeling this whole thing on the university writing center. So, just like in a university writing center, they'll be drawn from our students right here in the high school. I'll choose our best writers, and I'll train them in how to tutor writing. I know exactly how to do it."

Again, Doc nodded, cleared his throat, and looked away for a moment. I could see he liked the idea, but I knew what was coming next, and again, I was prepared for it. And I knew it would be the last major hurdle to clear.

"Well," he began, "it's a great idea. It really is." He paused. "But there's the budget to consider. I just don't think we can find any money for this. How much were you thinking?" And he looked at me intently, because money is always the make-or-break factor in new ventures.

And, dear readers, this brings us to *the most important ingredient in the creation of your writing center*. It's also (I shamelessly admit) my most brilliant innovation in a brilliantly innovative process. Ready for this? Here it is:

The budget is zero.

Nada.

Your writing center will cost the district precisely *nothing*.

You will create, open, and maintain a fully functional writing center in your school library on a budget of *zero*. This is the single most important ingredient of the writing center model I developed, and—make no mistake—this is the *only* reason it was approved by the administration. And this is the reason it will be approved by *your* administration. Very few people will say "no" to something that's free, especially when it's necessary, wonderful, run by someone else, and makes the district look good. I explained this to Doc.

"The budget is *zero*," I told him. "Nothing. We'll have a fully functional writing center in the high school, and it will cost the district absolutely *nothing*." I looked in his eyes and saw that I had his full attention.

"Okay," he said, "how will it cost nothing?" The conversation was still pleasant, but his question and his tone had grown a bit serious. It had gone quickly from a friendly chat into something that might be just a little important.

"Simple," I responded. "The writing center will be located here in the library, right? But really the writing center is not a 'location.' It's a *process*. Think about your own writing center, and the materials you used in it. You probably used . . . tables, chairs, computers, printers, pens, pencils . . . stuff like that. Right?"

"Yes," he said, and nodded. "That's pretty much it." And I could see he was starting to understand this new concept. I continued.

"Think about it. A student shows up to the library writing center because he wants help with a paper. He sits with a tutor, and they talk about the paper—what to do, how to start, how to revise. It's a conversation. It's a transference of knowledge. A library is the perfect place for a conversation like this. And talking doesn't gobble up any resources."

"Right," he nodded. "I see what you mean. But the tutors," he said. "How will you pay them?"

"Community service hours," I said. "Letters of recommendation. Stuff like that. Kids love being involved in cool clubs like this. There will definitely be incentives and perks. I know exactly what to do." I kept stressing my knowledge and experience, with the implied suggestion that I knew what I was doing, so this wouldn't become a headache for him, or for anyone else.

"Alright," he said. He cleared his throat and (for the first time) looked just a little uncomfortable. "But, Tim . . . you know we can't pay you for this. It's just not in our budget." He watched my reaction.

"I know," I said. "That's okay with me. This will be great for the kids, so I'm willing to do it for nothing." And it's true. To this day, I have not made (or asked for) a penny as director of the Writing Center. I do it because it helps the kids, and because I love doing it.

Doc looked around the library, thought for a moment, smiled a little, and nodded again. "Okay," he said. "Write me a proposal for the writing center. Alright? Write a formal proposal. Get it to me, and I'll take a look at it. If it looks good, I'll pass it along to the principal."

And with that, he looked around the library one more time, shook my hand, and left.

YES! I was thrilled. My writing center was in motion. But I still had work to do to make this a reality, so I began writing a proposal they couldn't refuse. I knew this statement was important (and would be looked by several sets of eyes), so I took my time with it and crafted a rather elegant and persuasive two-page document. I worked on it for about two weeks, on and off, writing, revising, editing—all standard and important parts of the writing process. I made sure it was well-written, mechanically flawless, and, above all, persuasive. In my proposal, I focused on several important topics: the function of a writing center (don't assume that people know what writing centers are, or what they do); how it is necessary for students' success; its budget of zero; the library as the logical place for the writing center; and my own qualifications and experience in creating and running a writing center. The following is the actual proposal I submitted, with minimal changes made for the sake of privacy:

*

PROPOSAL

SCHOOL LIBRARY WRITING CENTER

Submitted by Dr. Timothy Horan

For the past several years, I have been deeply interested in creating a *writing center* in the High School, based in the Library Media Center.

As a former teacher of high school English, I recognize the crucial role which writing (and clear communication) plays in a student's success in college, as well as in the workplace afterwards. Additionally, as a former adjunct university professor of English and Composition, I can also testify to the difficulties which most students face when confronted with college-level writing assignments.

In addition to improving students as writers and preparing them for college, our High School Library Writing Center will represent a natural complement to the International Baccalaureate (IB) program. By focusing on the entire *process* of writing (from initial brainstorming through final editing), the students will gain an understanding of writing as a dynamic process that is both methodical and organic. To put it simply, the writing center will seek to transform students into *writers*.

While I was pursuing my doctorate in English at St. John's University, a professor of Composition there began to plan and create the university's first writing center. He personally selected me to be the writing center's first Assistant Director, a post

I held for several years. In this position, I performed hundreds of university writing tutorials, thereby gaining deep experience in the dynamics of the one-on-one writer's conference. More important, I had the unique opportunity to assist with the creation of a university writing center, the training of writing tutors, and the management of day-to-day operations of a writing center. I believe strongly that this experience has made me uniquely qualified to create and manage a school library writing center.

Like college writing centers, the writing center I envision will utilize *peer tutoring* in the format of the one-on-one writer's conference. Students will be selected to be tutors (or "writing associates") based on their writing abilities, scholastic performance, enthusiasm for writing, and, of course, their willingness to help transform other students into writers. All conferences will take place during the day in the high school library, under my personal supervision.

In terms of *cost*, the expenses necessary to start (and run) our school library writing center will be minimal: a smoothly functioning writing center represents an active transference of *knowledge* and *skills*, rather than a consumption of resources. Any materials required (pencils, paper, computers, etc.) will be minimal, and will be freely available to our students as part of existing library services. As you can see, the writing center will draw upon services already provided by our library, but will elevate them and make them more widely available to a broader segment of students, albeit in a new and different format.

I believe strongly that a writing center at our High School will improve our students' writing abilities, overall academic performance, and success in the IB program. More important, it will impart to them skills and knowledge which will assist them not just in college, but throughout the rest of their lives.

*

I wrote and revised and proofread—over and over and over again. When I was happy with the proposal, I submitted it to Doc, and then waited.

A week went by, then two, then three. I was very excited about the writing center, but I went to work every day and tried not to think too much about it. I was starting to get a little antsy toward the end of the third week, and I was wondering what was happening with my proposal, when the principal asked to see me. She's a friendly bundle of energy, and when I walked into her office, she had my proposal sitting on her desk.

She looked up from it. "I got your proposal for the writing center," she said. "I love it. This would be great for our students."

Well, this was off to a good start. "Thanks!" I said. "This will really help them."

And then she said, "There's just one problem you might run into."

Uh-oh. I sat down. "A problem?" I thought I had solved all the problems. What could this be?

"I see here that . . ."—she looked at the proposal—". . . your tutors will all be high achieving students, right?"

"Yes," I said. "Our tutors will be our best students, and our best writers."

"Right, that makes sense," she said. "But remember, these students are all over-achievers. They are just non-stop busy. So some of your tutors probably won't have lunch periods," she said. "Their schedules are very full, so I'm not sure when they'll be able to tutor."

"Oh," I said. "Right." I looked at her and nodded, and thought about this new development. This was a great point and was the only obstacle I hadn't anticipated. But I'm an eternal optimist, and a pretty good problem solver, with a stubborn streak like you wouldn't believe, so I decided to keep going. My school would have a writing center, even if I were the only tutor. And really, problems like this are not too surprising. When you're breaking new ground (as we were), obstacles spring up, and you must find ways to vault over them. It happens. And you keep going forward, no matter what.

"I understand," I said. "But I'll be a tutor. If they don't have lunch, they can tutor during study hall, and after school, and—if they're really ambitious—they can tutor before school. I'm always here early, so I can help with that. So I think we can get good coverage for the schedule." I let all this sink in. "I believe we can do this. If it's okay with you, I'd like to start selecting my tutors, and then we can see exactly when they're available. And we can take things from there." I looked at her expectantly.

She looked at me, and she smiled at me and nodded. "Okay let me know how it works out," she said, and looked at her watch. "Oh, gotta go!" she said, and gathered some things off her desk and disappeared down the hallway. I was thrilled. My writing center was *happening*! It was very exciting, and it was fun doing something new and unprecedented.

And it was time to select and train my tutors.

But let me pause the story here for a moment. Those first few years were glorious fun and magnificent mistakes, but this isn't the place to revisit those early exuberant stutter-steps. So instead of telling you what *doesn't* work, I'll just tell you how to hire tutors and put your team together. Do all of the following things:

- First, make it your goal to hire about 20 tutors. This is a large but manageable number and will give you good coverage on the schedule. If your school is large, you might even bump it up to 25 to allow for natural attrition. As a general rule, I suggest having at least 10 tutors in your writing center. Or, for the more mathematically minded, you might consider about 1 to 2 percent of your student population, but no fewer than 10 tutors.

- Select your tutors during the month of May, or thereabouts. You will be asking English teachers for their best writers, and, by May, they'll definitely know who they are.

- Although you choose your tutors in May, *train* them in September. This way, you will avoid the dreaded "brain drain" that occurs during the summer. With your superb training fresh in their September minds, your tutors will be sharper and more effective when they begin tutoring.

- Choose your tutors from *two grades*. And choose about 10 per grade. If you're a middle school librarian, choose about 10 tutors from the sixth grade, and about 10 tutors from the seventh grade (in September, they will be seventh and eighth graders). If you're a high school librarian, choose about 10 tutors from the tenth grade, and about 10 tutors from the eleventh grade (in September, they will become juniors and seniors). Choosing tutors from two grades works very well. You open up the pool of talent, virtually doubling your chances of getting the best people. It also provides more coverage on the schedule and will give you a "continuous body" of experienced tutors in the writing center. All of the above works very well, so please understand it thoroughly.

- If possible, hire some tutors who speak other languages fluently. If you have a strong immigrant population, try to have tutors who speak their languages. I learned this from personal experience. Here's what happened.

One day during that beautifully unwritten first year, a teacher sent a boy to the writing center to get some help with writing. I'll call him "Xiang." Xiang had just arrived from China, and he seemed like a very nice kid. The thing is, he spoke almost no English. He knew perhaps 20 words of English, and that's not an exaggeration. I tried speaking with him and working with him, but he simply looked at me and smiled. I honestly didn't know what to do. I wanted to help him in some way, but how could I teach him to write in English, if he couldn't even *speak* English? After giving it some thought, I located a simple text, accompanied by clear illustrations, and I had a tutor perform some reading and language exercises with him. It went fairly well, but it was certainly not a perfect solution.

It was a difficult situation, and I thought about it quite a bit. How could I better help Xiang? One day, he communicated to me that he had a question, but he just couldn't articulate it, and he got a bit frustrated. And just then, another miracle happened. I noticed a certain boy in the library. At a table, way in the back, sitting with a friend. I knew him a little, and I knew he spoke Chinese, so I asked him to be my "translator" for a few minutes. He agreed and asked me what dialect Xiang spoke, and I said, *oh boy, I don't know, but let's try anyway*, and I paired the two up, and they were shy at first, just a couple of kids meeting each other. "This is Xiang," I said to my translator. "Please introduce yourself." He did, and Xiang was thrilled, and it quickly became a session of Chinese spoken rapidly and beautifully. Smiles and laughter, and two new friends in the world talking and having fun. It was a great thing to watch.

As you can imagine, this ended the tutorial (how could I compete with *that*?), and I made a graceful exit. *Very interesting*, I thought. Yes, very interesting indeed. And I vowed, right there, to hire a few tutors every year who could speak other languages besides the ones we teach in school. So this became part of the process when selecting tutors, and I recommend you do it also. Hire some tutors who are fluent in other languages.

Now, when it comes to the actual selection, I mentioned earlier that you will be approaching English teachers. This works very well. So when the month of May comes around, you should approach teachers of Honors English and Advanced Placement (or whatever are the highest academic courses in your school), and ask them about their best writers.

But the tutors you select must have other qualities besides being good writers. They must also be willing to learn, have good social skills, enjoy helping others in a "volunteer" capacity, and must be reliable. Oh, yes. You're hiring peer tutors to perform a function, but they'll also be representatives of the writing center and will be instrumental in creating its reputation, for better or for worse. But let me digress for a moment here about your tutors, because they're one of the best parts of running a writing center.

I've been a classroom teacher of high school English, and I've been a librarian, so I know a little about both gigs. I love being a school librarian, but one thing I miss about classroom teaching is making a strong connection with students. As a librarian, I certainly connect with students every year. But it's different. You don't get to know them in the same way that a classroom teacher does. You just don't. However, being a writing center director allows you to make a terrific connection with a group of wonderful students every year. And this is one of my favorite parts of directing the writing center. You get to coach an all-star team every year, and you play a prominent role in their education and experience. And not many people can make that claim.

When I was ready to start compiling my list of all-star tutors, I approached (with pad and pencil) several English teachers. I always grab them for a few minutes when they're on hall duty, or when they're in their classrooms on prep periods. I prefer doing this in person rather than through email. I suppose email would work also, but for this, I prefer face-to-face communication. I start by explaining what I'm doing, and then I ask them a few questions. That first year, a typical exchange went something like this:

"Hi Kate. Are you teaching AP this year? With eleventh graders?"

"I sure am," she says. "Why?"

"Well, I'm starting a writing center, and I'm selecting tutors. The whole thing will be peer tutoring, like a college writing center. So these tutors will be teaching other students how to write."

"Oh, ok," she says. "That sounds like a great idea."

"Thanks," I say. "So, I was wondering if you could give me the names of your best writers. I'm looking for, maybe, your top five?" Kate nods her head and thinks. "But these students really need to be two things: they need to be good writers, but they also need good social skills. They'll be tutoring other students, and we want things to be pleasant. We want repeat customers in the writing center."

"I understand," Kate says, and thinks a moment. And I get ready to jot down names (which are all fictitious here).

"Ok," Kate starts, "Susan McKay is very good. Great personality, very popular. And Shawna Wilson is terrific. She's a little shy, but a great writer. I think she'll be good. Jimmy Castillo is a very good writer, and a really nice kid. And, let's see . . . oh, Alexa Lee is terrific . . . she likes to be called 'Lexie' . . . and . . . let's see, one more . . . well, Dan Swerski is an amazing writer, when he turns stuff in."

I pause in my note taking. "When he turns stuff in?"

"Yeah," Kate says. "He's not the greatest with deadlines. I really have to stay on him. But again, his writing is terrific. He's a natural."

"Okay Kate," I say, "Thanks very much. I'll let you know how it goes."

And I walk away and cross Dan's name off my list. He's out. His talent sounds good, but his irresponsibility doesn't. I'm looking for a mix of talent, social skills, and responsibility, but in this case, responsibility is more important than talent. Responsible students can be trained to tutor writing. It's a hard-nosed attitude to be sure, but our writing center tutors must be completely reliable. This is a crucial point. Honestly, the only cardinal sin a tutor can commit is showing up late for a tutorial, or (even worse) not showing up at all. At all costs, we must avoid the tutor who never shows up for a student. We *never* want a student to wait for a tutor who (Godot-like) doesn't show up. This will quickly destroy your writing center's reputation. And although Dan is out, I now have four solid candidates. I repeat this visit with several other teachers, and, in a short time, I have a list of over 20 students. So far, so good.

Next, I had to personally recruit my tutors. This is an important step and must be handled well, because they always have the power to say "no." I decided that the best approach would be to speak with each student individually, to give them some compliments, to describe being selected as exclusive and a high honor (which it definitely is), and to mention some of the perks that come with being a writing center tutor. The first time I did this, I have to admit, I was a little nervous. I was asking busy kids (many of whom I didn't know) for volunteer work, and I just wasn't sure how they would respond. I looked up their schedules, and then met with them, one by one. Most of the time, I waited outside their classrooms before the end of the period, and, when the bell rang, I approached them as they exited the classroom. With very little variation, these short meetings all went like this:

"Hi! Are you Susan McKay?"

"Yes," she said nervously.

"You're not in trouble," I said, and smiled. (When I approach students, I often start the conversation with "You're not in trouble." It's a great stress reducer for both of us). I continued. "You know me, right? Dr. Horan, librarian extraordinaire?"

She smiles and nods.

"Good!" I say. "I want to invite you to join something."

"Okay," she smiles again.

"Well, besides being the librarian, I also run the writing center. Do you know about the writing center?"

"No," she says, cautiously.

"That's okay," I say. "It's the greatest thing in the world. It's in the library, and it's a place where tutors help other students with their writing assignments."

"Okay," she says again. "That sounds good."

"Oh, it's great. Every year, I invite our best—*best!*—students to be tutors in the writing center. And you come highly recommended by your teacher, so I want to ask you if you'd like to be a writing center tutor." I smile at her, and I let this sink in. I could see she was interested, and probably a little flattered about being asked. "This is very prestigious, and really, it's an honor just to be asked. I only ask the best students. Think you might be interested?"

She nodded and smiled again. This was going well.

"Great!" I said. "You'll be tutoring other students in writing. It's lots of fun, and you'll love it. You get community service hours for tutoring, and, if you want, I can write you a letter of recommendation for college. Also, you'll learn a lot about writing, which is always good. And there's one other thing: whatever college you attend, it's going to have a writing center. If you want, you can walk in and apply for a job as a writing center tutor, and tell them that you have experience. Still interested?"

"Yes," she said, smiled, and nodded her head (wow, that was easy!). And then she worked up her courage to ask an important question. "So . . . how much time will this involve?" Yes, it's a very important question for these students, who are all overachievers, who are all busy, who are all precociously aware of the precious nature of time.

You'll probably be asked this question, and you must handle it well, or your tutors will be scared off. "Really, not that much," I assure her. "It will be pretty low-impact. I can't predict exactly how much you'll be tutoring, but you can always say 'no.' Really. If you're too busy to tutor, or you need to study for a test, or, *whatever*, just tell me, and that will be fine. You won't have to tutor. You never have to tutor if you don't want to. In the writing center, you never have to do anything you don't want to do. And that's a promise." This is a very important point in several respects. First, we want *willing* tutors. An unhappy tutor is a resentful and ineffective one. Also, keep in mind that when students walk into the building, their primary responsibility is their own education, and we must support that. The writing center is an *accessory* to their education and school experience, it is not their primary responsibility. I let all that sink in. "So, are you still interested?"

"Yes!" she said, and seemed really happy about it. I love this part. It's the coolest thing in the world to see young people get excited about the writing center.

"Great!" I said. "I'm so happy to have you on board. Can I get your email address? When I have the team all set up, I'm going to set up a group email, and I'll let everyone know about the meetings. You're gonna love this!" And she jotted down her email address, and I thanked her, and told her we'd have a meeting within the next two weeks. She was thrilled, and I'm sure she went home and told her parents about it (good press for the library, right?). This enthusiastic acceptance has become the norm. That first year, every student I asked—*every single one*—was thrilled to be a part of the writing center and joined the team. And since then, I have had very few refusals—only two or three out of 50 or 60. And the students who refused were probably just too busy.

So at this point, I was in a good place: I had administration's blessing to create a writing center, and I had an all-star team assembled. My next goal was to hold group meetings with my new writing center tutors, and begin training them in the dynamics of the one-on-one writer's conference. For fledgling writers, it's the most effective writing instruction in the world.

And it's what I'll be discussing in the next chapter of this book.

Chapter 3

THE TUTORIAL: THE MAGIC TRIANGLE, THE ICE-BREAKER, AND THE INTERVIEW

Intrepid explorers, we are approaching the inner sanctum of the writing center: the one-on-one writer's tutorial.

The writing center tutorial is a wonderfully effective form of teaching and is often called the "one-on-one writer's conference," or sometimes just the "writer's conference." For purposes of this book (and for the sake of simplicity), I will be referring to this simply as the "tutorial." The tutorial is where learning takes place, and it is the shining centerpiece of your writing center.

Before we proceed, I want to clarify some terms that you will encounter repeatedly as you read this book. Whenever I use the word "tutorial," I am referring to two people sitting down in your library and talking about writing. One person is providing assistance to the other. In this book, the term "tutor" refers to the one providing instruction, while the term "student" refers to the one receiving instruction. *Tutorial, tutor, student.* These three terms are important, and you will be seeing them over and over, so please understand them well. The *student* needs help on an assignment and therefore comes to the writing center. The *tutor* instructs the student. When they sit together and discuss the student's assignment, that is a *tutorial.* Simple. I will be using these terms often and consistently.

Without a doubt, the tutorial is the single most important ingredient of your writing center. The tutorial is where learning occurs, and it is, literally, the writing center in action. Its importance cannot be overstated. It is the "bullseye" of your writing center's target, and everything else in your writing center orbits around it, relating to it and supporting it. The tutorial is the heartbeat of your writing center, so you need to understand it deeply and completely. Remember, you are a tutor in your writing center, but you are also the director. This means that you will not only be tutoring students, you will be training tutors in the art of the one-on-one writing tutorial. So you need to understand it very deeply.

If you're nervous about training your tutors, don't be. I will tell you everything you need to know, and you won't start training them until you have read (and reread) this book thoroughly and understood all of its principles. (And feel free to teach from notes during your first few meetings with your tutors. That's what I did.) As I teach you the principles of the writing center tutorial, you will simultaneously be learning how to train your tutors. It's two for the price of one, because the praxis and pedagogy are entwined.

Every year, when I train my new tutors, I think back to (and draw upon) my own training and experience as a writing center tutor. Although this was in a university writing center, I find that many similarities exist between the concerns (and struggles) of university students and their younger counterparts. You'd be surprised, but it's true, and it makes sense. In many cases, they're only separated by a few years, so they're more alike than different. They're all human beings struggling at the complex task of learning to write. So, as I train my tutors, I recall and utilize my own experience as a tutor in a university writing center.

When I first began tutoring, it came to me quite naturally, but I made my share of mistakes. And that's how I learned. When something worked, I repeated it. When something didn't work, I avoided it or changed my approach. I was constantly asking myself *What's working here? What's not working?* As I grew into a seasoned tutor, I began to develop my own style of tutoring, complete with a "checklist" of things to do during tutorials. Along the way, I found that some of the "theory" of writing began to be displaced by practical application. And, as my experience deepened, I found myself developing real-world techniques that made my tutorials highly successful in a measurable sense. I began to help students to a greater extent, and I began to make fewer blunders. I continued to refine and use these techniques, and I can tell you from firsthand experience that they *work*.

After a time, I was able to help my students immediately and concretely during tutorials. Honestly, it became very easy for me. I was also able to give them simple, understandable methods they could use when they wrote independently, away from the writing center. Most of these university students were young, ambitious, hardworking commuter students who went from campus to work. They weren't "writers" per se, or ethereal ivory tower types. They were tough, young New Yorkers who valued quick, tangible results over abstruse composition theory. And I gave them what they wanted and needed. Through working efficiently on the papers they brought with them (which were typically due in a few days or weeks), I was able to help them improve their assignments greatly. More important, however, I was able to teach them writing techniques that they could actually use in the real world. It felt great, and they always appreciated this.

As you tutor, you should always stress *practical application and pragmatic results over theory*. Always. And by "theory," I'm referring to the psychological and organic processes of writing and the ways in which compositions develop and grow. These are important topics to be sure, and personally, I find them very compelling. And because they can assist your development as a writer and a tutor, I will be covering them, to an extent, in this book. However, in the writing center, they are only important to the extent that they inform and assist the tutoring that takes place and the development of the students who come to the writing center for help. Did you catch that? Let me rephrase it: in the writing center, *theory is only important if it directly helps instruction in a "real-world" sense.*

There may be times when you want to explain the deep processes of writing to tutors or students (and certain students may be curious about it), but these instances should (and must) be related directly to the actual task of teaching students how to write. In other words, if something won't directly help a student learn to write, then you probably shouldn't be doing it. Therefore, in this book, my discussions of writing will nearly always be pragmatic in nature, practical and concrete. And I hope that this makes my book somewhat refreshing and unique. When I tutor, I do my best to keep my explanations and techniques very simple at all times. Why make things unnecessarily difficult or complicated? I love simplicity, and the concept of simplicity is deeply embedded in my life. I find that the best ideas in the world are the simplest, and I'm always suspect of things that can't be described well in a single sentence.

The one-on-one writing tutorial in the writing center employs something called "peer tutoring." This is when students tutor other students. This is valuable for several reasons. First, imagine for a moment that *you* (the adult librarian) have become a highly skilled tutor of writing (and if you tutor regularly, this will happen sooner than you think). You tutor students in your library whenever you are asked, and whenever you are available. And then imagine that word spreads through the school that students can come to the library and get help with their papers, and that it's a pretty cool experience. This is good. And more and more kids start coming to the library to get help on their papers. All of a sudden, you can no longer handle the traffic. And you wish you could "clone" yourself.

Well, *presto*. Welcome to the writing center.

By correctly training tutors, you have effectively cloned yourself. Now, instead of one of you, there are *20* of you: 20 highly skilled writing center tutors offering writing instruction in the library. Kids are getting the help they need, and your life gets a lot easier.

But there's another reason that peer tutoring works well. And this is because many students will feel more comfortable receiving instruction from another student. They've done their best for the past few years at avoiding adults, and they don't want to change things now. In cases like this, peer tutoring will feel social in nature, sort of like they're "hanging out" with another student. And remember, the library is a highly visible place. When they're working with another student, they won't feel self conscious in front of their peers, and it won't look like they're receiving extra help or "remedial" assistance (and these are definitely *not* what the writing center is).

However, many other students will wish to work with *you*, and you only. They will want to receive help from an adult, a "real" teacher, and they will gladly sit with you and learn from you. Perhaps they trust only adults with their schoolwork and their educations. Perhaps they are extremely shy, have been ostracized for some reason, or have been bullied. You don't know, but you're there for them also. I have had many students who would work only with me. When students first come to the writing center, I always try to pair them with another student. This is my first course of action (your tutors *want* to tutor!), and it should become your first course of action also. *Always try to place a student with another student.* (Eventually, when you gain experience as a writing center director and learn the personalities of your tutors, you will be able to successfully "pair" certain tutors with certain students, so that personalities will "match," and the tutorials will be more pleasant and productive.) But, as I said, certain students have insisted on working with *me* only. And that suits me just fine, because I love to tutor writing, and I always try to give students what they want and what they need.

It's always nice when students "adopt" me as their writing tutor. You'll enjoy this, and will develop a wonderful rapport with them (and, occasionally, with their parents). I came to understand their learning styles, and they came to understand my teaching style, and working with them was always a terrific experience. It even got to the point that some of them would stop by the library for a "chat." On a few rare occasions, I received gifts from these students, along with profuse gratitude for how much I helped them. It's always nice when it happens. It's a reminder that we're teachers, as well as librarians.

And this brings us to the process of actually training your tutors in the rudiments of the writing center tutorial. How, exactly, do you do this? I'm going to tell you that now, in practical, real-world terms. First, you start by recruiting your tutors. Remember earlier, in Chapter Two, when I discussed "recruiting" your tutors? I said that you would approach them individually, tell them about the writing center, then invite them to be tutors. When they accept (and most of them will), you'll ask for their email addresses. This is a very important detail, and, initially, it will be the primary way in which you reach out to your tutors. You absolutely must get the email addresses of every single tutor you recruit. Get them during that first meeting; don't leave it for later. And as you go through this process, do your best to stay supremely organized. Make a chart with two columns: one for their names and one for their email addresses. And then have your tutors fill it out, one by one.

So, let's say you recruit 20 tutors. This means that you now have a list of 20 names and email addresses. Make a *group email*, then contact everyone. It's a very efficient mode of communication. Now remember, these students probably don't know you at all. It takes time to build up trust, and many of them aren't used to receiving emails from adults, especially teachers. It will take time for them to get to know you, to trust you, and to get used to emailing an adult. That's okay. If they're bashful about emailing adults, they need to get over it, and I explain this to them, in pretty much those exact words.

Once you have made your group email with all of their email addresses on it, send them a "welcome to the writing center" email. The subject line should say "Writing Center," and the message should convey how happy you are that they have come aboard. But also include a polite request for them to respond and let you know they received your email. You're setting up a path of communication, but you're also tiptoeing gently into their worlds. So you need to proceed cautiously.

When you send this initial email, you'll see the responses start to trickle in. Give it a few days, and then send a second email scheduling your first meeting. (And take note of who is responding back to you, and who isn't. This may shed light on levels of interest and commitment.) On the day before your first meeting, send out a *third* email to your tutors, reminding them of the meeting. Remember, this is all new for your tutors, and when the day ends, it will be quite easy for them to pack up their books, and do whatever they normally do. Old habits are hard to break.

Your first meeting will take some preparation, but not too much. First, you'll need a time and place to meet. The time should probably be after school (that's how I do it), and the place should definitely be somewhere in the library. This will convey that the library and the writing center are joined together; one is a part of the other. Plus, the library is just a great place to meet. But choose your meeting location within the library carefully. I'm lucky. My library has a small computer lab attached at the back, accessible through a door. It's like a small classroom, complete with tables, chairs, and a computer and projector. The computers in the room are laptops that are kept locked in a cabinet, which means the tables are all clear. It's a perfect place to meet and talk. If your library doesn't have such a setup, you'll need to choose a good location. A corner or "far off" space will work well, because you need to focus energy and minimize distractions as much as possible.

When I meet with my tutors after school, the library is open and being supervised by another teacher, so everything works very well. I'm not holding a meeting and running the library at the same time, which would be very difficult. If you are the only librarian after school, I might consider having another teacher supervise the library for you, or I might even close the library so that you can run your meeting and train your tutors. I hate to close my own library, but sometimes it becomes necessary. And you don't really *need* to be near a computer and projector, but if you have them, you might use them from time to time, for various purposes.

When you hold meetings, you should always have some sort of agenda or clear goals to accomplish. However, please go at the pace of your tutors. You're giving them new information they will be using in the real world, and they need to really understand it. Remember, their students will be depending on it. Please don't feel as if you have to cram their training into a certain number of meetings. Their training and learning will arc over several meetings. Let it take as long as it takes. When you hold your meetings, be very structured, but go at the pace of your tutors. And, when the "teachable moment" happens, go with it. Some of the best learning will occur during these unexpected incidents, because they're always authentic. They're what the moment calls for.

At this point, you may be wondering how many meetings you should hold and how much training you need to do with your tutors. It's impossible to say precisely (lots of variables here), but if you want a general rule, I will say this: about 10 sessions of training is a good number. At a bare minimum, you might be able to prepare tutors adequately in five sessions. Maybe. But to train a tutor properly and thoroughly, 10 sessions will work much better. But no matter how many meetings you hold with students, they must all be productive, and must give your tutors new knowledge. And even when training is complete and the writing center is in operation, you should still hold one meeting each week, for the sake of group cohesion and morale. More on that later.

When you're having meetings, always try to have things ready before your tutors start arriving. This will make you look interested and organized, as if the writing center is important to you. For all of your meetings, push some tables together (perhaps two), to make a big square. And then put chairs around the tables. This will create a somewhat democratic (and "Socratic") feeling, unlike the traditional classroom "sage on the stage" setting where you are at the front, dispensing wisdom. Try not to make it feel like a "tenth class," because it's been a long day, and the kids don't want that. Although you are in charge and running the meeting, this seating arrangement will suggest implicitly that you are all equally important, and your tutors will appreciate this. You are all tutors in the writing center, and you all have an equally valuable role to play. As for materials, put lined paper and pencils on the table, and that's it. Don't put this stuff at every chair. Have it all on the table, and when your tutors start to arrive, greet them with a smile and say "grab some paper and pencils." This is important. I do this for a very specific reason, which I will explain shortly.

Make sure you take attendance at every meeting, including your first one. Place an attendance sheet on the table and, when they begin arriving, ask them to sign it. This will accomplish two goals. First, it suggests that these meetings are important, and that their presence there *matters*. Second, by noting their attendance patterns, you will be able to gauge levels of involvement and degrees of training. After attendance is complete and your tutors are seated, I would begin by conveying how happy you are that they have agreed to be tutors in the writing center. I would also convey that they are doing something wonderful and unselfish, and that they will love being a tutor (you're a leader, so do your best to motivate your people). And explain to them in simple terms exactly what a writing center is, because they definitely won't know. But keep your explanation simple.

Tell your tutors that a writing center is a place where students can come to get help on their writing assignments. This help is individualized, one-on-one peer tutoring, and *they* will be doing the tutoring. Explain to them that this is the noblest thing in the world, and that they'll never know the impact they'll be having on students' lives. *Most students can't write. And they need to learn how to write.* Period. Every year, I tell my tutors that *they* might be the difference between a student graduating and not graduating. And I mean it.

As you interact with them, be positive and upbeat, smile a lot, and try to motivate them as much as possible. Remember, the writing center is not (and should not be) a grim place; it is a place of happiness and helping others. (The teaching profession has become a bit grim in the last few years, hasn't it? Let's all start trying to have fun again.) Also convey to your tutors that they have (in every sense imaginable) an open door and lots of freedom, because tutoring in the writing center is strictly voluntary. They're busy, and they will definitely be wondering how much time and commitment this will require of them, and how it will impact their academics. Given a chance, the brave ones will ask you about this. Tell them that they can leave the writing center at any time. They can tutor as much or as little as they want. They always have the power to say "no." They make the final decisions on their levels of involvement in the writing center. Students love hearing this; it gives them high degrees of freedom and autonomy.

But be careful how you say this. My first year, I made a mistake. During my very first meeting, I said something like "If you don't want to be a tutor, that's okay, because I'll get someone else." And when I said it, the atmosphere in the room went flat (you know what I mean). It didn't come out the way I meant it, and I immediately felt awful. It sounded as if I said "Stay or go; you're all disposable," and that's certainly not what I meant. What I *meant* was this: "If you find that you can't fit the writing center into your schedule, and that you need to leave, I'll understand, and I promise I won't be angry. I know you're all very busy, so if you need to leave, please let me know. And please don't feel as if you're leaving me empty-handed, because eventually, I will be able to hire another tutor in your place." Yes, that's what I meant. And now, I say that to students, slowly and clearly. I explain it, because they need to really comprehend that they're all valuable members of the writing center, but they're not "trapped" in it. In fact, it's a privilege to be invited to be a tutor in the writing center. And now, when I explain this to them, I always include a statement that affirms their individual worth. I say "But I really hope you all stay with the writing center." It's important for them to hear this, and it always goes over well. They like hearing it.

I also explain to my tutors that they have been hand-picked for the position. They will be doing a very special kind of tutoring that involves a special kind of person (I'm a big believer in positive reinforcement). I tell them that, in the first few meetings, I'll be showing them exactly how to do this new type of tutoring. I also say that we'll eventually make a schedule, and they'll all be on it (the schedule is very important, and I'll be discussing this later, in Chapter Seven). I also tell them we'll be having meetings once a week (even after training is complete) and that we'll end every meeting at three o'clock sharp, no matter what. And I have never broken this rule. This is a very important detail. Have you ever been to a meeting that drones on endlessly, when you're hungry, or have things to do? It's an awful experience. Tell your tutors when meetings will start and end, and then stick to it. It will boost attendance at meetings, and it will increase their trust in you, and in the writing center.

In deciding which day is best to hold a meeting, I always take an informal "hands up" survey to find out which day is best for the tutors. Among the tutors in my school, this is usually a Friday. And if you have kids who can't make meetings because their schedules are too busy (and you definitely will), offer to meet with them one on one in the library, to get them caught up. Find out if they have any free periods, or if they can chat with you after school on any days, and perhaps even before school. And structure these meetings like writing tutorials (it builds good habits, and it works well).

And if they absolutely can't meet with you at any time—if they're just too busy—I would ask them (gently and politely) if they think they'll have any time to tutor. And if they don't, I would suggest (again, very gently) that they might be too busy to be writing center tutors. Belonging to a club but having no involvement in it doesn't make too much sense. It will be a distraction for them, and will create unnecessary stress in their lives. In cases like this, it's usually best for the student to leave the writing center, and it's probably time for you to hire another tutor. I always try to handle these exchanges with tact and gentleness and smiles, because the student hasn't done anything wrong. And keep in mind that the student will take this meeting to bed with him that night, and that he'll be thinking about it, over and over. *Did I do something wrong?* So please handle these exchanges carefully and tactfully.

After the basic logistics of meetings are completed, I ask if anyone has questions, and I wait (the mythic "wait time" of teacher world). Americans typically dislike silences in social situations, and you might see kids begin to shift nervously. That's okay. If wait time lasts more than about five seconds, I smile, make a beckoning gesture with my hands, and say "Come on, this is all new, I know you have questions!" And if there are questions, I answer them. And if there aren't any, I begin to explain the basic structure of the tutorial. And this is where things get really interesting. And lots of fun.

I start by stressing the simplicity of the writing tutorial. In terms of materials, your tutors need to bring only two things to the tutorial: *lined paper and pencils.* And that's it. Sound familiar? Just a few minutes earlier, you asked each of them to grab the lined paper and pencils you put out. This was a physical illustration of a principle which will (we hope) help them to remember to always bring these two important ingredients to tutorials: lined paper and pencils. I prefer pencils because they suggest (and this is very subtle) a "casual" feel and an invitation to abundant revision. They're also an acknowledgment of the fact that we all make mistakes, and mistakes are allowed (even encouraged) in the writing center. We learn through making mistakes, especially when it comes to writing.

The lined paper is for the tutor (and sometimes the student) to take notes. Your tutors should make notes during every single tutorial, and these notes are extremely important. The student will take the notes home, use them, and depend on them (and I'll be speaking more on this later). Next, explain to your tutors that the writing center tutorial has a basic and simple physical geography to it that involves the tutor and the student. And I use the term "geography" very deliberately, because the seating configuration is physical, is very important, and must be strictly orchestrated. It's not terribly important *where* the students sit, but it's extremely important *how* they sit. Here's what I mean.

Let's say a student comes into the library to be tutored. The tutor greets her, gets lined paper and pencils, and they choose a place to sit. Typically, this will be at an available table in a quiet section of the library, or (during busy periods) wherever there is room. Because a writing center tutorial is an exchange of ideas, it can take place almost anywhere. Nevertheless, *how* they sit at the table is very important. They need to sit *next* to one another. More specifically (and again, this is *very* important), if the tutor is right-handed, she should sit to the student's *right* (with the student to her left). This way, when she writes explanatory (and supporting) notes, the student can see the notes (and ideas) as they develop. Likewise, if the tutor is a lefty (like yours truly), he should sit to the student's *left* (with the student to his *right*). Does this make sense? Think about it. I'm a lefty. If I'm writing something with my left hand, the person on my *left* can't see the notes because my left arm is blocking them. However, the person on my *right* can see the notes as I write. This basic configuration is very important to the success of the tutorial, and (although simple) you must stress this arrangement to your tutors. Over and over. We want them to really internalize this concept. It's simple, but extremely important to the success of a tutorial.

Keep in mind that a student will likely be a bit nervous during her first trip to the writing center and will probably want to sit *across* from the tutor. She is unconsciously striving to feel safe by erecting a barrier (the table) between her and an unknown that may be dangerous, or (at the very least) unpleasant. It's perfectly normal. However, if this happens, the tutor should sit next to her, or ask her politely to change her seat, and give a reason for the request. I usually say something like "Would it be okay if you sat in this seat *here*? I'm a lefty, so it works much better if I sit on your left." I have done this hundreds of times, and I have never been questioned on it. Not once. However, it's always preferable to do this *before* they sit down, so I try to reach the table first. I choose my seat (on the left), and I point to where I want her to sit, and ask her very politely if she would sit there, and I give a reason for my request. Again, I have never encountered a bit of resistance with this request. They always sit where I ask them to sit. I think that part of this compliance is because it suggests that I *care* about what happens during the tutorial. I'm not there with an "okay, whatever" attitude; I'm there to help them out. It's very important to me.

Now that the two major players are arranged and sitting, there is one other component vital to the success of the tutorial, and that's the student's writing assignment. Remember, if a student is coming to the writing center, he is coming because he is working on a specific assignment, and he needs help with it. Period. A student will almost never come to the writing center just to talk about writing. (And if it ever does happen, I'll do my best to give the student what he needs. I'll talk to him about writing, and I'll give him some ideas on what [and how] to write. And then I'll ask him to come back soon, and show me what he wrote.) So we have our tutor and student seated at a table, ready to begin a tutorial. Picture it; see it in your mind. And now add in a third major player, and that's the student's writing assignment. And this completes the major ingredients of the tutorial. Tutor, student, writing assignment. This is the triumvirate of the tutorial.

The student's writing assignment (hereafter referred to as the "assignment") should always be on the table (literally) and is always the focus of the tutorial. Always. It will be in the form of a description of the assignment (the teacher's handout or from the student's memory) or a working draft that the student has written. Later, the assignment will be accompanied by notes generated during the tutorial. And still later, it will become the actual paper as the student composes it (with the assistance of the tutor). Thus the geography of the writing center tutorial is in *the form of a triangle*. I call this the "magic triangle": the tutor on the right (if she is right-handed), the student on the left, and the assignment is in front, where both can see it. I want to stress this, because it's very important and is a major factor with regard to the learning that takes place during writing center tutorials. *The physical geography of the writing center tutorial is a triangle.* Embed this firmly in your memory. And, during those first meetings, I always demonstrate this physically to my tutors.

I do this by asking for a volunteer (with the assurance that no one will get embarrassed). And one always steps forward. Remember, they're at the beginning of their writing center journey, so I sneak in as many lessons as possible, as often as possible. After my volunteer steps forward, I tell them "Here's how you start a tutorial." I grab some lined paper and two pencils, I hold them up, and I say "I have my lined paper and pencils." I wave them in the air. I then smile at the volunteer, and I say "Hi, welcome to the writing center. Let's go grab a seat over there." We then sit down at a table highly visible to the group, and (as I'm a lefty) I make sure that the "student" is sitting on my right. I put the notepaper in front of us, where we both can see it, and I pick up a pencil in my left hand and wave it in the air dramatically. "Look. I'm a lefty. My student is sitting to my right. Here is my pencil. I'm getting ready to take notes." I point to the lined paper. "Here is her writing assignment." I point to the three major players: "Do you see how we're sitting? We're in a triangle. This is the magic triangle: *tutor, student, writing assignment.*" I put my left hand on the paper, still holding the pencil: "Look, I'm getting ready to write on her draft, or to make notes." I make dramatic scribbling gestures with the pencil. "She can see what I'm writing. She can watch as I make notes. And I talk to her as I make notes. Do you see? It works!" I smile; I do this all with a very light touch. The mad scientist in his laboratory, that sort of thing. And the kids laugh, but they learn too.

Once the magic triangle is established, the tutorial proper begins. And this is where things really do get magical, and it's one of my favorite things in the world. I mentioned earlier that I developed certain techniques, and I used the term "checklist" in performing these techniques. This is accurate, but a bit reductive, so you might prefer to think of the tutorial as following a "pattern." I think that's better. There are things that the tutor should do during every single tutorial, in a specific order. After arranging the tutorial in the correct geography (the magic triangle), the tutor should begin instruction. But she should begin instruction subtly, with *social contact.* This is very important. There is a *social* component to these tutorials as well as an academic one, and it must not be overlooked. After setting up the magic triangle, we move into the second major component of the writing center tutorial, and I call this the "Ice Breaker."

This is two or three minutes (at most) of social interaction and easy banter designed to help put the student at ease. This is especially useful during early tutorials, as the students get to know each other, and trust is established. They should exchange names, and the tutor should project a persona of friendly enthusiasm (smile, make eye contact, use the student's name). This will convey that the writing center is a friendly place and, more important, a *safe* one. Then a few verbal exchanges of a friendly nature, such as "So, do you belong to any clubs?" or "I think we were in the same class once." Stuff like that. This is easy social interaction, and chances are that students will be better at this light chitchat than I am.

However, as your tutors become more seasoned and skilled, their seemingly innocuous chatter can also be a good way of gathering information useful to the tutorial. In an effort to gain a better "holistic" understanding of the student and his academic needs, the tutor should transition toward such questions as "What grade are you in?" and "What courses are you taking right now?" If the tutor is comfortable with the situation and the student, he may ask more revealing questions (of a "surrogate" nature), such as "What's your favorite subject?"; "Which is your *best* subject?"; "What do you want to be when you grow up?"; and (possibly) "How do you feel about writing?" These are a great way to better understand the student and his relationship to writing and to school in general. And, for the savvy tutor, the answers to these questions will shed a great deal of light on the student academically. As always, the goal is to construct a tutorial that is tailor-made to the student's needs and learning style. But be prepared for the student to be guarded and quiet during early sessions. This is new for him, and he will be cautious, but trust will develop along the way.

Developing a social rapport is also crucial in motivating students to come back for subsequent visits. We definitely want "repeat customers" in the writing center; this is where we do our best work. If a student comes in for a single visit, the session will unravel like a formality, and (to be honest) not much is going to happen. However, if he comes into the writing center for multiple visits, wonderful things will happen. And happen amazingly fast. In terms of numbers of visits, I can offer this: when the student is working on a particular paper, *about three to five visits is optimal* (but five is really best). It depends on the complexity of the paper and on the student's abilities and levels of motivation. Also—and this is very important—*the student should always work with the same tutor*, if at all possible. They will develop a comfortable rapport and will begin to understand each other's styles. And sometimes friendships develop, which is always nice to see. And if all goes well, you might make a repeat customer for the next several years, as he works his way through different grades and different assignments, and, in the process, turns into a writer. It's almost miraculous what the writing center can do, and it's a wonderful thing to see.

After the social "ice breaker" is complete, the tutor will transition (smoothly and naturally, we hope) to the third major component of the tutorial. I refer to this as the "Interview." This is a crucial ingredient, and it's where the tutor begins to get a clear idea of the assignment. Remember, the student has brought an assignment with him, and he wants help with *that* particular assignment. To put it simply, in order to help the student, *the tutor needs to know what the assignment is.* Don't look for great complexity here; it's old-fashioned common sense. If the tutor doesn't understand the assignment, she can't help the student with it. And in order to understand the assignment completely, the tutor must ask the student specific questions about it. She simply cannot help the student if she does not thoroughly understand the assignment.

However, it has been my experience that many new tutors "freeze" during this portion. They become assailed by self-doubts and are plagued by worries that are the bane of every new teacher: what *do I do? Am I doing the right thing? What if I run out of things to say? What if I say the wrong thing?* I remember one time I was training a university student to become a writing center tutor. We were in the final stages of training, and we were doing mock tutorials (yes, you'll be doing these also; I'll cover this later). This particular student was very bright and well-mannered, but when it came to the "interview" portion of the tutorial, he froze. He didn't know what to say, and he was absolutely terrified. It was written all over him, and I sympathized with his discomfort. Fortunately, the mock student and I were his only audience that day. I broke in and spoke with him gently, and said this: "Ok Dan, you're doing well, but I can see that you're a bit unsure about what to do next. Honestly, this is very easy stuff, and you're going to be a star, I can tell. Think about it like this. Let's say you're sitting next to your friend in the cafeteria. And he turns to you and says, 'Dan, I need to write a paper, but I don't know what to do. Got any suggestions?' What would you say to your friend?"

Dan thought a moment (still unsure of himself) and then said "I'd probably say . . . 'What's the paper about?'"

"YES!" I shouted and pumped my arms in a cheering gesture, and we all laughed. "That's it! You need to get information on her paper, and you need to write it down." I handed him some paper and pencils. "Ask her questions about her paper, and make notes as she talks. This is easy stuff, Dan. And the questions are all *common sense*." I continued to work with Dan, and I'm happy to say he matured into a very good tutor. And that night, I revealed to him one of the biggest secrets of a successful and pleasant writing tutorial. Ready for this? Here it is:

It's a conversation.

Got that? A writing tutorial is a *conversation*. You talk to each other. And you're talking about writing. And you even have a conversation piece: the student's assignment. But this conversation must be artfully constructed. It must be a give and take. The tutor cannot be the one doing all the talking. He must ask questions, of course, but he must also be a good listener. And listening is an art form that must be consciously cultivated. I find that, among Americans (today especially), listening is a dying art form. Have you noticed how often people interrupt each other before a sentence is concluded? Or when someone speaks, the other person is not really listening, but is thinking of what he'll say next? This is obvious if you watch any talk show. Most people don't truly listen anymore, and I dislike this. It's become the norm for people to spout aggressive one-liners at each other, and it's very uncivilized. I find that, when I close my mouth and listen to people, they have very interesting things to say, if I listen carefully.

I tell all this to my writing center tutors. And, as usual, I throw in an old joke. I tell them "Look at how you're designed. You have two ears and one mouth. That means you should listen twice as much as you talk." This always gets a laugh, and it makes pretty good sense too, if you think about it. I then tell my tutors that they need to listen to their students, *really listen*, to *everything* the student says. The tutors need to let their students talk, and they need to listen to their students, because *the tutorial is about the student*. Period. The student is the important person during the tutorial. Not the tutor. The tutor will ask questions, offer suggestions, and provide guidance, but the only things that matter are the student's paper, and (more important) what the student learns about writing.

When teaching my tutors the Interview portion of the tutorial, I draw upon my experience with Dan, and I say this: "Think about it . . . if a friend approached you for help on a writing assignment, what would you do? You'd probably start by asking him a bunch of questions. And these would all be rooted in common sense, and designed to get *an overall sense of the assignment*." And right there, during the meeting, through a combination of leading questions and brainstorming, my tutors and I develop a list of questions they should ask during every tutorial. And I write these on the big notepaper I have stuck to my easel. As you read these questions, please note how they are all anchored in common sense, and how they proceed logically and in complexity. During the Interview portion of the tutorial, you (and your tutors) should ask your students (at minimum) the following questions:

When is this assignment due?
What course (or subject) is this paper for?
What is the grade level?
Who is the teacher?
How long does this project have to be?
Are you required to use research? How many sources?
Does this need to be in MLA (or some other) format?

And this brings us finally to the big money-makers:

What, exactly, is the assignment?
Do you have a copy of the description on you right now?
Did you jot down any notes about this assignment? Can I see them?
Is there anything you can think of that I need to know about this assignment?
Have you started writing the assignment yet?
If so, did you bring a draft of your writing with you?
If not, have you decided what you are writing about?
Etc.

Look at those questions. See how simple, basic, and intuitive they are? Nevertheless, they yield lots of crucial information, and are designed to give the tutor a clear idea of the student's writing assignment. These are the questions your tutors should be asking their students, especially during early sessions working on a project. And—this is very important—as the student responds, the tutor should *jot down the information on the notepaper*. A clear picture of the assignment will quickly start to develop. This is very important, so I want to reinforce it: *your tutor must ask these questions, in pretty much this order, and he must jot down notes as the student is answering*. In a very short time, he will understand the assignment quite thoroughly, and will be better able to help the student.

This is a good place to take a breather, and talk about something different.

Up to this point, I have been talking about what writing centers are, and what they do. Now, I want to talk about what they *don't* do. It's just a few things, really, but they're all important, and they're all related to transforming students into writers. And you will find these rules at all properly run writing centers. First, writing centers aren't a "proofreading" service. For example, you might encounter a student who walks in and says, "This paper is due next period. I was wondering if someone could take a look at it and fix the grammar and stuff." We don't do this. Ever. When this happens, I politely say "no," and I explain to the student (tactfully) why we don't proofread. Although it would improve the paper and probably yield a higher grade, it wouldn't teach him how to write. However, I tell the student about the writing center, how helpful it is, and I invite him to bring his next paper to us, because we can definitely help him learn to write. I try to never miss an opportunity to turn kids into writers.

Nevertheless, there are times in which tutors will help with proofreading. When a student has come to the writing center for successive visits (perhaps five), proofreading becomes a legitimate part of the writing cycle. This is a part of "editing," and it's a valuable part of the writing process, so we need to teach it. But when proofreading is isolated into a lone "clean up" step, it's a shortcut and a quick fix that yields no new learning for the student. So we don't do it.

Similarly, we also don't allow "drop-offs." A student cannot drop his paper off to be "corrected" while he goes and eats his lunch. Again, it would probably improve the paper, but not his writing skills. For a student to learn about writing, he needs to be present at a tutorial. We also don't guarantee higher grades. While visits to the writing center usually result in higher grades on writing assignments, the grade remains an exclusive transaction between the student and his teacher. So, to sum things up, here's what we *don't* do: we don't proofread, we don't allow drop-offs, and we don't guarantee higher grades. But there's one more thing that we don't do, and it's the most important one of all: *we do not "write" papers for students*. And when I train my tutors, I explain this to them very clearly and decisively.

The writing center provides critiques, guidance, and suggestions for improvement, but we certainly do not (and must not) write papers for students. Providing too much input is really the only serious blunder a tutor (or writing center) can make. So every year, I tell my tutors very clearly that they are not to write papers for students. Ever. In other words, they should not be contributing to the *content* of a paper. They are to assist with the overall *process* of the paper, providing input with planning, organization, development of ideas, mechanics, research, and the general structure of an essay (etc.). But the *content*—the information contained in the piece—remains solely the student's responsibility. The tutor can engage in collaboration and modeling (to a limited extent), demonstrating to the student how to write sentences and how to structure paragraphs (etc.), but *the student must write the paper*. It must remain exclusively his work and his intellectual property. If it's not, we're doing him a great disservice. He won't learn to write, and he won't feel a sense of pride and ownership when he hands in a completed paper.

All of this brings me to an extremely important point, and it's something that should become one of your guiding mantras. To run a writing center properly, we need to embrace a very important principle, which is expressed in the mission statement of my own writing center. Here it is: *The Writing Center does not "fix" papers; we create writers*. That's our mission statement, and that's our purpose. This is an extremely important concept and is the backbone of any properly functioning writing center, on any level. We're not there to "fix" the paper that the student is working on, which would be easy enough. If we did this, we would be targeting a *symptom*, rather than a root *cause*. The student's paper is not the goal. The paper is a *vehicle* used to attain a goal. And that goal is teaching the student how to write.

If we teach students how to write, then the by-products of bad writing will eventually disappear on their own. But make no mistake, students' papers do improve through writing center tutorials, and it would be easy for an uninformed outsider to get the impression that we're there to polish papers for a quick fix and a higher grade. This is most spectacularly *not* the case. We're not there to "fix" papers; we're there to transform students into independent writers, so that they can go off to write independently, for their other classes, for college, for their eventual careers, and for their lives in general. It's very important work that we do in the writing center, so let's not minimize it.

The concept of "creating writers" rather than "fixing papers" will be a reliable guide as you train your tutors and develop your own writing center. And it will be a reliable guide to your tutors as they begin tutoring. As your tutors begin teaching students, they must always ask themselves this question: *will this help the student learn to write?* If the answer is "no," then they probably shouldn't be doing it.

In the next chapters, I will cover the fourth and final major component of the tutoring process: *Teaching*. I will go into greater detail about how to train your tutors, and I will describe effective tutoring techniques and how to help any student with any writing assignment. As you and your tutors embark on this adventure and compose the narrative of your writing center, I want you to keep something in mind, especially when things get difficult: you are pursuing a noble goal that will change students' lives. You are not fixing papers; you are creating writers. And in so doing, you are giving your students a lifelong gift of wonder and beauty.

Chapter 4

THE TUTORIAL: THE BIG THREE: TOPIC, FOCUS, ORGANIZATION

Remember the three major components of the tutorial that I described in the previous chapter? There is the *geography* of the tutorial (the magic triangle), the social *ice-breaker* (where students get to know each other a little bit), and the *interview* portion (where the tutor learns about the student's writing assignment). In this chapter, we are going to move from the interview portion to the final major component of the tutorial. I refer to this next component as the "Teaching" portion, and this is where the actual instruction takes place. And sometimes, original writing is generated here also. It's a great place to be. So, as you can see, there are four major parts to a writing tutorial:

1. Geography
2. Ice-Breaker
3. Interview
4. Teaching

And that's it. Look at that short list. Doesn't it have a nice feel to it? It's logical, it's doable, it's understandable. The teaching portion is, of course, an extremely important part of the tutorial. Although every part of the tutorial is indispensable and plays a necessary role in teaching students how to write, the teaching component is really the most important, because this is where the student's paper gets looked at, discussed, and improved. It is also where the student learns to write. From the student's point of view, it's the biggest money-maker. His vision, with regard to writing, will be naturally quite limited. His immediate concerns are improving the paper, finishing it, handing it in, and hoping for a decent grade. We're assisting with all these things, but really, we're teaching him how to write.

The instructional portion begins after the interview portion is completed. Once the tutor understands the assignment, she can then begin teaching the student. However, the tutor's next moves will depend on what the student brings with him. This is very simple, because the possibilities are quite limited. There are really only two things a student can bring to a tutorial:

1. He can bring a clear description of the assignment, and nothing else. This may be the teacher's handout, notes he generated during class, or a description from his memory. This is pretty common. In a case like this, the student has not started writing yet (he has no draft), so the tutor will help the student from "scratch."

2. He can bring an assignment description *and* a working draft that he has written. This is very common. In these cases, the tutor will help him revise the draft into successive drafts.

These two things are different and will require differing approaches by your tutors. Nevertheless, they are not as different as they might appear, because they are all part of the writing process, which is a sequential cycle. And once your tutors learn the entire process and understand it well, they will be able to teach any student who comes into the writing center, regardless of where he is in the cycle.

As you begin training your tutors, you should explain to them the *types* of papers they will encounter in the writing center, because this will affect how they conduct a tutorial. This is not very difficult, because (generally speaking) there are only five different types of writing projects in schools:

1. Personal Narrative: For example, "Describe a life-changing experience that you've had." This will be drawn from personal recollection or reasoning, and will not require research.

2. Informative Essay: Here, you will teach your reader about something (or someone) important, such as Nikola Tesla, the Amazon Rainforest, the Stock Market, the Civil War, etc. This will usually require research.

3. Analytical or Interpretive Essay: For example, describe and discuss the impact of social media on students' lives, or analyze the symbolism contained in *The Scarlet Letter*. This will usually require research or a primary text to analyze.

4. The Academic Argument (sometimes called the argumentative or persuasive essay): Here, you will discuss a controversial issue (such as school uniforms, climate change, etc.), *choose a side*, and then argue your point. This is often a formal research paper, but it can also be drawn solely from personal views.

5. Creative Writing: Here, you will compose a fictional piece, such as an original short story, poem, or play. You won't often encounter this in the writing center, but if you do, please hold a tutorial and talk to the student about his or her writing. This will not require research, unless the writer deems it necessary, for some reason.

When tutors learn the type of paper the student is writing, they can provide better assistance. For example, let's say a student is supposed to write an *argumentative* essay on climate change. *Is climate change really happening? And if so, are humans responsible for it?* However, he has begun writing an "informative" essay on the subject, merely defining and describing climate change. The informed tutor can spot this misunderstanding and help the student write an essay that addresses the task very precisely.

Once tutors can identify different types of papers, they can help their students write thesis statements. This is very important, so you'll need to train your tutors how to do this. It's not terribly difficult. First, what exactly is a *thesis*? A thesis is a central *idea* that drives a paper. A thesis *statement* is a sentence (or two) that says exactly and clearly what a paper is about. It's a fairly simple concept, but many students have trouble understanding and formulating thesis statements. Here's what I tell them: think of a thesis statement as *an answer to a question*. This means that *every paper a student writes is an answer to a question*. The question must be worth asking and must be designed to generate a meaningful paper. I call it the "essential question." Therefore, before creating a thesis statement, *the student must know what question he is attempting to answer*. Once he understands this (with the help of a tutor), he can begin formulating (again, with the help of a tutor) a viable and focused thesis statement. Let me give you some examples.

With regard to the five types of papers I listed earlier, we're most concerned with the first four (you won't often encounter creative projects in the writing center, and when you do, they won't need thesis statements). Here are some examples of essential questions and corresponding thesis statements for the first four types of papers.

1. Personal Narrative:
    a. Essential Question: What was a life-changing experience that had a great effect on you?
    b. Thesis Statement: Winning the state championship in soccer was a life-changing experience and had a huge effect on my life.

2. Informative Essay:
    a. Essential Question: What is the Amazon Rainforest, and why is it important?
    b. Thesis Statement: The Amazon Rainforest is in South America and contains a great diversity of plants and animals. It is important for many reasons.

3. Analytical or Interpretive Essay:
    a. Essential Question: What is the impact of social media on students' lives?
    b. Thesis Statement: Social media are ways that students can communicate with each other through the computer. There are many different types of social media, and these have had a great impact on most students' lives.

4. Academic Argument:
    a. Essential Question: Should middle (or high school) students be made to wear uniforms to school? Why or why not?
    b. Thesis Statement: Middle school students should not be made to wear school uniforms, and this is for a variety of reasons.

See how it goes? Writing good thesis statements is not too difficult. The keys are clarity and simplicity. If the essential question can't be answered in a simple sentence (or two), then the question probably needs to be revised and reconfigured.

Ideally, a thesis statement should be a single, simple sentence that is understandable, and should even sound "conversational" in nature. You should be able to speak it aloud and have others understand what you're talking about.

And where should the thesis statement be placed in an essay? Well, it goes in the introduction, of course. But within the intro, it usually goes in one of two places. The thesis statement can be the *very first sentence in the piece*. I encourage my own students to put it there (I love the honest simplicity), and this is what I often do in my own academic writing. However, some teachers prefer it to be the *last sentence in the introduction*. And if the teacher wants this, that's what we do. Both ways have their merits and are very effective if handled well.

So, when should the tutor help the student devise a thesis statement? There's really no right answer to this question. Sometimes the student will be passionate about a subject, and know what he wants to write about. He may believe deeply, for example, that "the voting age should be lowered," and he wants to write a powerful essay arguing this point. Other times, however, the thesis will emerge clearly as the student works on the paper. (Remember, as we write, and papers develop, we learn, we make discoveries, and the papers often begin making demands of us and "want" to be about a certain unanticipated topic.) But with or without a thesis, the tutor should commence the instructional portion of the tutorial with a consideration of *topic*.

Your instruction is geared toward a specific essay, so your tutoring pedagogy should spring from a well-conceived (or well-understood) *topic*, because that topic is the foundation of the student's essay. What is the essay about? If the student has written a draft, I ask him what the draft is about. If he has an assignment description but no draft, I ask him what the paper needs to be about. If he has choice, I ask him what he wants it to be about. And if he has nothing (no paper or knowledge), I tell him we need to find out what his paper is about.

In any case, I urge you to start the instructional portion with the issue of *topic* (I sometimes refer to this as "subject"). It's a big issue and is the foundation of any piece of writing. *What is the essay about?* And here, I want to give you the first rule of writing, and it's a masterpiece of simplicity: *every piece of writing must be about something*. You're probably saying to yourself "Well, of course; everyone knows that." Well, let me tell you, they *don't*. They definitely don't. Or they haven't thought of it in these clear and simple terms. And nobody taught me this either; I developed it through years of studying, writing, and teaching. This is a gem of knowledge that, while appearing to be simple, is crucial to producing a meaningful piece of writing. When you explain this to your students (and your tutors), you're giving them a bit of wisdom that will assist all of their writing. Trust me on that one. And I keep this in mind during all of my own writing. For example, what is this book about? *It's about helping school librarians create their own school library writing centers*. Period. One thing, one tidy sentence. I may digress at times, but ultimately everything here is related to creating writing centers (or the act of writing, which is part of the main topic).

But let's take this "simple" idea one step further: *every piece of writing must really be about one thing, and one thing only*. When you read a nonfiction book, or a newspaper article, ask yourself what it's about. Try to isolate the main subject, and you will nearly always come up with one central topic. And if you don't come up with one thing, that means the article is lacking focus (which is a problem) or you haven't read it carefully enough.

Reinforce to your students that every piece of writing needs to be about a single and clearly specified subject, because most of them won't know this. I remember, when I was tutoring in the St. John's University writing center, when I was new and developing experience, students would often bring me a draft they had written. They would put it on the table, and, to start the tutorial, one of the first questions I would ask (quite casually) was, "What's your paper about?" And the students would pick up the piece they had written and start reading the first few sentences. I remember thinking this seemed a bit odd to me. Something wasn't right. This didn't tell me what the piece was about, and it gave me no clue as to their interaction with the paper or the subject. So I changed my approach.

The next time, I turned the paper over—physically turned it over on the table, so that we were looking at the blank back page—and I asked "What is this piece about?" And they would pick the piece up, turn it over, and start reading me the first few sentences. *Hmmm*, I thought. *Interesting.* I went home and thought some more about this. Why were they doing this? Why couldn't they talk about something they had just written? Why did they always start reading their paper to me? I could easily read it myself. Once again, I changed my approach.

The next time, I turned the piece over, and *put my hands firmly on it*, palms down, in a "don't touch this" gesture. I smiled at them (a bit mischievously, I suppose), and asked "What is this piece about?" And you know what they said to me, most of the time? It was shocking, really. Over and over, student after student looked at me and said this: "I don't know."

Think about that. I was astounded. I never forgot it, and it changed my entire approach toward tutoring. These were bright university students, who had been working diligently on a paper, and *they couldn't tell me what the paper was about.* And the reason was because they didn't really *know* what the paper was about. They were writing blindly, flailing in the dark, on some subject related to the course, but there was no actual interaction with the material, no relationship with it, no true comprehension, and no new knowledge generated (in the student's mind *or* on the paper). And there was an unspoken hope that if they wrote enough, they might say the right thing and receive a passable grade. This is an awfully lonely and frustrating place to be. You compose a paper, you don't know what it's really about, you don't learn anything, and so, at the end, you can't possibly feel proud. There's no payoff when the paper is completed, except for relief that this strange and unpleasant task is now complete.

For me, this was a profound revelation and was an insight into how deeply students need clear and simple writing instruction. They *need* it. We can't assume that they know anything about writing correctly. So to every single student I teach—every single one—I say, "Every paper needs to be about something." And I let that sink in. It's a wonderful bit of information to know and helps make sense of the entire process of writing and the reasons why human beings engage in the difficult task of writing in the first place. It's understandable, and students love hearing this simple bit of wisdom. They get it. When I see the light go on (the eyes have it), I mention Part Two of that statement: "And every piece of writing should really be about one specific thing . . . and one thing only." And I let that sink in also.

As you help your students find and develop their topics, please keep in mind the assignment and what it calls for (which you learned during the Interview portion). *The essay topic must be aligned with the assignment description.* This is simple, but it's extremely important, and it's deceptively easy to make a crucial mistake here. For example, let's say your student brings you a draft. You must read it and ask yourself "What is this about?" and the follow-up question "Does this topic fit the assignment description?" By now, these probably seem like no-brainers. However, let's say this particular assignment requires students to write about the theme of "dreams" or "loneliness" in Steinbeck's *Of Mice and Men*. However, the student has written an essay on the Great Depression, or she has written a biography of John Steinbeck. If this happens, then the student must start over, no matter how good the essay is. And you must explain this to the student. As you read each piece, try to determine what it is about *and* if it is addressing the assignment description. As usual in the world of writing, however, this is a bit more involved than it sounds. Let's consider another example.

Let's say that another student brings you a different essay. The required topic of this essay is a history and description of the Globe Theatre. This means that the essay must be about the Globe Theatre; there is no question about that. As you read the essay, you notice that the student does include information on the Globe Theatre, but the majority of the essay is on the life of Shakespeare, with another substantial section a summary of *Macbeth* (which the student has recently read). In this case, we have a student (and an essay) that doesn't know what it is about. Is it about the Globe Theatre? Is it about Shakespeare? Is it about *Macbeth*? It is addressing the assignment description *only partially*, and it is lacking focus (a grievous sin in academic writing which I will talk about later). These are problems, and you must help the student align her essay with the assignment description.

This sort of thing is very common and is usually born of a fear of "not having enough to say." The student believes *I can't possibly write a three page paper on the Globe Theatre. I don't know enough to write for three pages!* For the student, generating writing is extremely difficult, and three pages seem like three light-years. He freezes and simply does not know what to say. In reality, students have a great deal to say, certainly enough for a three-page paper. And they can buttress this with academic research. They won't know how to do these things, of course, but that's what the writing center is for. We're there to teach all aspects of writing.

At times, you (and your tutors) will need great and sensitive insight into helping students discover what their essays are (and should be) about. Some assignments are quite open-ended and will allow the student to choose a topic for the essay. If a student brings a draft for which he chose the topic, again try to determine what the essay *is* about, and what it *needs* to be about (and these are two different things). In cases like this, it's a bit more complicated than it sounds, because very often the student thinks the essay is about one thing, while the essay "wants" to be about something else. And that "something else" is often a better and more meaningful topic.

I once assisted a student with his college application essay. The prompt was rather generic, something like "Tell us about yourself." The student wanted to go into business, and his essay read like a resume. *I had this summer job; I had that part-time job; I took these courses; I hope to do such-n-such*. It was flat and uninspiring. But I noticed something. There were a few spots of interest in his piece. Dr. Ahrens used to refer to these as "hot spots," and nearly every piece of writing has a few. In several places, this student referred to his father. His father was a successful businessman, and he respected his father tremendously. He worked with his father at times, doing different things, and accompanied him on several business trips to interesting places. And at one point in his essay, he indicated that he admired his father, and that he hoped that he too could be a success. Just like his father.

Bingo.

Here was the "soul" of his essay, and its true topic. This essay was not about the student's background or his experience (which, by nature, is going to be rather dull). It was about his relationship with his father. It's human, it's meaningful, it's interesting, it's universal. Virtually every person on the planet has some sort of experience or interest in the parent–child relationship. And in the student's essay, this human drama was playing out against a backdrop of business. It was perfect subject matter, and I pointed this out to the student. Of course, he was interested, and a little surprised. It was as if his subconscious had bubbled to the surface, demanding to be heard. And I think this is pretty close to the truth, more often than we realize—especially when we're writing. (I have a theory that when we do our best writing—especially when we write fiction—we're using the same part of our brain that generates our sleeping dreams. Our conscious thinking shuts down, and we begin to "dream" our stories, our thinking, our writing. So of *course* it's going to be imaginative and true to our deepest feelings and fears.) So this student's essay wanted to be about a father–son relationship. I explained this to him, and I worked with him over successive tutorials, probing, asking questions, offering suggestions, and the finished project was wonderful—scholarly, interesting, meaningful, poignant, and deeply human. It was a tremendous success.

But let's consider yet another variation of this. Let's say the student comes to the writing center and has to write some sort of essay in which he has substantial choice. He will usually show up with a vague idea which he thinks the teacher will "like," or he has absolutely no idea what he wants to write about. When this happens, I try to help the student find a topic. "The topic is there," I tell him, "floating around; our job is to find it." Another abstract idea, akin to Michelangelo believing his sculptures were already inside blocks of marble, and his job was merely to release them. It's just one way of looking at things. But I will say this: when we find the topic, we know it. It feels right to the student, and to the tutor.

In helping students find topics, I always look for a balance between academic viability and personal interest. This puts us at the start of the writing process, which is a good place to be.

So the student and I engage in something called "brainstorming." Brainstorming is a very important early step in the writing process, and you will use it during many tutorials. When the writing topic is not specified, brainstorming will often be the first step in commencing the teaching portion of the tutorial. It's very important, and to do it well is difficult. It requires sensitivity, skill, observation, and, above all, deep listening. We're not *telling* the student what to write about; we're helping him choose a suitable topic for his essay. We're leading him on a process of discovery. It's always best if the student arrives organically at his own essay topic; we're just there to coax it out of him. Here's how I do it.

Armed with my lined paper and pencils, I begin to ask him probing questions, and I jot down his answers. These are designed to get a sense of him as a person. Who is this student, really? What is different or interesting about him? What are his likes and dislikes? When we know these things, we can usually help the student find a topic which he likes, which interests him, and which is academically viable. Here are some of the questions I ask:

> *What is your favorite subject in school?*
> *What is your best subject? In which subject do you get the highest grades?*
> *Do you belong to any clubs, or groups, or sports in school?*
> *What do you want to be when you grow up?*
> *What are your favorite things to do?*
> *Do you have any hobbies?*
> *What is your favorite book? What did you like about it?*
> *What did you do this past summer?*
> *What will you be doing this next summer?*
> *Do you have a "dream," or some sort of goal you want to accomplish in life?*
> *Etc.* Things like that.

At this point, you may be thinking this looks similar to the Interview portion. Well it is, and it isn't. Both components involve asking probing questions for the purpose of gaining information to teach your student how to write. However, please note that the interview involves getting information on the *assignment*, while brainstorming involves getting information on the *student*, in order to help him select a topic. The methods are the same, but the goals are different, and the focus is narrower and more personal. Nevertheless, brainstorming takes place after the interview, so, at times, these two components may blend seamlessly into one another. That's okay. If this happens during your conversation, let it. When a tutorial begins to exhibit its own organic energy, and it seems productive and on-target, go with it, see where it leads you. It's common to piggyback brainstorming on top of the Interview.

As I brainstorm with the student and ask questions, I jot down the answers (along with my thoughts and observations), and, above all, I *listen* to the student. Let your students talk, and listen to what they say. And, based on his answers and reactions, sometimes these questions lead to other, more revealing questions, which lead to revealing answers. I do this, I take my time, and after a few minutes, a pretty clear picture begins to form on the page. It's magical process, and I love this part of the tutorial. I start to get a sense of who the student really his, his likes and dislikes, his passions, his interests and dreams. I am always, *always* able to come up with a topic of interest to the student. Whenever the student is allowed choice, it's very important that he choose something that he likes, or is interested in. When he has some personal involvement with the topic he's writing about, he will learn more, enjoy the process, write better, and generate a more interesting essay.

And now I want you to take a deep breath. I have been giving you a lot of information in this chapter, and I want it all to sink in. So at this point, you may wish to take a break, because I'm getting to something extremely important. Remember, this long and meandering discussion has ultimately been about the instructional portion of the writing center tutorial. We have now arrived at the point where we look at the student's draft. You will be doing a great deal of this in the writing center, so I want you to understand it thoroughly and deeply. It's a beautiful dance. You will develop a feel for this process, and I challenge you to fall in love with it. This is where you will help a great many students, directly, immediately, and more than you can imagine. You will be doing this a lot, and it is, arguably, the single most important thing you and your tutors will do in the writing center.

You will be reading and critiquing drafts for every student who comes (more than once) to the writing center. Whether you help a student get started with a first draft, or whether he brings a first draft with him to the writing center, you will be reading his work. Every student who comes to the writing center will be producing original writing (under your tutelage), and you will be taking him through successive drafts and revisions. This is an inescapable part of the writing process and is built into writing center instruction. However, it has been my experience that most students come to the writing center with a draft already completed. These students are usually sheepish, and the drafts are usually a mess. And so, as a tutor, what do you do? You read his draft, interact with what he has written, talk to the student, and offer critique and suggestions for improvement. And you make lots of notes on his draft, which he will look at later.

Picture the scene. You're sitting there, with the draft on the table in front of you. You have your lined paper on the table, and pencil in hand, ready to do business. The student is seated next to you, expecting you to give him solid direction and guidance. But what exactly do you do? And what if it is badly written, as it probably will be? Here's what you do: have fun, enjoy, discuss the draft, and teach your student how to write. Working on messy drafts is one of the areas in which the writing center shines brightest, and it is where you and your tutors will do your best (and most appreciated) work. But to do this well requires an understanding of students and what's going on in their minds. I suppose some would call this adolescent psychology, but I just think of it as trying to understand students and where they're coming from. If you do this, you'll connect better with students, and they'll learn more, and you'll both have a pretty good time.

As you perform the tutorial, try to understand the experience from the student's point of view. When you (and your tutors) are dealing with a student's draft (reading it and critiquing it), keep in mind that *how* the tutor approaches the draft is extremely important. At all times, she must treat it with respect, no matter how poorly written it is. And she mustn't let the student know that his piece is weak, because that would be a great discouragement. It will take time and experience for you and your tutors to get really comfortable and adept at handling students' work, but don't lose heart; you'll grow into the position. But I'm here to help get you started on your journey, and if you do the things I describe here, you'll do a wonderful job right from the beginning. Listen closely and read carefully, because I'm about to divulge all my secrets. Here's how it works.

When the student brings a draft to a tutorial, the tutor will look at it and make suggestions for improvement. The draft becomes the focus of the tutorial, at least for a time. But understand that when the student hands his draft to a tutor, he will be very nervous. It's a reluctant act of trust. He knows he's not a good writer. He's worried about being embarrassed, about looking "dumb" in front of a peer (or you), and about having another student (or you) think poorly of him. I have heard this from many students, and I always explain this to my tutors. We're all human and fragile. We are stung by insults and hurt by slights (adults included), and tutors must be very sensitive to the act of trust that is occurring during writing center tutorials. So I give them some very important instruction on this topic. You will do well to remember this and to implement it also. Get ready, because this is important. I always tell them this: "When you start reading the student's draft, give the piece of writing some *compliments*. And do it soon. No matter how bad it is, give it some compliments."

As you read the piece, don't leave the student sitting there as if he's on trial (because this is how he'll feel). This is an extremely important (and useful) bit of advice, so please burnish it into your heart and pass it along to your tutors. I give compliments all the time when I'm tutoring, and you wouldn't believe the relief it generates and the shy smiles it draws. *Oh wow, maybe it's not so bad, after all. Maybe I'm not such an idiot.* Please give compliments. Please. Your students will thrive on these.

When devising compliments, I usually look for something specific. I point to a certain passage and say something like "I really like what you say here," or "You make a really good point here," or "This is a great description." If I can't find anything specific, my compliments are always more general in nature: "Okay, it looks like you're off to a great start," or "This is going to be a really interesting essay," or "This is really good for a first draft. I can't wait to see where you go with this." The students immediately become happier and more motivated, their levels of confidence and interaction go up, and we increase the likelihood of repeat visits. Compliments are a very powerful technique in the writing center.

But what exactly does the tutor do with the written draft? He reads it in front of the student, compliments it, talks about it, asks questions about it, and makes notes on it (in pencil). You and your tutors must do all of these things during every tutorial.

However, the notes are most important for the student, because he'll be depending on them later. And here, I want to be very clear about something. Writing center tutorials generate two different kinds of notes, and both kinds are extremely important. There are the notes that you will be writing (in pencil) on lined paper. These are generated most often during early tutorials, and they involve information-gathering and planning (the interview, brainstorming, miscellaneous notes about the assignment, etc.).

The other type of notes comes later, after the student has written a draft (or two, or three). You will read his draft and write notes directly on the draft. In pencil. These notes are also extremely important and will form the basis for corrections, editing, and successive drafts. The student will be depending on these notes, so they must be clear, simple, and effective. For the student, these notes are a lifejacket in an ocean of uncertainty. However, before writing on a student's draft, always, always ask "Can I write on this?" This shows respect for the student (and his work), and the answer will always be an enthusiastic "*Yes*," because the student knows he needs them. So again, when you look at a student's essay and offer suggestions for improvement, *always make clear and understandable notes*. Always. This is new and difficult information for the student, and he will simply not remember what you tell him.

When going over an essay, some tutors ask students to read their work aloud. Don't do it. This is a mistake. The student is very self-conscious about his work, believing (perhaps rightly so) that it is substandard. Being "forced" to read his paper aloud will be a humiliating experience for the student, and we'll lose him. He'll never come back to the writing center.

So you will sit there and read the piece, line by line, with your pencil in your hand, complimenting the piece, discussing it, making notes, and asking questions. And here I want to reinforce an important point that I have made several times before. You are teaching writing, but the piece is the *vehicle* through which you teach writing. The piece will definitely improve, but the important thing is that the student learns to write. So as you make suggestions for improvement, always explain to the student what you are doing and why you are doing it. And make sure you always explain to the student that your notes are *suggestions*, and he is free to implement them or to disregard them. It is *his* essay, exclusively.

But I can feel you growing impatient. You're thinking "I'm a librarian, not a writing teacher. What, *exactly*, do I (and my tutors) *do*?" Not to worry, I'm getting to that right now. First, read through the piece with a pencil in your hand. On that first read-through, you may wish to make notes on the piece, or you may wish to simply read through, ask questions, and see what's there. It's up to you and the piece of writing. And here's another very important suggestion that you really need to implement, especially during those early sessions, when you are reading a draft for the first time.

When you first look at a draft, you need to commence your instruction by focusing on the "big" things. In early tutorials, you should ignore such "small" issues as grammar, punctuation, spelling, and "mechanics"; you'll get to these later. This is a stupendously important principle, so I'm going to say it again: *start by looking at big things first*. And by big things, I am referring specifically to these three elements, which I call the "Big Three":

1. Topic
2. Focus
3. Organization

When the Big Three have been adequately addressed, you will proceed with subsequent tutorials and successive drafts, and you will work increasingly on the "smaller" things, such as development of ideas, transitions, grammar, punctuation, spelling, word choice, clarity of language, sentence length, etc. It's sort of like walking in a funnel, toward an end that gets increasingly narrow and polished. Or, to resurrect a metaphor that I used earlier, imagine Michelangelo chiseling a sculpture out of marble. He started with the general shape of the figure, and worked on increasingly finer details the closer he drew toward completion—strands of hair, fingernails, irises. And last, he polished the marble to a magnificent, shining luster—a procession from big to small. Do the same thing in your tutorials.

If you look at my list of the Big Three, you'll see that the first thing on the list is "Topic." This is the biggest issue. It's where you help the student select an appropriate subject for his essay, and I already covered this earlier in pretty good detail. So let's assume now that the student has chosen a good topic for his essay, and you are reading the first draft that he composed for it. At this point, you're going to start looking at focus and organization. Look at focus first, because it's bigger than organization, and *we're proceeding from bigger to smaller.*

Focus is closely related to topic. In simplest terms, focus means that the writer chooses a topic to write about, and then *sticks to that topic, and nothing else.* And that's it. Remember how I said earlier that the essay must be about "one thing, and one thing only?" Sticking to one topic will yield a focused essay, and this is a good thing, so the writer should keep focus in mind as he composes. With everything he writes, he should be wondering "Is this somehow related to my central topic?" If it's not, it should probably be omitted. Keeping an essay focused on one central topic is good for two basic reasons. Most young people aren't used to considering issues in their full depth and complexity, especially when those things are academic in nature or are outside the range of their normal experiences or interests. Writing focused essays is a way of introducing the complexity of the world to students, of peeling back that first layer of appearance, and seeing what lies beneath. But focus is also good for the reader. When people choose to read, it's really for only two purposes: to enjoy themselves or to learn something (or, ideally, both at the same time). Focus helps with both of these things. By sticking to one subject and developing it thoroughly, the writer prevents confusion in the mind of the reader and enhances comprehension and enjoyability.

And this brings us to the third member of the Big Three, and that's *organization.* Every piece of writing must be organized clearly and logically. This way, the reader can follow the writer's line of thought and the development of his ideas. And just as focus is the single-minded child of topic, organization is the ordered sibling of focus. As you can see, the Big Three are all related to one another. There are no firm lines of demarcation among the three; they all blend into one another and do different (but important) jobs. When the writer pays attention to all three, it renders essays readable, understandable, and enjoyable and helps to prevent confusion in the mind of the reader. But employing organization is good for the student-writer also. It teaches him to organize his thoughts, to think clearly, to develop ideas, and to approach complex issues thoughtfully and methodically. Those are the benefits of organization. Now, what exactly is it?

To put it simply, organization refers basically to two things: the *content* that is chosen for a piece, and the *order* in which it is presented. When a writer chooses a major topic for his essay, he must naturally choose supporting materials to help explain his subject. These are often in the form of examples, explanations to the reader, or illustrative anecdotes. I refer to these as "subtopics." I am getting to something quite elemental here, and extremely important with regard to writing essays. And indeed, this is the solution for students who are plagued by the horror of not knowing what to say, which results in the practice of inflating essays with insipid padding. Students have a certain term for this practice, but I won't use it here. You can probably guess what it is.

I really want you to understand this, so I'll explain it as methodically as I can, by using concrete examples. Organization is the inclusion, progression (or order), and development of ideas in an essay. When you choose the major topic of your essay, you should immediately begin thinking of related examples, or *subtopics*, that you will use to help explain your topic, and introduce it to your readers. And I suggest trying to come up with *three* examples. I call this the "Rule of Three," and it's an extremely effective method.

Whenever I approach any sort of academic writing, I immediately think in terms of the number *three*. Three is the minimum number needed to examine any topic in reasonable depth and is a manageable (but thorough) number for middle and high school students to use. When I explain this to students (or tutors), I tell them that "one is an example, two is a pair, three is a *pattern*." I have used the Rule of Three with my students (and myself) in a multitude of papers, and it is always successful. However, keep in mind that, like all things associated with writing, the number three is not absolute. Like the outline (which I'll discuss in the next chapter), it is intended as a guide and is a way to ensure that a topic is explored in a reasonable depth. And as you read this book, you will see the number three many times. And this is not an accident.

Now, what exactly are subtopics? They are just what their name implies: they are the smaller offshoots of a larger topic, relevant representatives of smaller categories of that topic. For example, let's say a student is writing a paper on the solar system. There are bunch of subtopics that would work well here, but here are three good ones: *the sun, the planets, their satellites.* That would provide an interesting and informative paper. Or suppose the student has to write a paper on the desert environment. Possible subtopics could be drawn from the following list: a definition (and characteristics) of "desert," different types of deserts, different deserts around the world, desert-dwelling societies, oases, animals that live in the desert, plants that live in the desert, rain patterns in deserts. You'll note here that I gave you eight subtopics. You can either pick your favorite three, or, if you want a longer and more thorough paper, you can use as many as you want. They're all good subtopics and will teach the writer (and reader) about deserts.

When choosing your subtopics, always try to make them relevant and interesting. They should be related to your topic, they should be "good" choices, interesting to read, offered in appropriate amounts (not too long and not too short), and presented in a logical order. I know that sounds difficult, like juggling five beanbags, but it's really not too difficult. Most of it involves research, imagination, and good old common sense. Let me give you a very simple example.

Let's say a student has to write a three-page biography of Thomas Edison, and that he is required to use research. So we have a clearly defined topic: *Edison*. And if he writes about Edison and nothing else, his paper will be *focused*. So far, so good. But now we need to start thinking about *organization*. This means the writer needs to choose appropriate subtopics about Edison and then present them in a logical order. So the student needs to do some research, and he needs to read his sources.

Of course, the writing center should help the student with his research (because our students don't know how to do it). This is a crucial step in the writing process (and a valuable teachable moment), and we shouldn't miss it. The tutor will show the student how to do research, and together, they will locate and pull about three biographies on Edison (print, online, or both). When it comes to research, three is a good number, as it provides reasonable depth. We then direct the student to read his sources and to underline (or highlight) interesting passages in each. And he comes back to the writing center the next day, with his sources highlighted in yellow (and earns a nice compliment for working so hard). So what does he do now? How does he weave this information into an essay?

Here's what he should do (with the assistance of the tutor). And this is what I always tell my students and my tutors: start by thinking in simple terms. Try to pull out (or decide upon) *three subtopics* that are simple and concrete, and let common sense be your guide. In this case, we might encourage the fledgling writer to choose these for his subtopics:

1. Edison's early life (birth through teen years)
2. Edison's middle life (young adulthood through middle age)
3. Edison's later life (middle age through elder years, up to his death)

See how easy that is? It's clear, and the organization is *chronological*, which readers can follow intuitively. It's very simple. This would yield a competent essay that would be, in many respects, a summary of the writer's sources. There is nothing inspiring or interesting here (in terms of its construction), but if it's done well, the writer would learn a bit about Edison, a bit about writing, and probably receive a decent grade.

But let's take it a step further. What if we got a bit more ambitious and challenged the writer to increase the complexity of his simple essay? In order to write a better and more meaningful essay, we might include the element of *evaluation*, which will allow the student to generate some original thought and original writing. Original thought is always a fantastic goal for a writer to pursue. With our help, the student might generate the following three subtopics:

1. Brief biography of Edison (presented chronologically, from birth to death)
2. Edison's most important inventions (choose and discuss about *three* of them)
3. Edison's death and legacy (how do his inventions impact our lives today?)

This will yield a better and more meaningful essay. It will challenge the student to interact with his material, to think about things, to evaluate knowledge, to think inferentially, and to reach his own conclusions. Through writing an essay of this nature, he will learn much more—not just about Edison, but also about thinking and writing. An essay of this nature will be more interesting (to him and to his reader), and it will certainly be much more original than its earlier chronological (and summative) counterpart.

However, please note how both essays are organized with a beautiful simplicity and are designed with common sense. When a student understands this, organizing essays will become very easy. Think of it as giving three simple directives to your students:

1. Choose a major topic for your essay.
2. Stick to your major topic and write about nothing else (this will keep your essay focused).
3. Choose three large subtopics that are related directly to your major topic (this will keep your essay organized).

As you guide your students in becoming writers, tell them to always keep things simple and *human*. Essays are written by humans, for humans. Don't be dazzled, confused, or bamboozled by tangles of flashy details. Urge your students to keep their writing simple, understandable, and doable. When it comes to choosing subtopics, tell them to go for elements that are simple, concrete, and "chunky" (I like that word). If something is *chunky*, the student can grab it and understand it and write about it. For fledgling writers, the road to completion is paved with simplicity.

Now, let's look at a more difficult example. Let's say that I had to write an essay on an *idea*, such as "Education." Write about an *idea*. It sounds so dry and dusty, doesn't it? I mean, where can we possibly go with this? It's an important topic, of course, but what student would find it interesting? Most students aren't really jazzed about "Education." Also, this topic is intangible, like a puff of smoke, and the prospect of writing an essay on this would be a nightmare for most young students. What would they do? They would undoubtedly engage in such safe platitudes as "Education is great, it teaches you about history and the world. It's interesting to learn new things." And a few more tortured sentences, until they quickly run out of steam. And then they sit there, staring at the computer screen, in utter misery, wondering what to say. It's a terrible place to be. So how would we direct the students to plan, start, and complete a difficult essay of this nature? An essay on an abstract *idea*? And is there a way to make this interesting to them, as well as to the reader?

If I were given this essay, here's what *I* would do.

I would immediately search for three concrete, chunky subtopics, related to Education. Concrete means it exists in the real world. Chunky means one can grab it or see it or talk about it. Here are some groups of three subtopics that would work for an essay on Education: books, teachers, schools; middle school, high school, college; Math, Science, English; reading, writing, technology; bachelor's, master's, doctorate; and so on. See how easy it is to grab three chunky topics for an essay?

Always try to anchor your discussions to concrete entities in the real world. People can understand real-world references and can usually identify with them.

But if I were writing this essay, I would base it on my own life and my own experiences, and use those as a springboard into larger and more universal discussions on the topic (I talk about my own experiences a lot, because there's nothing in the world that I know as well). We're all experts on ourselves and our lives, and we find ourselves endlessly fascinating (or we should). I think this egocentricity is forgivable (we're all human), and it can certainly improve (and provide material for) our writing. If you're interested in your subject, then your reader probably will be also. And the reverse is true, in most spectacular fashion: if you're bored by what you're writing, don't even ask about the reader; he's already snoring.

In choosing "personal" subtopics for this hypothetical essay on Education, I would try to be surprising, interesting, and deeply human in my choices. People like encountering the undeniably human when they read. It makes us feel less lonely in the universe to know that there are others like us who think, feel, and experience the same things we do. As I chose my topics, however, I would be careful to stay close to my major topic, which, in this case, is Education. Having given it some thought, my subtopics for this hypothetical essay would probably be these:

1. *Being taught by my parents as a very young child.* My father teaching me to swim, by tossing his gold watch into the deep end of the pool, and me swimming down to get it, thrilled to hold it up, dripping and shining in the morning sun, and him smiling at me. "Good job!" he said. "You did it!" When I'm a teenager, he teaches me good carpentry. My mother consoling me after the death of a beloved dog and explaining to me that it's part of life. And it's supposed to hurt, real, real bad. For a long, long time. Maybe even forever. And how we'll never forget him. And oh, how I still miss him. So, so much.

2. *My formal education.* College and making new friends. Studying in Europe, and falling in love. We walk the canals of Venice, holding hands, and whispering to each other. The city of Venice is a glimmering movie set, and nothing is real in the shimmering dusk. Our first kiss is very late at night, by a deserted canal, while moonlight dances the water. In one year, she will break my heart. Later, it's grad school, and studying 12 hours a day. Exploring the beauties and mysteries of literature, a doctoral thesis on Shakespeare.

3. *Life experience.* The military. Work and career. Marriage and divorce. Starting over in my thirties, buying a log cabin on a lake, and doing all the carpentry myself. I build a library in my house. A new girlfriend. A knowledge of broken hearts (they never really heal, despite what you've heard. But you can still find happiness). A rumination on the beauties of formal education, and the unmercies of life experience. A conclusion that life and school are not incompatible (despite what you've heard). Both are necessary to understand the world, and our roles in it, just a little bit.

That's how I would do it. (And now you know a little more about me. As you've chosen to spend this time with me, I think that's okay.)

But students don't have the benefit of life experience, so how might we direct a student to write an essay like this? Here is your first practical application; think of this as an exercise. But I'm not grading you.

Ready? Deep breath.

Let's say you have a student sitting in front of you. Her name is Emily. She is a fictitious (but realistic) compilation of many students I've helped in the writing center (and I named her after one of my favorite poets, Emily Dickinson). Emily is a nice kid. She's very polite and a little shy; she has dark hair and wears glasses and has braces, and she has to write an essay on Education. And she's lost; she has no idea what to do. Your job (as tutor) is to help her locate (about) three subtopics for her essay and to assure her that she can do it. These subtopics (you tell her) must be related to the main topic (Education). They should also be concrete, meaningful, and (ideally) somewhat interesting to the writer, and to her reader (which is her teacher). And they need to be presented in a logical order. Toward which subtopics would you guide our Emily? And in what order should she present them? Take a minute and think about it. And then jot down your answers (preferably, my dear reader, in pencil, on lined paper). Take your time, and think clearly and logically. And don't worry, this isn't graded. Do this now, and come back when you are finished. And no peeking at my answers below. Go.

I'm here. I'm waiting for you. Take your time.

Well? Did you come up with any subtopics? Was it difficult? If so, then you're probably overthinking it. Remember, keep it simple and human, and listen to your inner, friendly voice of common sense. Personally, I would probably guide Emily toward these three subtopics:

1. Describe several (perhaps 3) things that your parents taught you.
2. What is your favorite subject in school? Why is it your favorite?
3. What do you want to be when you grow up? What education is required for this job?

Note how each topic is concrete and chunky and is part of the Emily's world. She can grab ahold of each, and talk about it, because she understands it. She also finds these topics meaningful and interesting. Look at what we have here: parents, school, and future career (notice that it's not terribly different from my own hypothetical essay about Education). What could be better than anchoring an abstract essay to concrete elements in a student's life? Every student has some interest and experience in these things and will enjoy (to some extent) writing about them. Also note the order in which I placed them:

1. Parents (her first teachers)
2. School (her present state)
3. Career (her future)

Thus we have a simple, (chrono)logical organization: *past, present*, and *future*. It's understandable, and it makes sense. How did you do with the exercise above? Don't worry if you had a tough time with it; this takes practice. Keep going; you will definitely develop a feel for it. And don't forget our Emily; we'll continue helping her in the next chapter.

I've given you a lot of information here, and this chapter's getting a bit long. So this seems like a good place to take a break. Go and do something fun, maybe take a walk, and think about the stuff we just covered. When you come back, I'm going to present you with something that you and your tutors will rely upon and use over and over. It's humble and it's beautiful and you've known this thing all your life. And now, dear readers, I urge you to embrace it, and I challenge you to fall in love with it.

Chapter 5

THE TUTORIAL: THE BLUEPRINT AND THE LIMESTONE

The first year of my writing center, I was training that initial group of pioneering tutors when one of them asked a simple but important question. This student (I'll call her "Taylor") put up her hand and asked "What if we're looking at a paper, and it's just completely messed up?" It was a great question, insightful and prescient, because many of the drafts they'll look at will indeed be "completely messed up."

I nodded my head and smiled. It was a light bulb flash for all of us, a terrific teachable moment that I utilize to this day. I abandoned my plans and gave my tutors an extremely powerful and pragmatic instructional technique that I knew they'd be using all the time. I stuck some blank poster paper at the front of the room, and, with the help of a black magic marker, I began teaching them the simple beauties of the *five-part outline*.

This is what I was hinting at in the last few lines of Chapter Four: the outline. It is a fantastic technique that you and your tutors will use for virtually every student who comes to the writing center.

The outline model I use isn't the traditional "five-paragraph essay" (which you may have heard of); it's a five-*part* outline. This means that it's composed of five major parts, which *may or may not become paragraphs*. I had developed (and used) this outline format while tutoring university students, so I knew that it works extremely well. And one of its strongest attributes is this: it can be *expanded or contracted* to suit the abilities and needs of the student and the assignment. It's a great way to organize information and to get started, and it gives fledgling writers a powerful framework on which to hang thoughts and ideas. Properly implemented, it will teach students the structure of the academic essay, and will assist greatly with focus and organization. It will allow them to compose an essay that is basic in structure, but thorough in scope.

I have met some teachers of composition who don't like outlines, believing that their structure is too rigid, that it squashes creativity, and that it stuffs original compositions into something analogous to a cookie cutter. And I understand their concerns. But the outline I conceived, and the way I implement it, is very different. The method I developed allows for (and respects) the fluidity in the composition process. As the student writes, he will make discoveries, draw conclusions, get inspired, and realize he knows things that he didn't know he knew. So a "paragraph" on a topic may turn into several paragraphs on the same topic. And he may decide to include another topic (or two), which will turn his essay into a six (or seven)-part (or paragraph) essay. And this fluidity is my favorite thing about it, because, although it's an outline, it allows for expansion and great creativity.

But along with room for creativity and discovery, my method also includes a great deal of structure, and this is really the best thing about outlines. Remember, when students come to you, they will have no idea how to write an essay. Their thinking will be disorganized and confused, their thoughts and ideas a swirling tangle of chaos. Their minds are a tornado of ideas, and some of these ideas are good, and some are bad. And none is organized. And this leads us to the big secret of outlines: *they impose order and structure onto a student's disordered thoughts*. Order and structure. These are good things, and very necessary. Think of it from a student's point of view. *What should my paper look like? How do I start?* The possibilities are literally infinite. An essay can take a multitude of shapes, and this is one of the essay's greatest challenges. It's a vast blank canvas. And, like Hamlet, the student will be frozen into inaction, unsure of what to do, or what steps to take. Give him an outline.

By helping students construct an outline, you are organizing their thoughts—swirling, chaotic, incomplete—into a structure that is clear and manageable. Capture the tornado, and put it in a bottle so it can be viewed and studied and developed. You are imposing order onto disorder and giving their thoughts a clearly defined form. Initially, the outline will be imperfect and inchoate, but it will be something to look at and work with, something to alter and improve. It's a codified and concrete starting place; there it is on the lined paper, right in front of him. *Look at the outline. What's working? What's not working? What's missing? Let's adjust it until you like it. It seems to be shaping up nicely*. And the tutor offers guidance, suggestions, and leading questions the entire time.

And now, I want to take you back in time. Come with me. I want to put us both in that room, several years ago, when I was training my tutors after school, when I began teaching them the spartan beauties of the five-part outline. See the tutors, tired but eager learners. See the blank poster paper, stuck to the whiteboard with masking tape. See me standing there, tired but happy, with a magic marker in my hand. I'm talking to my tutors, and I'm going to teach them about constructing outlines with their students. And you're standing in the back, listening carefully, and maybe you're taking notes. Part of this will be me speaking to my tutors on that day; part of this will be me speaking to you now. Here's what I said that day:

"Okay, Taylor had a great question. You're going to see lots of papers that are really messed up, so one way to help these students will be to organize their ideas in the form of an outline. But I have a specific outline that works really well for the writing center, and I call it the Five-Part Outline. And one of the best parts of this outline is this: *it works whether or not the student has written a draft.*" I pause and let this sink in.

This may seem complicated, but really it's very simple, and I explain it to my tutors. If the student has not yet started writing, the outline is a *planning* tool and becomes a map for her to follow. However, if the student has written a draft, the outline works like a miracle. The tutors will read the draft, make notes on it, and determine what's working and what's not. They will then (re)organize the material onto an outline by putting in the good stuff and discarding the rest. When doing this, the tutor should look for the major topic of the essay (*What's the essay about?* and *Is the topic aligned with the assignment description?*). He should also locate (and extract) three subtopics, and any relevant examples, and then write them on the outline. My goal is always to keep as much of the student's draft as possible, so that he will retain a sense of ownership for the essay. This process is simple and highly effective. I explain all this to my tutors, and I begin showing them the five-part outline.

On my poster paper, I write the word "Title" at the top, and I drop numbers one through five, below. It looks like this:

Title_____

   1.

   2.

   3.

   4.

   5.

I pause and point to this tidy blueprint. "See? The essay is already taking shape. I have just created a framework on which we can hang our students' ideas. Write this in pencil, on lined paper, for all the students you tutor. Now, these five things may be paragraphs or they may become larger sections of an essay. We don't know yet."

I explain that having five sections is not an absolute; it's a starting place designed to impose order and structure onto a jangling jumble of possibilities. We start with five, but we don't actually know if we'll end with five. It could be more; it could be less. It depends on the complexity of the topic and the skill and motivation of the student. But start by creating a five-part outline and do it in front of the student, *whether or not she has written a draft.* And while you do this, get used to communicating something about the fluidity of the outline (and the composition process), and tell your tutors to communicate it to their students also. Tell them that "Anything we do today can be changed. This is just a rough outline. If you don't like something, let me know, and we'll change it."

This is a powerful affirmation, and students love hearing it. Remember, it's not *your* essay; it belongs completely to the student. And I always add, "This is one of my favorite things about writing: we can do whatever we want. Add, subtract, change, start over. We can do anything when we write; it's the most forgiving thing in the world." Students love hearing this too. It's a great stress-reducer, and it's empowering for them. But it's also true. Writing is wonderful like that; it's the ultimate blank canvas, allowing us to paint any picture we want.

Next, I explain the function of the introduction and the conclusion. As always, I keep it simple, and I write the word "Introduction" next to number one, and the word "Conclusion" next to number five. I explain that the introduction tells the reader what the essay is about and also contains the thesis statement (and here, I begin explaining thesis statements). The conclusion tells the reader what she's just read, a bit like a summary. It's pretty simple, and, in a sense, the introduction and conclusion tend to be a bit similar, like matching bookends. But let's take this a step further. Remember earlier when I said that every paper needs to be about something? It's true, and I meant it. Now, let's relate this to introductions and conclusions: every paper raises a question in the *introduction*, explores the issue in the *middle section* (I prefer this term to the moniker "body"), and then provides an answer to the question in the *conclusion*.

So, in a sense, the introduction is the place where the writer *poses* the question (remember, I call this the "essential question"); the middle section is where the writer *explores* or *explains* the issue being examined; and the conclusion is the place where the writer *answers* the question. And if the question has been answered in the middle section, the conclusion provides a tidy summary of the essay and mentions the answer one more time, in a brief, snappy, memorable format. This is for the benefit of the reader, because we learn through repetition.

Now, here, I want to give you a very important tip, and I want you to pass this along to your tutors. Follow my logic. The introduction tells the reader what the paper is about; this is a given. However, the composition process is fluid and dynamic, and the writer makes decisions, performs research, makes discoveries, and reaches conclusions as she writes her paper. This means that, as we compose, we very often start writing on a certain topic and end up writing on another, different topic. It's very common. Now, let's take this one step further.

When a paper "wants" to be about something else, when it starts making its own organic decisions, urging you to explore in a different direction, then get behind the paper and follow along and see where it leads you. Your writing will be better, and the paper will be more natural, interesting, and energetic. And this means something else, and it's something important, so listen carefully: *we don't really know what a paper is about until we're finished writing it*. I described this in the Introduction by using a metaphor of growing tomatoes. You don't know what a tomato plant (or a paper) is going to look like until it's fully developed.

And this raises an enigmatic question: if we don't know what our paper is truly about until it's finished, then how can we possibly write a fitting, accurate introduction? We can't. *Yet*. So I exhort you to give the following directive to your tutors and have them teach it to their students: *write the introduction last*. It's very simple and extremely effective. I feel very strongly about this, so let me repeat it: tell all your tutors and all your students to *write the introduction last*. Some teachers may disagree with this (it's hard to break long-standing habits), but it makes perfect sense to me, given the wild nature of composition and when we're teaching fledglings how to write essays that contain sparks of life and spontaneity.

When students start an essay, they should begin by *writing the second paragraph first*. It's counterintuitive, but still wonderfully effective and efficient. If they write the introduction first, bad things will happen: they will feel beholden to it, and it will squash creativity, and the paper will feel flat. Or, when they end the paper, their original introduction will no longer fit, and they'll have to write it a second time. Or they'll just leave it alone, and it won't fit the paper. So *write the introduction last*. When they finish writing the paper, they will then know what the paper is truly about. And they can simply pull the introduction out of what they have already written. It's very easy this way. I therefore suggest writing the paper in this order:

1. Middle section (starting with the second paragraph)
2. Conclusion (some summary here; what is the answer to the question asked by the paper?)
3. Introduction (thesis statement. What is the paper about? What question are you asking?)
4. Title (make it short, interesting, and accurate)

As you can see, the students' final task will be to choose a title. The title should be fairly short and should say exactly what the paper is about. And this is why I suggest writing it last. What better time to choose a title than when you're looking at the completed whole? *Aha! Now I see what my paper is about!* And titles should contain two elements: the subject and the writer's "angle," or point of view. Let's say I'm working with a student who is writing a paper on the Amazon rainforest. "Okay," I say to her, "What's the paper about? Is it just information about the Amazon rainforest? Or will you be focusing on some specific point?"

"Well," she says, "I believe we need to preserve the Amazon rainforest. So I want to write about that."

"Okay," I nod, and I think to myself *academic argument.* "Sounds like a good topic." And we're off to explore this world of twilight mist and to argue for its continuing existence.

In this case, the *subject* is the Amazon rainforest. The student's *angle* is that it must be preserved. Put together, these form a central idea, or thesis: *we need to preserve the Amazon rainforest.* The title might therefore read "The Amazon Rainforest Must Be Preserved." And that's it. It's a good, clear title, and we know what we're getting into. Don't overthink titles; they should be short and simple and accurate and clear and catchy. There are no tricks to titles, or there shouldn't be, for fledgling writers. A simple, accurate title is a kindness to your reader; don't leave her guessing. Tell her in clear terms what she's about to read. There's no reason to turn an essay into a puzzle or to make the reader work harder than he has to.

Once my tutors begin to comprehend the overall flow of a paper, and the order in which it should be written, I move them toward a subject of extreme importance: *subtopics*. Subtopics are the backbone of an essay, and they need to understand this concept deeply. Remember, in the previous chapter, when I asked you to select three subtopics for Emily's essay on Education? (I finally suggested *parents, school,* and *career*). Well, look at numbers two, three, and four on our developing outline. Your three subtopics will go there, sandwiched between the Introduction (number one) and the Conclusion (number five). And now, let's invite Emily back. I write her subtopics on our developing outline, and now it looks like this:

Title_____

1. Introduction (contains thesis statement)
2. First subtopic: parents
3. Second subtopic: school
4. Third subtopic: career
5. Conclusion (think "summary" here)

Emily's outline is shaping up very nicely, and my tutors are looking at it with great interest. Things are starting to make sense to them. At this point, I stress that the subtopics *may or may not represent individual paragraphs.* Please understand this. Each subtopic *may* be covered adequately in one paragraph or it may blossom into several paragraphs. We won't know until we're further in the writing process. As the student writes and thinks and performs research, she may decide upon additional subtopics, and the five-part essay may expand into six or seven sections, which should be appropriate for most school projects. The outline may also be reduced to four sections and perhaps even three. But certainly no fewer than three. An essay, if it is to be an essay, requires, at the minimum, an introduction, a middle section, and a conclusion.

The concept of subtopics is fairly simple, but it is extremely important. During this portion of my tutors' training, I proceed slowly, and I always use concrete examples. I begin by using the Thomas Edison analogy I discussed in Chapter Four. I then do an exercise with my tutors in which I name a few simple topics, and then I ask them to come up with three good subtopics for each. For example, I ask "Can you think of three subtopics for a paper on *ocean life*? Jot them down." I also ask them to "List three subtopics for a paper on *ancient Egypt*." I give them a few minutes to scribble their answers (in pencil, on lined notepaper), and their responses usually include things like "mammals, fish, crustaceans" and "the Nile, the pyramids, King Tut." These are all good (clear, simple, and relevant) and would be effective for these assignments. Next, we discuss the best *order* in which to present these subtopics, and this makes for a nice lesson in organization.

However (I tell my tutors), if the student has already written a draft, we will work "backward." Instead of going from outline to draft, we will proceed from *draft to outline.* We will read the student's draft, locate relevant subtopics (and any supporting examples), and then plug them into an outline. Does this make sense? These are fairly easy concepts, but they are immensely important for your tutors' (and students') academic development.

When the tutors get a firm sense of subtopics—what they are and how they are used in an essay—I explain that they will be frequently helping students choose subtopics for their essays. To do this, they will brainstorm with their students. And one effective method for brainstorming is a graphic organizer which I call the "wheel" (illustrated in Figure 5.1). It's very simple and very helpful. I start with

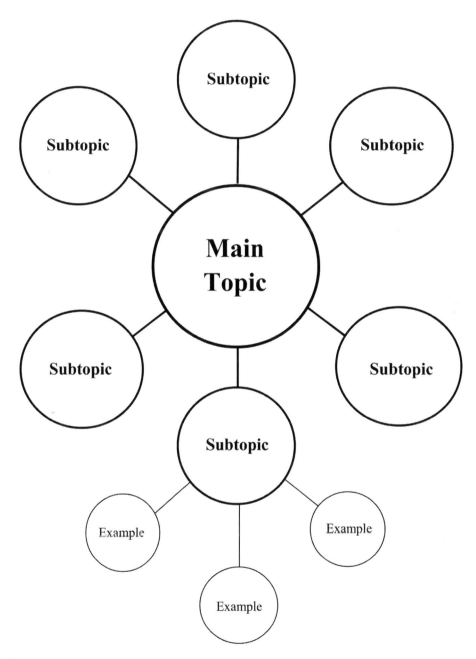

Figure 5.1

a blank piece of paper. I write the main topic in the center, and I circle it. I then draw "spokes" (perhaps six or eight) coming out from the center. At the end of each spoke, I put another (empty) circle. And it looks a bit like a wheel.

When I use the wheel during a tutorial, I ask my student to try and think of several subtopics that are associated with the main topic. We brainstorm together (I use leading questions here), and I write these subtopics in the empty circles. So the subtopics are "circling" the main topic like planets around a sun, which is a good place for them to be. If necessary, I can also draw spokes and circles emanating from the *subtopics*, and write in three illustrative examples for each subtopic (but this usually comes later [and I did it once on the illustration, on the bottom]). Many students benefit from this sort of visual presentation; it helps with their thinking and comprehension (I get this; I'm a visual learner myself). When the graphic organizer is filled out satisfactorily, I ask the student to look at it and choose his favorite three subtopics, and to think of the best order in which to present them. It's a very effective method for generating ideas for an essay, and it also assists with focus and organization.

When your student has chosen his subtopics, it is time for something of extreme importance: teach him how to write a *paragraph*. This is crucial instruction, and its significance cannot be overstated. Most people (including adults) don't know how to write paragraphs, because they don't really understand them. Your tutors may be able to construct a passable paragraph, but they probably won't know how to *teach* them. First, what is the purpose of paragraphs? They're a mental break for the reader, a place where she can rest a moment and soak up what she has just read. They're also an organizational tool, breaking up discourse into smaller, focused bits that we can more easily understand and digest. Who wants to read page after page of text with no break? I sure don't.

But paragraphs do more than just give us mental breaks. They are vital to any piece of writing. They are the limestone blocks in the cathedral of meaning. And this brings me to the ultimate secret of paragraphs: *every paragraph must be about something*. And let's take this one step further: *every paragraph should be about one thing, and one thing only*.

Sound familiar? It should. In the previous chapter, I said nearly the same thing about writing in general. I said that "every piece of writing must be about something" and that "every piece of writing must really be about one thing, and one thing only." And now I'm saying something very similar about paragraphs. Now, let's draw a natural conclusion from this information: *a paragraph is like a miniature essay*. Do you see? It must have a topic, and it must be structured and organized and composed of certain specific elements. But most important is a paragraph's *topic*. It must be clearly defined and specified. Make sure you explain this to your tutors and to your students. As they write (or tutor), they should be able to point to any paragraph and say what it's about, clearly and decisively. And it should be about one thing only. And they should be able to express that thing in a single word or a short sentence. If they can't express the topic of the paragraph clearly and succinctly, it probably means that the paragraph is lacking focus, and that it needs to be rewritten. Or perhaps split into two smaller paragraphs. I want to stress this once again: *every paragraph must have a clearly defined topic.*

When you're tutoring, you need to help your students with their paragraphs. Here's what you do. Once the student has chosen her three subtopics, write them on the outline. Let's say we're still working with our favorite student Emily, and she's excited about her essay. Below is Emily's developing outline. Note that Emily has suggested a title, so I jotted it down. It's a *working* title, and it should really be more specific and descriptive, so I remind her gently that she may end up changing the title. But it's not bad for a start.

Title: *My Education*

1. Introduction (contains thesis statement)
2. First subtopic: Things my parents taught me
3. Second subtopic: My favorite subject in school
4. Third subtopic: My future career
5. Conclusion

See that? It's shaping up into a nice essay: friendly, human, focused, and well organized. And now comes the next part: outlining and developing each subtopic. Now, we know that each subtopic may be a single paragraph or it may blossom into several paragraphs. However, when I *teach* this, I always begin by treating each subtopic as the basis for a single paragraph (this is simple, and students find it comprehensible). So that's what I'll do here. For the sake of simplicity and teaching, I will treat each of Emily's subtopics as the basis for a paragraph.

Remember that I described (in Chapter Four) the "Rule of Three"? And remember how I said above that each paragraph was like a miniature essay? Well, let's take that a step further. Now that we have assigned subtopics to each section, we need to start developing our subtopics and discussing them in detail. In order to do this, we will apply the rule of three to each subtopic. This is important, so I want you to really understand it.

When developing subtopics, *or paragraphs*, you should choose and discuss (about) *three examples* that describe each subtopic (or each paragraph). I think you see that we have a pattern emerging: three subtopics for the essay and three examples for each subtopic (or paragraph). This is no accident. If the Rule of Three works for essays, it also works for paragraphs. And this is because (as I said above) paragraphs are like miniature essays. Now, let's go back to our student Emily. She's been waiting for us very patiently, so look over my shoulder as I explain all of this to her.

I want Emily to start developing her subtopics into effective paragraphs, so I talk to her, I give her guidance, I ask leading questions, I listen (and listen and listen), and I jot down her responses, in pencil, on lined paper. My goal here is to *help Emily come up with three examples for each subtopic*, or a total of nine illustrative examples. See the structure of her essay developing: *we have three subtopics. Each subtopic will become a paragraph. And each paragraph will be developed with the use of three supporting examples.* It's pretty simple, really.

Here is what I say: "Okay Emily, this is shaping up into a very nice essay. What I want to do now is to come up with about three examples for each subtopic. These will help you tell your story." And I jot down the letters A, B, and C under each subtopic. I make sure she sees what I'm doing (I'm a lefty, so she's sitting on my right—we've got the magic triangle) and that she knows why I'm doing it. I explain things very clearly and simply, and I always encourage questions, because every tutorial is a text that is constructed collaboratively.

I then say to Emily, "Let's look at your first subtopic, which is about your parents teaching you when you were very young." I then ask her several leading, probing, questions: "Can you remember some specific things they taught you? Can you think of any specific *times* when they taught you? Can you think of something you learned that was really cool? Can you come up with, say . . . *three* different examples?" I ask these questions gently, I smile. And if she's having difficulty, I may use a wheel graphic organizer to help her visualize her recollections and the potential flow of the essay. I might write her examples directly on the wheel we used earlier (remember, I did this on my illustration, above) or (if I want more space) I may start a new wheel graphic organizer for each subtopic. In either case, the subtopic will go in the center, and the examples will emanate out from it, like moons orbiting a planet. As always, everything I do is done with a spirit of gentleness. Our students think better when they don't feel "pressured," so I always do my best to create a low-pressure environment. The warm, fuzzy librarian guy who helps kids with writing. That's the persona I wear, and it works for me, and the kids seem to like it. They respond well to it.

After a few minutes, and a few more leading questions and prodding, Emily has come up with three good examples. And I jot them down on the outline before we forget them. I do the same with the other subtopics (writing everything on the outline), and I make a few notes by the introduction and conclusion. By the end of the session, we have our nine examples, and our outline is looking good. In fact, it's nearly complete. I then ask Emily to look at her outline, and to look for the "soul" of her essay. *What's it really about?* And I ask her if she can come up with a more specific title. She does. Here is what the outline looks like now:

Title: *My Lifelong Education* (it's a pretty good title)

1. Introduction (contains thesis statement. Write this last. What is this essay really about? What question are you asking?)
2. First subtopic: Things my parents taught me
   a. First example: how to swim
   b. Second example: how to play soccer
   c. Third example: how to draw
3. Second subtopic: My favorite subject in school
   a. First example: English (describe it, say why I like it)
   b. Second example: My favorite book is *Of Mice and Men* (describe it, say why I like it)

      c. Third example: My favorite English project was writing a short story (describe it, say why I liked it)

   4. Third subtopic: My future career

      a. First example: English teacher (describe it, say why I want to do this)

      b. Second example: Describe how much college and education I'll need

      c. Third example: Interview my English teacher about her job (ask her three questions)

   5. Conclusion (summary, restate main points. What was this essay about? What is the answer to the question I asked in my introduction?)

See how nicely Emily's essay is shaping up? It looks terrific. She looks at it and reads it. She's thrilled. *So that's what an essay is supposed to look like!* She has a definite plan now, and she's not flailing in the dark. I've seen (and you'll see) kids positively beaming at this point. Although the outline is a collaboration (you'll coax it out of your students), they can take ownership for it and feel rightfully proud. And deeply relieved. Emily's outline is very good, and it should yield a very good essay. The topic is clear, and the outline is focused and organized. But it's also very human. It obviously means a great deal to Emily, and she is very excited about it (heck, I would be too). And this means that the reader (her teacher) will probably like the essay also.

At this point, I begin teaching Emily how to weave this information into well-written paragraphs. This is a magnificently important component of instruction. Please be aware that you will probably be the first (and possibly the last) person to teach your student the beauties and basics of writing a paragraph. So do it clearly, and do it well, and your students will own it forever. In my entire life, I was never taught how to write a paragraph. I learned through trial and error, through practice, through observing paragraphs as I read, and through figuring things out on my own. Your students will not know how to write paragraphs, so take them all through the basics of writing paragraphs and make no assumptions about what they might already know. Here's what I do.

I start by telling my students that they need to weave the outline into a smoothly written text and to think about it (and do it) one paragraph at a time. This is very important, but it's not terribly difficult. First, how *long* should each paragraph be? No more than *two or three paragraphs per page.* When an essay is printed (let's assume in Times New Roman, 12-point font, always a good choice), a paragraph should be no longer than half a page. Any longer than that, and I would consider splitting it up into two smaller paragraphs. But don't make them too short, either. Printed out, paragraphs should be no shorter than about a third of a page. I always tell students this, and for a visual, I use my hands on a sheet of printer paper. This size of the paragraph is between my forefingers (on top) and my thumbs (on bottom): two for longer paragraphs, three for shorter paragraphs. This is very valuable knowledge for fledgling writers, and my fingertip display helps them understand it.

Next, I tell my students to remember that each paragraph has a topic. *We covered that before, remember?* They nod. I then tell them something very important: in the first sentence of the paragraph, *they need to tell the reader what the paragraph is about.* This is very important. The first sentence of a paragraph is called the *topic sentence.* The topic sentence tells the reader what the paragraph is about. This assists with readability and comprehension. And again, I remind my students that a paragraph is like a miniature essay. An essay starts with an introduction. Similarly, the topic sentence is the "introduction" to the paragraph. And keep the topic sentence simple and clear. For Emily's paragraph on "Things my parents taught me," the topic sentence might read as follows: "My parents were my first teachers, and they taught me many things." And that's it. It's simple. It's nice. Don't overthink it. Don't overdo it. It also tells readers what's following next. Don't keep them guessing; just present the information clearly and simply. Don't make the reader work harder than he has to.

Now that we have the topic sentence, we need to discuss the three examples that support and explain the topic of the paragraph. Suggest to your student that *each example might be discussed in about three sentences.* Three subtopics, three examples for each subtopic, three sentences for each example. Three, three, three. Yes, when it comes to writing, my favorite number is *three.* But as always, this number is a guideline, not an absolute. Students need this sort of imposed structure as they're learning to write. Codified structures are a great starting-off point on which to hang their ideas.

At this point in the tutorial, I will ask Emily to begin writing the "Parents" paragraph (and not the introductory paragraph; remember, she will write that last). We have already written the topic sentence, so let's start weaving Emily's examples (swimming, soccer, drawing) into a paragraph. And tell her that she can often introduce her examples by simply stating "For example" (why overlook the obvious?). For example, if Emily has a case of writer's block (or low confidence), you might *model* writing the sentences which describe her swimming anecdote. Develop them in front of her (with her input) and narrate the process as you scribble, in pencil, on lined notepaper. After a few minutes of collaboration, these sentences might read as follows:

> For example, when I was eight years old, my father taught me how to swim. We were camping at Lake George, and we went down to the lake every morning. My father was a very good swimmer, and after three days of lessons, I could swim by myself in the deep water.

See how easy that is? After that, I ask Emily to try and do the other two examples (soccer and drawing) by herself. *You can do it!* As she sits there and writes, *during the tutorial, in front of me,* I tell her to use the passage on swimming as a guide (students find exemplars like this extremely helpful). Emily reads the passage over, thinks a moment, and begins writing about the wonders of soccer and drawing. I watch for a moment. Emily is doing well, so I leave her for a few minutes so that she can think and write in privacy. When I come back, I read what Emily wrote. I give her some compliments, and I make some suggestions and notes on her draft. The bell is about to ring, so I tell Emily to do the same thing with her two remaining subtopics. Weave them into coherent sentences. And *try to do this tonight, while it's still fresh in your mind.*

When Emily comes back a few days later, I look at her work and give her some more compliments, and she gives me a shy smile. Again, I give her some suggestions for improvement and make notes on her draft. But I tell her that, although her paragraphs look great, they aren't finished yet. She needs to start thinking about how she is going to *end* her paragraphs. And, because paragraphs are like miniature essays, they should end with a type of "conclusion." Like the conclusion to an essay, the final sentence in a paragraph will sometimes offer a tidy summary of the paragraph. And often, the last sentence in a paragraph is a *transition* to the next paragraph.

Transitions can be short (often a single sentence), but they do a bunch of good things. They assist one paragraph in flowing smoothly into the next paragraph, and they signify that one paragraph is ending, and a new one is starting. They also improve style, helping to make writing appear polished and elegant. And they improve the unity and continuity of essays, making them appear to be one long flowing stream of discourse, rather than a choppy patchwork of bits cobbled together. In this way, they are very helpful to the reader. They help his thoughts flow smoothly, and they assist with comprehension and an enjoyable reading experience.

As I teach Emily about transitions, I encourage her to think about her current paragraph (her parents as teachers) and her next paragraph (her favorite subject in school). What transition could she use as a "bridge" from one paragraph (or subject) to the other? How can she "blend" these two paragraphs together and avoid "choppiness" in her writing? I ask some leading questions (*What do they both have in common? How do they differ?*), and I help her write her first transitional sentence. And, dear reader, here is your second test (ungraded, as always). Take a moment and see if you can come up with a snappy transitional sentence for Emily to use at the end of her "parents as teachers" paragraph, to help it flow smoothly into her "favorite subject in school" paragraph. Go ahead. Take a few minutes, and write down your answer. In pencil. On lined paper. You can do it.

I'm here, waiting for you.

Well, how did you do? Was it difficult? There are lots of transitional sentences that would work in this case, but here is a good, simple one to end that paragraph: "I learned a lot from my parents, but that was just the beginning of my education." See? Easy. And now, I want to start wrapping up this discussion on paragraphs, and I want to give your third "test." I want you to generate Emily's sentences for her other two examples, soccer and drawing. I did the example on swimming (see above); so feel free to use that as a reference (if Emily can do it, you can do it too). Go now, write your sentences, and provide at least three sentences for each example. Scribble your heart out, preferably in pencil, on lined paper.

I'm waiting, patiently.

You're back. Did you do it? Was it tough? If it was difficult, you're probably overthinking the task. This is fairly easy material, but please don't get discouraged, because it does take practice. And now, I want to put Emily's entire paragraph together. As you read it, note all the parts of the paragraph as you encounter them: the topic sentence, the three examples (each developed in three sentences), and the closing sentence, which is a transition. And note especially how all the parts come together, flow smoothly, and work harmoniously to create a warm glow of meaning:

> My parents were my first teachers, and they taught me many things. For example, when I was eight years old, my father taught me how to swim. We were camping at Lake George, and we went down to the lake every morning. My father was a very good swimmer, and after three days of lessons, I could swim by myself in the deep water. When I was a little older, my parents taught me how to play soccer. They both played soccer in college, and they were very good players. I play on my school team, and last year I scored two goals. My mother also taught me how to draw. I love drawing animals, and my favorite animal to draw is a dog. I drew the picture of the dog below (that is my dog, Sparky). I learned a lot from my parents, but that was just the beginning of my education.

That's a good paragraph. It's simple, but it's well constructed and clearly written, with examples that are chunky and concrete. And Emily (even though fictitious) emerges as endearing and likeable. How could anyone not like our Emily? And this is a good thing. When we read, we are spending time with the author. And it's always pleasant if we "like" the person we're with.

Please read Emily's paragraph over and take a close look at it. Note that it adheres to the big three: it has a clearly defined topic, it's focused, and it's well organized. Also note that it follows the pattern of an essay. It starts with an introduction (topic sentence), it has a three-part middle section (three examples), and it has a conclusion (transitional sentence). Writing strong paragraphs is fairly simple, but it's an immensely important part of learning how to write. So teach it well to your tutors and students.

Now, let's put everything together. I began this chapter with a discussion of the five-part outline. I discussed the structure of the essay. I covered how to construct effective and efficient paragraphs. All these things are integral parts of learning to write, and they must all work together. To illustrate this concept, I am now providing you with a highly detailed outline that combines everything I discussed in this chapter. Take a look at it, and note how everything works together to create a focused, organized essay.

Look at the outline below. It's simple and clear. Read it over carefully, and note its structure and flow. It contains the entirety of the basic academic essay and the basic structure of a reliable paragraph format. Are things beginning to make more sense now? But wait; I know what you're thinking: you can make "skeleton" worksheets for your writing center, print out a hundred, and have them as a resource for your tutors to use. It will make things quick and easy. I suspect some of you may want to do this, but please don't. It would be a mistake.

Title_____ **(include subject and angle)**

1. Introduction (Write this last! Thesis statement. What is this essay really about? What essential question are you asking?)

2. First subtopic:_____(what is this paragraph about?)

   a. Topic sentence_____

   b. First example:_____(about three sentences)

   c. Second example:_____(about three sentences)

   d. Third example:_____(about three sentences)

   e. Transitional sentence_____

3. Second subtopic:_____(what is this paragraph about?)

   a. Topic sentence_____

   b. First example:_____(about three sentences)

   c. Second example:_____(about three sentences)

   d. Third example:_____(about three sentences)

   e. Transitional sentence_____

4. Third subtopic:_____(what is this paragraph about?)

   a. Topic sentence_____

   b. First example:_____(about three sentences)

   c. Second example:_____(about three sentences)

   d. Third example:_____(about three sentences)

   e. Transitional sentence_____

5. Conclusion (summary, restate main points. What was this essay about? What is the answer to the question you asked in your introduction? What do you want your reader to remember?)

I know the idea is tempting and has its merits. *Just keep a stack of blank outlines handy, and tutors can fill them out for students.* I see the draw; the prefab convenience is enticing. But like all quick fixes, it also has powerful drawbacks. The main problem with using skeleton worksheets in the writing center is subtle, but resounding: It makes us look like a "factory," where we churn out impersonal products in a cookie-cutter format. But (you may be thinking), isn't the essay format I describe in itself a cookie-cutter? *No*, it's definitely not. The essay format I describe applies *structure and organization*, but it also allows for great fluidity. It respects the composition and development process as being extremely creative and open-ended. Providing skeleton worksheets to students in the writing center would inhibit their creativity and stunt their growth as writers. The difference between an outline that is constructed collaboratively and a skeleton worksheet is the difference between a blank canvas and a paint-by-numbers worksheet. It's structure versus stricture.

The process I describe of building the outline with the student allows for fluidity with regard to the student's motivation, knowledge, and skill. If we use a five-part skeleton worksheet, chances are we're going to see a bunch of five paragraph essays, and this will severely limit the writerly growth of students. But if we use my open-ended approach, we're going to see a bunch of wildly different essays composed by wildly different learners.

My approach also, by its nature, takes into account *differentiation* (essentially, this means teaching individual students according to their individual abilities, styles, and needs as learners. I'll be discussing this in greater detail in the next chapter). A skeleton worksheet suggests that we view the composition as a *product* to complete, and "here is what it should look like." My approach (with its pencils, blank note paper, and open-ended essence) views the *process* as the most important thing, respecting (and teaching) the composition as a complex entity that grows and develops in a roiling forum of great possibility. And it is the arena where knowledge is generated and true learning occurs. And remember, this is extremely germane to the mission of the writing center: we don't "fix" papers; we create writers.

But there is another benefit to burying the skeleton sheet, and this is a psychological one. Adolescents are very conscious of themselves as individuals, and they want to be seen as unique and special. So why not honor this? When we (tutors and students) construct an outline (and essay) from scratch, it sends a variety of constructive messages to the student. It tells him subtly that we respect him as a unique learner and we respect his developing essay as being completely original. The student and his essay haven't been put on some sort of production line; they are part of a genuine, spontaneous, human conversation, and we're not sure how this thing will end. Or what it will look like. But we're there to help him out and teach him how to write. We're there to show him that writing an essay is not a punishment.

Learning to write well is an opportunity for the student to construct meaning and to create beauty. It also allows the student to explore a world that is rich, pulsating, and immensely complex and to impose order upon it. At its deepest levels, it provides the writer a chance to learn about himself, to connect with others, and to feel a bit less lonely in an unfamiliar world, and a bit more welcome in a vast, unfolding future.

Chapter 6

THE TUTORIAL: TIPS, TECHNIQUES, AND MOCK TUTORIALS

Every year, as I train my tutors, one of them asks me "What if I don't know anything about the subject of the paper? How can I help the student?" It's a great question and a terrific teachable moment. My tutors are nervous that they don't "know everything," and I get this. If a student comes to them with a topic on which they're unfamiliar, what will they do? How will they teach it?

It's simple. We don't teach *what* to write. We teach *how* to write.

Not long ago, I worked with a student who was writing a high-level paper on the Beatles and their impact on society. This was fun for me. I'm a Beatles maniac, and I know a lot about them and their music. Around the same time, however, I was working with another student who was writing a paper on the development of prosthetics. Although I know virtually nothing about this topic, I was able to help both students, and to the same degree. And more important, my basic methods didn't change from one student to the other. How? It's because I didn't teach the students *content*. I taught each student *process*. I taught the structure of an essay, how to organize information, and how to develop ideas.

To help explain this concept to students, I perform an exercise with them. I call this the "Mystery Topic." Every year, I do this during a meeting, and it's part of their training. For the purposes of this unique instruction, I ask them to sit at tables, with lined paper and pencils, while I'm up front. I tape a piece of blank poster paper to the whiteboard where they can all see it. I'm standing there with a black magic marker in my hand, and we're ready to begin.

I smile and ask "Who thinks you need to know a subject well in order to help a student write a paper on it?" I wait. My tutors look around, and most hands go up hesitantly. I shake my head and wave my own hands. "No, never, perish the thought. No one can know everything. Except for *me*, of course. Just kidding. [My dry delivery always gets a good laugh.] You can definitely help a student without understanding the topic, and I'm gonna prove it here, today!" I jab my finger in the air, very dramatically. It's all done with satiric grandiosity and a light touch. We all have our teaching style, right? I continue.

"To do this," I say, "we're going to be doing a little role-playing . . . sort of. I'm gonna do this the way I do a real tutorial. So let's pretend this is a tutorial, happening here, now. This blank paper [I point to the poster] is my lined paper, and this magic marker is my pencil. I'm the tutor, and all of you are my students. I'm going to prove *once and for all* [gesturing like an angry magician] that you can run a great tutorial without knowing anything about the topic." I smile, I nod, I let it sink in. It's all in good fun.

"Okay," I continue, "I want you all to think of the most complicated, difficult, impossible topic you could possibly imagine, then write it on your notepaper, and then turn the paper over. And don't tell me what it is! Go ahead and do that now." I watch them thinking and writing and turning over their papers. Some of them are grinning a little. *What is he doing?* "Is everyone finished?" I ask. "Does everyone have a Mystery Topic? Alright." I pause. "I will now teach everyone in this room the secrets of writing a paper on a topic that you know nothing about. I can't possibly know what your topics are, but I'm going to teach you, *all of you*, how to write a paper on *your* topic . . . at the same time!" Again, the kooky magician promising wondrous and impossible feats. "So listen carefully, and watch closely, because you'll all be doing this in a week or two. Here we go."

I turn to my poster with my magic marker poised, and I come out of my role for a moment. "Okay," I smile at them [we're all having fun], "from here, I'm going to speak to you the way I speak to students during a tutorial. So I'm role-playing now. This is me at a tutorial. But you can ask questions at any time. Ready? I'm about to start acting." I begin speaking and writing on the poster, and this is what I say during tutorials. And remember, I'm teaching a bunch of unknown topics, simultaneously. As you read what I say, please remember the five-part outline I gave you in the previous chapter, because I'm going to use that as the basis for my instruction. My tutoring-persona-patter goes a bit like this:

"Sounds like a really interesting topic! You know, I think an outline might work well for an essay like this. I think we can do this topic in . . . let's see . . . I think about five parts will work well for this. I'll start jotting it down on here." I write the word "Title" at the top of the poster, and I then drop in the numbers one through five (leaving space between the numbers). My histrionic hesitancy suggests to the student that I am treating his paper with originality and fresh consideration, something which students always appreciate. But it *always* starts out with five parts.

I continue. "So you know that the first paragraph is the introduction and the last paragraph is the conclusion." I write the word "introduction" next to number one and "conclusion" next to number five, along with some notes. "And, you know the introduction says what the paper is about, and the conclusion is sort of a summary." I had previously given my tutors the outline format, so this is understandable to them.

"But now we have to figure what parts two, three, and four are about. Hmmm. . . ." I appear to be thinking deeply, as if making major decisions. This is carefully scripted theater, so I always know what comes next. "Usually, we put some subtopics here. Things that are related to your major topic. Can you think of, maybe . . . *three* subtopics for your essay? Subtopics are, you know, specific things that are a part of your topic. For example, if we were writing about baseball, we might pick these three subtopics: the history of baseball; the rules of the game; and the reasons why you love baseball." I turn to my tutors and come out of character for a moment. "Let's say that, during the *interview* phase, I discovered that the student is a baseball fanatic. It's always good to link instruction to a student's interests, if possible." And I go back into character, and continue talking.

"So, can you think of three things related to your topic? When you do, we'll jot them down." I write on the big outline: "First subtopic" next to number two; "Second subtopic" next to number three; and "Third subtopic" next to number four. "Can you think of any subtopics? If you can't, that's okay. We can work on those next time. And after you choose subtopics, I want you to think about discussing them through using specific examples. Specific examples are sort of, like, stories within the subtopic. And for this essay, I think that about . . . *three* examples for each subtopic will work well." And underneath each subtopic, I drop in the letters A, B, and C. "So, like we said earlier, let's say you're writing a paper about baseball, and one of your subtopics is the history of baseball. Can you think of three things about the history of baseball?" I turn to my tutors. "This is a leading question. We're trying to get the student to think and come up with his own answers. And if he's stuck, we can help get him started. Make sense?" They nod. And I go back into character.

"What about. . . . *who* invented baseball? *When* was it invented? *How* was it invented? These would be good examples to use for the history of baseball. So start thinking about your subtopics. And when you come up with three subtopics, try to think of three examples for each subtopic. If you come up with any, write them down on the outline. But I see that the bell is about to ring. We'll work on all of this next time. When can you come back in?" I raise my arms in a "*Ta-da!*" gesture, and that ends this exercise.

I grin at my tutors. "See? That's how you teach a paper when you don't know the topic." I point to the big outline I made. "Look at this outline. I kept it very simple, but it works. The student now has a guideline for his essay. It's basic; it won't overwhelm him. And all we need to do is plug in subtopics and examples. And make sure you give him the outline before he leaves! This is important, because he'll be looking at it as he starts his paper." Here is the outline I use for the Mystery Topic exercise. And remember, we're at the beginning of the writing process, so it's not highly detailed:

Title: _____

  1. Introduction (What is this essay about?)
  2. First subtopic:

  _____

   a. First example: _____

   b. Second example: _____

   c. Third example: _____

3. Second subtopic: _____

   a. First example: _____

   b. Second example: _____

   c. Third example: _____

4. Third subtopic: _____

   a. First example: _____

   b. Second example: _____

   c. Third example: _____

5. Conclusion (summary)

I continue. "Now, think of all your Mystery Topics. See how this works? So remember, we don't teach *content*. We teach *process*. And if we do this, we can never be accused of 'writing the paper for the student.' It will truly be *his* work. See?" They nod. "So we don't need to 'know everything' to tutor in the writing center. As a matter of fact, whether you know the subject or not doesn't really matter. Your tutoring methods should always be pretty much the same." I let this sink in. "Questions?" I ask, but there usually aren't any. This "Mystery Topic" lesson always works well, and I recommend you do this with your own tutors.

Every year, I also show my tutors my three favorite teaching techniques to use during writing center tutorials. And now I'm going to give them to you, so that you can use them and pass them along to your own tutors. They are *modeling*, *scaffolding*, and *differentiation*. And they all work extremely well in the writing center.

Modeling (as I employ it) simply means demonstrating to students what to do and how to write. It also means generating writing samples that students can use later as exemplars. When I model, I make sure to proceed very clearly and patiently. I perform a specific task in front of students as an example of how the thing is done and what it should look like when it is completed. During tutorials, modeling incorporates both process and product. I do this a lot during tutorials, most often on the student's notepaper. For example, I might model how to write a paragraph.

With the student's input (and leading questions), I will write a clear and basic paragraph, explaining each step of its construction. And now the student has a well-written paragraph that he can use later as a model. This works very well. And if the student can't write a coherent sentence, I'll model how to write a sentence. I will give him whatever he needs. And I'll do it happily.

I also use scaffolding when I tutor. Scaffolding is the process whereby a teacher instructs a student, helps a student, then slowly distances himself from the student, as the student acquires skills and slowly becomes more and more independent. When I employ scaffolding in writing center tutorials, I try to follow a basic pattern, a sequence that can be divided into five basic steps. However, I keep things feeling casual and spontaneous, and the students don't know I'm employing sophisticated pedagogy. The steps go like this:

1. I begin by explaining the thing being discussed. I then physically *demonstrate* it to the student. He watches me perform the task, and I discuss each step of the task, allowing for questions and input (this step incorporates modeling).

2. I then ask the student to perform the task. I talk him through it, and I watch him do it.

3. The student then performs the task with me watching. I offer input if it's needed, and he asks me questions if he has any.

4. The student practices the task. I'm beginning to distance myself, but I'm available for help, if he needs any.

5. The student performs the task independently and well. He no longer needs my help. And when he has mastered the task, he has acquired new knowledge. He feels great and always gets a nice compliment from me.

Scaffolding is a really cool stealth teaching method that produces abundant growth in the student.

I also use differentiation during tutorials (I mentioned this briefly in the previous chapter). It is an extremely effective technique, and I use it all the time. The concept is really very simple. It means teaching differently to different kids. When you tutor in the writing center, you will have to adjust your instruction to the unique needs of each student. It is immensely helpful and boosts learning tremendously. And it's not as difficult as it sounds.

Although the basic tutoring methods remain the same in each tutorial, I differentiate my teaching for every student. My goal is always to give each student exactly what she needs, according to her grade, course level, ability level, experience, personality, likes, dislikes, learning style, and even her demeanor on a particular day. I am constantly "reading" my students, so that I can give them the best learning experience possible.

And how do you learn to differentiate in the writing center? You can start by simply being aware that each student has unique needs and a unique learning style. And you must try to teach each student the way he or she wants and needs to be taught. A good way to do this will be to practice the methods I describe in this book. I built differentiation into my version of the writing center tutorial, and it's woven into the fabric of the methods I've been teaching you. In Chapter Three, for example, I discussed the Interview portion of the tutorial. Here, you'll be asking your student a series of questions in order to understand the particular assignment. In Chapter Four, I discussed the "probing questions" you'll be asking your student. These are designed to help you understand your student as a unique individual with unique needs. All of these questions are designed to understand your student in a "holistic" sense, so that you can teach her more productively and give her the instruction she needs, in a way that she can comprehend.

At some point, you (or one of your tutors) will probably work with a student from another country, who is learning to speak English. When this happens, it's a vast exercise in differentiation. These students, commonly referred to as English Language Learners (or ELLs), pose a hearty challenge for writing center tutors. They all have differing abilities when it comes to English, and many of them are shy about speaking English, especially with adults whom they don't know.

So what do we do? We try to teach them how to write.

If possible, try to pair an ELL student with a tutor who speaks the same language. If you'll remember, in Chapter Two, I told the tale of Xiang, and I suggested hiring a few tutors who speak languages other than English. This is always a good idea and will increase the versatility and depth of your writing center. If you hire multilingual tutors, they should speak to their students in their native languages, and they should begin by explaining *concepts* to the student. The tutor can cover such topics as the nature of the assignment, the structure of the essay, how to perform research, and the purpose of research (etc.). This is very useful information, because not all countries and cultures structure their forms of writing in the same way that we do. I like the idea of explaining complex concepts to an ELL student in his or her native language. It's hard enough learning a new language; can you imagine trying to learn *subject content* in a new language too?

But if you can't align an ELL student with someone who speaks her language, you (or a tutor) will still hold a tutorial anyway. It's challenging, but do your best. Speak slowly and clearly, use a simplified vocabulary, and go at her pace to ensure comprehension. Try to have her understand the assignment and explain the structure of the essay to her. Remember, not all countries structure their essays the way we do in the United States. And an outline is a great way to teach the essay format. In other words, teach her the way you teach *all* students, but make sure you differentiate according to her linguistic abilities. And here, I want to offer you a very valuable tip: when your ELL student begins writing her essay, encourage her to *write the first draft in her native language*. This is a very good idea, for several reasons.

Writing in her native language will allow her to organize her thoughts and to capture her ideas. It will also allow her to learn the structure and flow of the essay format we teach in the United States. This will make the process of composition much easier and less daunting and will give her the satisfaction of a completed assignment. And, after it's complete, she can "translate" it into English. At this point, be advised that the student will probably wish to use some online translation software to translate her work into English, but you should discourage this.

She will learn more about the language and about writing by translating it "the old-fashioned way" (with thought and time and sweat). This will be a much richer learning experience. After she translates into English, it will, of course, be riddled with linguistic errors. This is to be expected. However, at this point, the tutor can look at her assignment and offer some assistance with linguistic difficulties.

But here, I want to pause for a moment. Obviously, the tutor is not allowed to "translate" the essay into perfect English. That would be a breach of ethics, and we don't do that in the writing center. However, the tutor can note *repeated* errors and work with the student on correcting those. At all costs, we want to protect the reputation of our writing center and keep its operations completely honest and transparent. To help with the challenge of tutoring an ELL student, I suggest communicating with the teacher who is providing her with English instruction (she will probably be taking classes to learn English). You can let him know about the student's progress and what you're doing with her. He will appreciate the information and can likely offer suggestions that will assist in this difficult task. And all of this is very constructive. It's great for the writing center and great for the students. Generally speaking, any form of collaboration between the writing center and the other instructional venues of your school is a good thing.

We're getting close to the end of your primer on how to tutor, so, before we move on, I want to give you some wonderful techniques that will help you and your tutors teach students how to write. I mentioned some of these earlier, but that's okay. As I tell my students, if I say something more than once, that means it's really important. Also, repetition followed by practice creates deep, long-term learning. I've been addressing lots of the "big issues" with regard to the teaching of writing, so I want to return to an intimate view of two people talking about writing. I want to revisit the one-on-one writer's conference in close detail and talk about some practical methods and techniques that work really well. I think this will help put the puzzle together and make more sense of what actually happens during a tutorial. And I'm going to present these in bullet-point format, because I think that will make a friendly and accessible resource for you to look at from time to time. And it will be a handy list as you train your tutors.

So, let's say a student comes to the writing center and you are going to tutor him. You greet him (with a smile), set up the magic triangle (complete with notepaper and pencils), do the social ice-breaker, and conduct the interview. You look at the assignment sheet and get a good understanding of the project. And now, you ask him a hugely important question: *What would you like to work on today?* Or, you might phrase it like this: *What would work best for you today?* (I actually prefer that latter version). Who wouldn't want to be asked that question? Think about how you would feel if you went to someone, in extreme need of something specific and important: wouldn't *you* like to be asked that question?

Asking these simple questions is one of the most important things you can do as a tutor and the answers will affect (and direct) the rest of the tutorial. Remember, the tutorial belongs to the student (as does the assignment), and *he will almost always have a clear goal in mind.* This is just a bit of common sense, because *the student knows what he wants and what he needs*, much more than you do. So *ask this question every time*. And then listen to the answer. And then give the student what he wants and needs. Ask it at the beginning of a tutorial, *every single time you tutor*. It's the equivalent of a physician asking you "Where does it hurt?"

So let's say you ask the student what he wants to work on, and he asks you to look at the three-page draft he has written. He hands it to you and says "I don't know if it's any good" (and I always appreciate this simple, self-deprecating act of trust). You can see that he's shy and nervous, so you smile at him and say "Okay, no problem" and pick up a pencil, and you start reading his draft. But what do you do next? Here's what you do:

- Read the draft, while the student looks on.
- Read with a pencil in your hand and ask him "Can I write on this?" He'll always say "Yes."
- Give it some compliments quickly, to reduce his stress level.
- Concentrate on the big issues first. I refer to these as "The Big Three," and they include *topic, focus*, and *organization*. You can address the smaller issues later, as he proceeds through successive drafts and you proceed through successive tutorials.
- During your first read-through, ask yourself the following questions:
  - What is the paper *supposed* to be about? What is it *really* about? These should be the same thing. If they're not, work with the student to get the paper aligned with the assignment.
  - Is the student sticking to the topic? Or is he including any extraneous matter that is unrelated to the main topic? Is he "padding" his essay with unnecessary verbiage?
  - Is the paper organized? Does the organization make sense? Can the organization be improved?
- As you read, feel free to address any obvious problems or mistakes, especially ones that the student is repeating over and over.
- As you read his paper, mark it up with notes and corrections. Make sure he can read these and make sense of them. This document will be his roadmap later, when he revises his piece into a second draft. However, as you mark his paper, explain what you're doing, and why you're doing it. These notes are *extremely* important to the student. He will be relying upon them *that night*.
- If you don't understand why the student did something, ask him. He may have a very good reason for it.
- If a passage doesn't make sense, circle it, and ask him if he can make it clearer. *Read it out loud*, so that he can hear how it sounds (our ears can often pick up mistakes that our eyes miss). Then *ask him to "tell" you what he's trying to say*. This is a very powerful technique, because most of us speak better than we write. Cover the passage with your hands and ask him to "say it out loud." Then write down exactly what he says, right on his draft. Chances are it will be excellent.
- Don't ask him to read his work out loud. This will embarrass him, and he will run from the writing center.
- This is a good time to tell him to *write the way he talks*. This is very important, so I'm going to say it again: tell your students to *write the way they talk*. This is a

wonderful technique, and I'm surprised it isn't taught more often. We all have lots of practice speaking, and most of us do it pretty well. Chance are, if a student writes the way he talks, it's going to be good and pretty close to his unique identity and his own unique voice. And he can always go back later to edit it. He can remove slang and casual language and make it sound more "academic."

- Similarly, tell him that, when he's writing and gets stuck, to simply "write" a passage by speaking out loud (even if to himself). This has a freeing effect and is a great way to beat writer's block: we're thinking, talking, listening, and trying out ideas, all at the same time. This is a good way to see what works and what doesn't.

- Tell him to get his *ideas* down on paper first and to worry about the *wording* later. And this is great advice for any writer: *grab your ideas and put them down on paper, before you forget them.* You can always go back later to edit and improve the readability and mechanics. *Ideas first. Wording later.* As writers, we can always tinker with words, but when an idea is lost, it's gone forever, like a fading echo.

- When you get to the end of the paper, give it another compliment, but then suggest that there is room for improvement. You might say, "Okay, this is very good for a first draft, and there's lots of good information here. But I think we can make it even better." And then begin creating an outline with the student.

- When a student's draft is "completely messed up," begin making the outline by using his messy draft as a basis. Keep him involved in the construction of the outline, use lots of leading questions, and stress that you're using his ideas (and his writing), but putting them into a different form. He must always feel a sense of "ownership" for his work. He must feel as if he *earns* the grades he receives.

- In cases like the above, you create the outline based on (and drawn from) the existing draft. In a sense, it's like working backward. You simply pull the good stuff out of the draft and leave the bad stuff behind. By doing this, you are assigning focus and organization to his draft, his ideas, and his writing.

- As you construct the outline, make sure you tell him that "Anything we do today can be changed. This is your essay one hundred percent, and *you* make the final decisions here." This is a very important message and a great reassurance to the student. Students love to hear this, and it's a great lesson in the fluidity of writing and the role of editing.

- Make sure the outline (and all notes you make) are *clear and readable.* They will be his lifeline later, when he goes home to put in the changes you suggested. Make no mistake, he will spend the evening staring at your notes as he edits his essay. Do not underestimate the importance of the notes you make for the student. He will depend on them, more than you think. You have just become a very important person in his life.

- Tell him to write the introduction *last* (I specified the reasons for this earlier).

- Remember, you (and your tutors) must not write the paper for the student. You will teach him the *process* of writing, but he is responsible for the *content*.

- You can tutor a student's *creative writing*, even when it is not related to his school work. These students are looking chiefly to share their work with another human being. They want an informed audience, so this is an act of trust. Honor it. Be supportive, express enthusiasm for it, give it lots of compliments. However, you should also ask questions about it and offer suggestions for improvement. Feel free to direct them to read certain literary texts and consider offering them creative writing prompts to use in the future. Invite them back to the writing center for future visits. Remember, we're there to create writers.

- Urge your tutors to keep you informed with regard to their tutorials. As an involved director, you should know everything that is occurring in your writing center. Feel free to ask them about their tutorials. *Hey, how'd everything go today? What did you cover? Where is your student in the writing process? Got any questions?* This is good for their continuing development as tutors.

- If a student resists your (or a tutor's) suggestions, the correct response is "Okay," and then continue with the tutorial. *Do not argue with your students.* It's stressful, and there's no need for it. It's *their* paper they're writing, and they make the final decisions about it, good or bad.

- Explain to your tutors that they may, at some point, encounter a difficult student, an unpleasant tutorial, or an uncomfortable situation. *This is extremely rare*, because most students appreciate the help they get in the writing center (especially if it comes from another student). But if a tutorial becomes unpleasant for some reason, the tutors always have choices: they can continue with the tutorial if they want to. However, they also have your full authorization to *end the tutorial immediately*. In any case, if something unpleasant or unusual happens, they need to tell you about it. And they should not work with the same student again during future tutorials.

- If your tutors encounter something alarming in a student's writing (for example, threats of harming oneself or others), they need to let you know immediately. And you should bring this information to your administration immediately.

- Explain to your tutors that students may confide in them about highly personal aspects of their lives (dating, personal struggles, problems at home, etc.). This is an act of trust, and they are to keep this information 100 percent confidential and tell *no one*. However, if there are questions of potential safety involved, they are to tell *you*. And you will alert the administration appropriately.

- When the bell is about to ring (or the tutorial is about to end), there are several things you need to do. First, ask him if he wants the notes. The student will *always* take them. I have done over a thousand tutorials, and I have *never* had a student refuse the notes. Not once.

- Encourage him to edit (or begin) his essay *tonight*, while your instruction is still fresh in his mind. This is very important, because (although he has the notes you made) he'll forget the fine points of the discussion you had with him.

- Try to bring the student back into the writing center. Say something like, "You're off to such a great start. I'd love to see where you go with this. Can you come in again this week?" And then walk with him over to the schedule book and schedule another tutorial. Agree upon a time to meet and write his name next to yours in the book (I'll be discussing the schedule book in the next chapter). Smile, give another compliment, and project a friendly attitude that suggests he's welcome in the writing center any time.

- As a director (and a tutor), please try to have students work with the *same tutor every time*.

- If possible, try to bring students in for multiple tutorials. Three to five tutorials on a project works very well. More than five tutorials on a particular assignment may indicate an unhealthy dependence or a reluctance to write. Five visits is optimal. If the student comes in for five sessions on a single project, the results will be spectacular.

- Continue to hold weekly meetings for your writing center after it opens. Ask your students about their tutorials, what went well, and what could be improved. Give them the opportunity to ask you questions about writing or tutoring. These meetings are great for team cohesiveness and morale and are a demonstration of good leadership.

- If you do all those things I discussed above, the tutorials you hold will be a smashing success right from the beginning, and you'll be teaching kids how to write.

And this brings us to the final part of your tutors' formal training: *mock tutorials.* Make sure you do these shortly before they begin their actual tutorials in the writing center. These are lots of fun. Like the Mystery Topic exercise, mock tutorials also employ role-playing. But the tutors will be role-playing with each other. Here's how it works. Let's say you have a meeting at your regular time, and your tutors start to show up. You explain to them that they'll be conducting actual tutorials very soon, but before that, you want each of them to conduct some *mock* tutorials. And how many is good? Because they're so busy and because we (as professionals) are always so pressed for time, I suggest that each tutor participate in at least *two* mock tutorials. But *four* mock tutorials is optimal, if that can be arranged.

And if your tutors can do four, try to have them do two tutorials in the role of *tutor*, and two in the role of *student*. Although they are tutors in the writing center, it's important for them to be on the receiving end of tutorials and to view a tutorial from the perspective of a *student receiving instruction.* They need to experience what it's like to be tutored, to see how it feels, and to get a sense of what works and what doesn't. Both roles are important and make for a wonderful learning experience. And I explain all this to my tutors. I always hold one mock tutorial per meeting (not two), so this entire training segment of four mock tutorials typically takes a total of four meetings. As meetings are about 35 minutes long, the time allocation is very realistic.

After explaining to my tutors exactly what's going on, I convey that this isn't a "test," it's a learning experience. And if they have any questions, they can break out of the role and just ask. We don't want our tutors to flounder, panic, or get stressed out. We want them to learn. So, let's say we're having our weekly meeting, and eight tutors show up. This is good, because we can have *four tutorials* occurring at the same time. If there is an odd number (let's say five or seven tutors show up), *I always cast myself in the role of student.* (You should do this also; you already know how to tutor.) I then designate four of them to be tutors and four to be students. When I do this, I go around the room, pointing to each, and saying "tutor, student, tutor, student, tutor, student," until they all have their roles. This is different, they're nervous, they're excited, they're having fun (and so am I). I make a note on the attendance sheet who played tutor and who played student, because, next week, the roles will be reversed. The tutors will be students and the students will be tutors. I then ask the "students" to leave the room for a moment, while I have a brief chat with the "tutors."

"Okay!" I say to my four "tutors." There is a feeling of energy in the room, trust me. "You're about to hold your first tutorial. It's exciting! Who has questions?" And I wait, but there usually aren't any. I speak to them slowly and calmly, like a coach who cares about the upcoming game.

"Now, just remember the things we talked about. Get your notepaper and pencils. Sit in the magic triangle. Do the ice-breaker, then do the interview to get some info about the project. Okay? *Magic triangle, ice-breaker, interview* (I count them off on my fingers). Then brainstorm with the student to nail down a clear subject. Then, time permitting, help your student construct an outline. This isn't a test; just do your best with it. And don't rush it! It's not a race or a checklist of things to get done. Some things will just have to wait until the next tutorial. Any questions?" I look at them. I wait. I smile.

They smile back at me. They shake their heads no.

"You are going to be the best tutors ever, I can tell!" I say.

And then I have them choose their students at random, by reaching into a jar, and pulling out a name (I prepared this earlier; it's a good way to go, mirroring the random nature of real-world pairings. It also helps prevent them from tutoring their friends, a very tempting option). Then I ask them to choose their seats and to "spread out" as much as possible (they will often want to sit at the same table, but today, we want some room among the tutorials). And then I go visit the "students," waiting patiently outside the room.

"My favorite students!" I greet them, and they smile. "Ready to get tutored?"

They're excited too. I hand each of them a piece of paper with their "assignment" detailed on it. I prepared this before the meeting and made copies. You should definitely do this. Prepare for the mock tutorials ahead of time; try to have every detail set. It's a complex and important activity done in a short amount of time, so it needs to be planned and choreographed very carefully. I tell the students to look at their papers (everyone has the same assignment) and we go through the assignment together. Here's what I say:

"Okay, you're all 'average' tenth grade students (if you're a middle school librarian, I suggest making them 'average' sixth graders). You've been given a fun assignment for English, but you're not sure what to do. You want to do well; you're just not a great writer. So you come to the writing center to get help. Here is the assignment: you must write a three-page paper, double-spaced, about your *favorite place*." At this point I look up at my tutors. "Okay? Your *favorite place in the world*. Think about it and try to really make it your favorite place. Try to make it as 'real' as possible. You need to describe the place and say what it means to you, and why it is important to you. It is due in one week. Okay? Any questions?" They shake their heads, and look at the assignment. "Let's go!" I say and we all enter the room, and I make a grandiose announcement. "Tutors, greet your students!" It's a lot of fun. At this point, the tutors greet their students, "introduce" themselves, and the pairs walk to the tables. There are pencils and notepaper at each place, the magic triangles are established, and there is a murmur of conversation in the room. So far, so good.

If we have an even number of tutors, and I'm not playing the role of student, I bounce from table to table, listening to their progress. You should do this too, if you can. I like to just sit and listen, but if a tutor is having a really tough time, I might break in very gently. I did this one year. The tutor (who was very bright) had a mild case of stage fright and was reading the student's assignment, staring at the paper, and saying nothing. I could see that she was feeling nervous, so I jumped in. "Lynne," I said (not her real name), "you want a hand? It's okay, this isn't a test; it's a learning experience." After thinking a moment, she sheepishly nodded her head *yes*.

"Okay," I said, "no problem. Remember, the tutorial is a *conversation*. So make some small talk with your student and then talk to him about the assignment. You might make a list of his favorite places. Try to come up with at least three and then have him pick his favorite one. And make some clear notes to give him later. And then start working on the outline. Remember? It's easy. You can do it," I say, and smile. "You're gonna be a star at this; I can tell." She seems a bit relieved, and I bounce over to another pair and watch what's going on there.

I spend some time at each table, watching their progress, and getting a sense of what's happening. When there is about 10 or 15 minutes left in the meeting, I stop the tutorials, because I want us to speak, as a group, about the experience. I want each person to speak for a minute or two, because this really helps the learning process. When I have their attention, I say "Okay everybody, so that's a tutorial! How was it?" I look around. They're all smiling a little.

"Now, I want to hear from a tutor." But I don't wait for a hand to go up; *I choose a tutor* and ask him about the experience. But I'm very careful about how I phrase my questions. I avoid "yes" or "no" questions, and I avoid "general" questions such as "How was it?" These questions often draw the one-size-fits-all answer "Good," which won't teach us anything. Instead, I always ask specific, open-ended questions, because these encourage complex thinking and reflection. Today, the first tutor I choose is named Rick.

"Rick," I say. "You were a tutor today. What did you feel went well?" Rick thinks for a moment and talks about his experience, and we all listen, and sometimes this leads to a brief discussion about tutorials. I then ask Rick the opposite (and perhaps more important) questions: "What did you find challenging about tutoring?" And "Is there anything you could have done better? Anything that you might change during future tutorials?" And again, we listen to his answers, and I offer positive feedback and helpful suggestions whenever I can. But Rick is on the spot in front of his peers, so I make sure to include compliments and lots of positive reinforcement. "Okay Rick, nice work today. Thanks."

I then turn to Rick's student, Jessica. The questions here follow a similar pattern. I ask "So Jess, you were Rick's student today. What did you feel went well? What worked for you?" She talks, and we listen, and I offer comments and interact when I see teachable moments. I then move on to questions that might make some students (especially Rick) uncomfortable. Essentially, these questions are *What could Rick have done better?* Of course, we're in a very sensitive (and public) territory here, so I'm careful about how I handle these questions and how I phrase them. I usually ask questions such as, "If you could do this tutorial over, what could be done differently? Was there anything 'missing' from this tutorial that might have been helpful? If you were to come back for a second tutorial, what would you ask for?" And Jessica talks, and we listen, and I offer comments and feedback when necessary, when I think it will help.

And that's how I do a post-mock-tutorial "debriefing." I keep an eye on the clock, and I question as many tutors and students as the time will allow. I try to get feedback from all of them. And then, next week, we repeat the entire process. But we switch roles: the tutors become students and the students become tutors.

As you'll be performing a series of mock tutorials (during four meetings, spread out over four weeks) with your crew, I want to give you some ideas for these four mock assignments:

1. Week One: Describe your favorite place. Include what it means to you and why it's important to you (we just did this one).

2. Week Two: Describe an experience you had that changed your life. Describe the experience, why it affected you so deeply, and how it changed you or your life.

3. Week Three: name and describe your "hero." This person can be real or imaginary. *It cannot be yourself.* Describe this person, why he or she is important, and what he or she means to you.

4. Describe your highest goal in life. Make sure to include a description of the goal, why it is important to you, how you might achieve this goal, and what attaining this goal would mean to you.

You'll note that all of these are prompts for personal narratives. These work well, because we're dealing with fledgling tutors, and these topics don't involve research.

Well, this concludes my primer on the writing tutorial. I hope you revisit these chapters in your quest to become a master tutor of writing. But there are other aspects of running a writing center besides tutoring. There are daily operations, public relations, and the use of technology, to name just a few. These are all very important to the life and functioning of your writing center. And in the next few chapters, you're going to learn about all of them.

Chapter 7

DAILY OPERATIONS: THE COLONEL, THE BINDER, AND A THING CALLED CELLY

After you set up your writing center, you will be the one to run it. You alone. And it will fail or succeed on the basis of your personality, your actions, and your commitment to it. I have been told by students—and I have noticed personally—that many school clubs tend to "dissolve" over time and fade, existing only on paper. Students in middle and high school tend to get very enthused about things in the beginning (it's novel, it sounds like fun, my friends are in it), only to "cool off" over time. They're too busy; they would rather be doing other things; they "don't feel like it," or it's "not for them."

Please understand that the laws of entropy are very strong when it comes to school clubs. And writing centers are no exception. Their natural tendency will be to fall apart. But if you are actively involved in the writing center, and if you demonstrate the proper leadership, you won't be the only one there. Do it right, and you will always have a cadre of interested tutors. And the flipside is true also. You will always have a few tutors who find that the writing center is "not for them," and this is okay. Don't hold it against them. If they don't like it, you should *want* them to tell you. I would greatly prefer one enthusiastic tutor to 20 glum ones. The writing center needs to be a place of happiness and willing involvement, not begrudging participation or reluctant membership. As I have explained to my tutors (and students), "the writing center is a happy place." And it needs to be.

So you will need to hold things together. You will have to be involved in your writing center every day. However, don't let this discourage you. Properly managed, running your writing center won't take too much time or effort. I attended a conference recently where I gave a presentation on school library writing centers. It was lots of fun, and I'm always jazzed about the interest this topic sparks among school librarians. The room was packed. And, when I was taking questions, one attendee asked me something interesting: "Does running your writing center conflict with your duties or take you away from running the library?"

"No," I explained. "It doesn't. After the writing center is set up and you train your tutors, the actual management of the writing center is pretty minimal. The only thing that can get a little time-consuming is when I tutor. But I only tutor when I'm available. And much of this is on my own time. I tutor before school, during my lunch, during prep periods, and after school. But this is only when I'm needed, when my tutors can't, and when I'm available. I always have the option of saying no."

And because I can choose, the writing center has never come in conflict with my duties as a librarian. It's a priority issue, and I'm very conscious of it. I'm fully aware that, when I walk into my building in the morning, my primary duties (the ones I get paid for) are to run a school library. I don't get paid to run the writing center. So, if there is any conflict between running my library and running my writing center, the library will win every time. But this doesn't mean that I esteem my writing center any less. It's just common sense prioritizing.

One powerful technique for keeping your writing center together is holding weekly meetings. Hold meetings no matter what, even when there's no breaking news to pass along. And always hold them on the same day, at the same time. Announce them the day before the meeting and again on the day of the meeting. This is good leadership and will convey a number of positive messages to your tutors: you take the writing center seriously, that it's happening and vibrant, that it's not going anywhere, and that you consider them to be valuable members of the team. These are all powerful motivators for young people (and for people in general).

Don't underestimate the psychological power of routine and expectation and interpersonal contact. I still hold meetings once a week. The turnout for these meetings tends to be a bit low, because my tutors are so busy. But that's okay; attendance is not the point. Leadership is the point. You're doing this to hold your writing center together. It's great for cohesiveness and morale.

Keep the meetings fast-paced and productive and don't keep your tutors longer than you have to. That's not fair to them. I have held many meetings that lasted only about five minutes (and some even less). I just talked to them and conveyed that the writing center is still happening, even though things have been a little slow (this is okay; in fact, a slow week can be a nice break for everyone). I'm a great believer in transparency, so sometimes I say, "Hi Everybody. Okay, I have nothing new to pass along. But I just wanted to see everyone, and see how you're doing. We're a team, so I just wanted to touch base." And I mean it.

But before they go, I ask a few open-ended questions such as, "Does anyone have anything I need to know about? Anything interesting going on? School trips coming up? Schedule changes?" And if they shake their heads no, I smile at them and say "Thanks for stopping by. I really appreciate all your hard work. I'll see you all next week." They like being recognized, and they always appreciate not being kept. And they run along, to their next club, or sports, or theater. They're involved in such wonderful things.

Running your writing center gracefully will certainly take savvy leadership on your part, and this process mustn't be underestimated. However, like most things, the better you get at it, the easier it gets. You must realize that *you* are the hub of your writing center, and, as I said earlier, it will fail or succeed on the basis of your personality alone. And this brings me to a very important point, which is also one of the mainstays of the writing center model I created: I believe passionately that *you should be the sole director of your writing center*, and this is for a number of reasons.

First, there are logistical considerations: you can be there to watch things and run the writing center every day. This is just common sense. A writing center, if set in motion correctly, doesn't require much management, but it *does* require management. And it certainly requires leadership. You will be there to organize tutorials, to answer questions, to solve problems, to be a tutor, and to make sure things run smoothly. By simply being there, you give the writing center a psychological focal point, an intangible feeling of solidity and weight. When you're a leader of an organization, there is just no substitute for being present.

But there are also intangible reasons why you should be the sole director. Can we talk? If you've been a media specialist for longer than a few hours, you must realize that school librarians aren't always esteemed as the highly trained professionals that we are. Many people simply don't understand us or what we provide for our students. I hate to say it, but some actually believe that the advent of the Internet and the quick fix of search engines have rendered librarians (and even libraries and books!) obsolete, and therefore disposable. You and I both know that this is beyond ridiculous. If anything, the recent explosion of accessibility to information (unprecedented in human history) has made librarians indispensable navigators in an expanding ocean of knowledge. There is just so much information out there, and so much of it is bad. But it *looks* good, and it's easy to get, and when it comes to information, most students don't know the difference between good and bad. And in steps the humble, wonderful school librarian.

But we're quiet about it, and the small miracles we perform every day don't make the papers. So there is an undeniable benefit to placing the writing center prominently in your library (where it clearly belongs) and making *you* the director. In addition to helping students, it will also have the wonderful corollary benefit of helping your library, and helping *you*. It will elevate the status (and visibility) of your library, and it will help showcase your skills as a multifaceted (and indispensable) educator of children.

This is very important to us, to school libraries, and (by extension) to education all over the world. Writing centers can help put school libraries (and librarians) more firmly and prominently on the map and help them stay there. We routinely help students find information, and we show them how to use it. And now—because of school library writing centers—we teach students how to *write*. And this is very important. Writing is a universal skill, stretching across (and relating to) all disciplines. Writing centers, I believe, represent the next step in the evolution of school libraries. Don't be quiet about your writing center or the things you do as director. Tell teachers. Tell your administration. Tell the parents in your district. Proclaim it to the world. Be like Chanticleer, harbinger of morning. *Allow your writing center to advocate for your library*. It's a great way to demonstrate to the world that school libraries and media specialists are indispensable for students' educations.

But there are other reasons why you should be the sole director. Your constant presence in the library (capable and friendly) will have a powerful cohesive influence on the writing center. By just being there, you are exerting leadership and setting a good example. There is a suggestion that someone is watching and "in charge" in case there is a problem. This gives students a sense of security and confidence in themselves, in the writing center, and in you. They're not flying solo; you're there to help, if necessary. Doesn't the captain of a ship belong on the boat and not someplace else? If you opened a small business (let's say a used bookstore), shouldn't you be there every day to run it? Wouldn't that be best for your bookstore?

Your constant presence in the library is good for operations and good for morale. If the director of the writing center were another teacher (let's say an English teacher) in a different part of the building, this would not be an optimal situation (no matter how capable he is). First, he is not in the library to watch things. He's also extremely busy and won't be able to tutor regularly (trust me on that one; I've been a high school English teacher). At best, he might pop in a few times each week to check on things. As the librarian *is* physically in the library, she can manage things much more directly and immediately. She'll also be able to tutor regularly and will develop experience and deep knowledge of the tutoring process. And, as the writing center is part of the library, she will very likely feel a true sense of "ownership" for it. The writing center will become part of library offerings and not a remote satellite for another department.

At this point, you may still doubt your own abilities, and you may be tempted to ask an English teacher to be "co-director" along with you, or perhaps assistant manager. *Don't do it.* This would be a mistake. You may also have teachers approach you and say "When I was in college (or graduate school), I tutored in the writing center. Do you need some help with this?" If this happens, you must politely decline, while avoiding hurt feelings or damaging the relationship. Say something tactful, like this: "Thank you so much for the offer. I don't need any help right now, but I'm sure I will in the future." It's vitally important that you remain the sole, official, and true leader in the writing center. However, don't be afraid to ask advice from your colleagues; this is a different matter entirely and can be highly productive. But be careful of others wanting to intrude on your space and exert "unofficial" influence. This will likely lead to resentment, conflict, and an uneasy working relationship. And it will be bad for the writing center.

In any complex venture, there must be one person solely in charge, one person who can make final decisions. It's extremely rare for two people to work together like Lennon and McCartney. It almost never happens. If you attempt to share power with another teacher, it will probably result in quiet friction and interpersonal power struggles that will destroy morale among everyone involved. People can feel it. And it will eventually destroy your writing center.

When I was creating my writing center, I was fully prepared to vigorously decline all offers of help. No one had the expertise that I have, and I didn't want to deal with "helpful suggestions" from people who aren't as knowledgeable as I am. This is a recipe for conflict and argument. I didn't need the stress, and I knew it would be counterproductive. *You, and you alone, should be the director and should make all decisions*. And I know what you're thinking: that I have lots of unique experience and you don't. That's true. But you have this book, and I didn't. I only had knowledge, experience, and a belief that this crazy thing was necessary and that it would work. And now I have written this book for *you*. And you can always contact me on the forum with questions, if you have any. Allow yourself to grow into the position. Be bold, take risks, and believe in yourself and your abilities.

As the sole leader of your writing center, you must be very conscious of the "vibes" you project as director. Where the writing center is concerned, you must always project affability and enthusiasm, and you must always convey that the writing center plays a very important role in students' lives and in the world. Because it does. I make an effort to be very approachable with my tutors, treating them more as colleagues than as students (perhaps more feasible in high school than in middle school). This works, because the writing center involves busy adolescents with short attention spans doing academic work in a *voluntary capacity*. There are other things they'd rather be doing, and, if you're not careful, they can lose interest and drift away. Your writing center will be held together on the basis of your commitment to it, your enthusiasm for it, and your involvement with it. Your tutors, and the students they teach, will believe in your writing center to the extent that *you* believe in it. Part of good leadership is being enthusiastic. True enthusiasm is contagious and is a great way to motivate people.

Being a leader is always difficult, and it's a deceptively complex thing, but I can offer a few techniques that have worked well for me. First, you will develop your own leadership style with regard to the writing center. Everyone's leadership style is different. It must be true to your personality and who you are as a person. I don't consider myself a natural leader, yet I turned into a pretty good one. My leadership is quiet and positive and deeply human. And much of this is thanks to the leadership training I received while serving as a commissioned officer in the U.S. Marine Corps. Many people I've met (in fact, most of them) believe that Marine Corps leadership involves "screaming and yelling."

No. Absolutely not. Quite the opposite.

This is an awful stereotype and a vast oversimplification born of popcorn movies and the basic training environment (where constant stress is imposed in a "toughening up" process). The Marine Corps produces the greatest leaders in the world, and, as an officer, I was taught the techniques of extremely polished, high-level leadership: the things that occur behind doors in successful mega-corporations. And most of these are common sense. Here are my ten favorites. I learned these in the Marine Corps a long time ago, and I still use most of them on a daily basis:

1. Leadership involves getting the *willing cooperation* of others.
2. A good leader *motivates* his or her people.
3. Your most important job is accomplishing the mission.
4. Your second most important job is taking care of your people.
5. Give clear directions and check up on things, but don't micromanage.
6. When there is a conflict, get both sides of the story. The truth is usually somewhere in between.

7. Praise in public, reprimand in private.
8. Whatever you say to a subordinate (good or bad), he (or she) will take to bed with him (or her) that night.
9. You don't matter. Your people matter.
10. Set the example.

See that? Lots of insight into human psychology, with no screaming or yelling. If you do those ten things above, you'll be on your way to becoming an accomplished leader (which is always a great thing for a teacher, librarian, or writing center director). Military leadership is professional and polished and highly efficient. It's very human and goal oriented and rooted in an understanding of people and the things to which they respond well. Anyone with a bit of designated authority can shout and posture and "force" people to do things. It's the easiest thing in the world. However, this always creates anger and resentment in the subordinates and is terrible for morale, motivation, and team cohesiveness. And the person receiving this treatment becomes demoralized and gets soured on the leader, on the job, and on himself. Poor leadership can have an extremely detrimental effect on any organization. But when good leadership is exercised, the result is respect for the leader, enthusiasm for the job, and a boost in self-confidence. People are happier and the organization runs much better. Truly good leadership is a wonderful thing, but it's very rare.

Years ago, when I was a young second lieutenant (the lowest rank for an officer), I pulled a duty called "Officer of the Day." This was a 24-hour task that required me to sit at a desk in our headquarters (a large, red, brick building, baking in the Florida summer). I had to stand and salute superior officers when they entered or left the building, answer the phone (very politely), sign visitors in and out, and maintain a log of activities. At night, I needed to check that all doors and windows were secured and locked, and that nobody broke into the building. I had to do this every hour and make a note in the logbook. It was all standard, low-level stuff.

Until the commanding officer (a colonel) walked in and stood in front of me.

To be a marine colonel is a fearsome thing. One more promotion and he'd be a *general*. I jumped to my feet and saluted him. "Good afternoon, sir," I said. I didn't know the colonel personally, and he made me very nervous. He was a tough-looking old bird, in his fifties, with a tight gray crew cut and an aloof demeanor, and I had never seen him smile. And he had legs like a thoroughbred. They rippled with muscle, and, even though we were all young and in very good condition, we had trouble keeping up with him on runs. He liked to take us on ten milers in the Florida jungle morning. We started on a trail and finished along a beach, and then took a swim in the ocean. That felt really good and also (I think) saved us from heatstroke.

Anyhow, the colonel stood in front of me and spoke to me for the first time, and he looked pretty serious. "Afternoon Lieutenant," he said. "Tonight, General Crest is coming to the base. He's arriving at 19:30, and I need to pick him up at the airport. But if he gets in early, he'll give us a call. And if he calls, you need to write down whatever he tells you. I'll stop by later to check. Understood?"

"Yes sir," I managed.

He nodded and went up to his office, and a bit later, he left the building. I saluted him again as he passed.

Well, the general's call never came. And at 18:00, I did my rounds, checking doors and windows. All secure. I was alone in the big building, and I stood there, listening to the silence. The door to the colonel's office was open, so I decided to have a peek. It was big and spartan, with a large desk at the far end, near a window. The whole thing was immaculately clean and immensely organized: books, flags, photos on the wall of previous commanding officers. I looked around and listened. Silence. *The colonel's office.* The building was empty, so I went inside. *What's it like to be the colonel?* I wondered. I stepped in a little further and looked around. *I really shouldn't be doing this*, I thought and walked over to his desk anyway. It was dusk, and a golden light filtered through the big window. The room smelled clean and somehow electric. I walked behind the colonel's desk; it was oak, or mahogany; leather chair; photos of a beautiful family; beautiful wife; beautiful children; and the colonel in the photos, smiling. I was just about to sit in his chair, when the colonel walked in, as silent as a fleeting thought. He was dressed in red shorts and a golden tee-shirt, and he was carrying a newspaper and a cup of coffee.

I was so shocked, I didn't even salute him. I jumped and stood there, frozen in terror. But he walked past me, very calmly, sat behind his desk, and opened his newspaper and took a sip of his coffee. He didn't even look at me, but just said "Did the general call?"

"No s-sir," I managed, stuttering a little. And then I remembered to salute him, and I left his office as quickly as I could. I went back to my chair and sat and scribbled his entry in the logbook, barely legible, because my hand was shaking so bad.

That's a true story. Looking back at it—at my own youthful silliness—I see a good lesson in leadership there. The colonel could have made a big deal out of my intrusion into his space. This was a serious no-no. He could have been very angry and placed me in big trouble, but he didn't. He didn't do anything, other than ask me about the general. And that's because he understood his people. He understood that young lieutenants are gathering experience and sometimes do dumb things. And he understood the mystique that he and his office held for young officers. I always appreciated what the colonel did for me that day. It's a small incident, to be sure, but I view it as an example of very good and insightful leadership.

As a leader, you will also need to keep your writing center organized and running smoothly. There are several ways to do this, and thankfully, they're all pretty simple. One of the first things to do is to make a daily schedule. This is very important. For me, the end result is a professional-looking binder marked "Writing Center," with some fancy clip art on the cover. A stylized hand holding a pen and scribbling on some lined paper. It's nice. Our schedule contains blank schedule pages and used pages, and the current week is always on top. This way, when I (or a tutor) open the book, the current week is right there, at a glance. When a student wants to make an appointment, we simply write him on the schedule. And when a tutor is going to be absent, we cross her off. This book is therefore a record of past tutorials and a schedule of future ones and is a convenient encapsulation of writing center activities. It's important, because it tells the story of the writing center for the current year. It's laid out clearly and logically, and it's really hard to make a mistake with something like this.

I always leave the schedule at our main desk. Tutors can check it any time they want, students can use it to sign up, and I can keep an eye on what's happening in the writing center. I'm at the desk a lot, so I'm usually the one to sign up students. I like this; it allows me to see what's going on, and it gives me a chance to "talk up" the writing center. When a student signs up for the first time, I usually say things like "Oh, the writing center is the greatest thing ever! You're gonna love it." And this always gets a shy smile.

But I know what you're thinking: a *binder*? A binder is rather old fashioned; wouldn't an online schedule be better? Perhaps. I could certainly make an online schedule and post it to the writing center webpage, and someday, I may do this. But remember, we're dealing with middle school and high school students, and there are privacy issues to consider, both inside and outside the building. And technology, seductive and slick though may be, isn't perfect or infallible. I love my binder system. It's simple, it's real, it's human. Sometimes it's good for students to walk into a library and speak with a real human being, rather than communicating through a keyboard. And my binder has not yet "gone down" because of power outages or Internet failures. Sometimes you just can't beat the old ways of doing things. My binder is undeniably efficient and reliable, so I'm sticking with it. It works.

And what's in the binder? The all-important daily schedule. You will need to make one of these, and I'll show you how I did it. Creating the daily schedule is deceptively complex, so you need to do this carefully. My school runs on a "Day One, Day Two" schedule, and these alternating days certainly impact tutor availability. If your school does something similar, you'll need to make two different weekly schedules to represent a two-week cycle in the writing center. But if your school has a single-day schedule, you'll only need to make a single weekly sheet, which is a little easier.

To make my schedule, I created a template using computer software. More specifically, I used a word processing program and created two "tables" (representing the two weeks) composed of multiple rows and columns. I called these "Week One" and "Week Two." During *Week One*, Monday, Wednesday, and Friday are Day One. During *Week Two*, Monday, Wednesday, and Friday are Day Two. I made six columns. The first column (on the left) is for periods during the day. The other five columns are for the days of the week (and are labeled as such). Each day is divided into ten rows. This represents our nine periods, with a "tenth" period after school. Later (when I print the schedule), I write the dates, in pencil, below the days of the week. This is the basic schedule. It's simple but very effective, and you can take a look at it on the next two pages. And when you make your own schedule, make sure you save a copy in your computer software. You'll be using it year after year, so having a template is a great time-saver. Now comes the task of talking to your tutors, finding out who's available when, and putting them on the schedule.

For this, you can approach students individually or in a group. I prefer to ask them as a group during meetings. It's efficient and it's easier. To do this, I bring two blank weekly schedule sheets to a meeting. Making the schedule is a little tricky. It's easy to make a mistake, so I proceed slowly and clearly. I begin by telling students that we're making the schedule, and I ask them to think about when they're available to tutor. This might be (I explain) during a free period, lunch period, study hall (I can get them released from that), or after school, or some other

Writing Center Schedule: Week 1

PER	MON (1) Date: /	TUES (2) Date: /	WEDS (1) Date: /	THURS (2) Date: /	FRI (1) Date: /
1					
2					
3					
4					
5					
6					
7					
8					
9					
After School					

Figure 7.1

Writing Center Schedule: Week 2

PER	MON (2) Date: /	TUES (1) Date: /	WEDS (2) Date: /	THURS (1) Date: /	FRI (2) Date: /
1					
2					
3					
4					
5					
6					
7					
8					
9					
After School					

Figure 7.2

period when they're available. I go period by period on Day One, and then period by period on Day Two. At the meeting, the scene typically looks like this:

"Alright," I say, "who can tutor period one on Day One?"

Katie and Ryan both raise their hands. "Okay Katie, I'm putting you down for period one on Day One." I write her name, in pencil, in every *Day-One-period-one* slot, for a total of five times (three times in Week One and two times in Week Two). I then write Ryan's name right underneath Katie's. But Ryan tells me that he won't be able to tutor first period on Fridays, because of "something at home."

"Okay, no problem," I say and erase his name from Day One, period one, on Friday. He's still on the schedule four times.

"Now, who can tutor period two on Day One?" And more hands go up. And I keep going through all the periods on both days until I have completed a first draft of the schedule.

See how it goes? The schedule, simple though it is, holds lots of information, certainly more than you (or I) can remember. It holds the students' basic tutoring schedule, but it also records their exceptions. For example, Darren can't tutor on Thursdays after school (Day One or Day Two), because he takes tennis lessons that day. Victoria would "prefer" not to tutor on Fridays after school (because the week is "just so long"). Maura can't tutor after school because of driver's ed. But she'll be finished in a few weeks. And her father's buying her a car, she tells everyone (quite proudly) and smiles.

When making the schedule, you want all the coverage you can get, so strive to write in as many names as possible, in as many boxes as possible. The more the better. Don't be afraid to "encourage" your students a little here. And, when the schedule is complete, I tape the schedule to the whiteboard and ask the tutors to find their names and to make sure we didn't make any mistakes. I always say "Let me know if I need to erase your name anywhere or write it in anywhere. Take a good look."

But when the students actually see their names on the schedule, they may start to feel a bit nervous. *Wow, this might be too much. I don't know if I can do this.* Remember, you're dealing with over-achievers who are extremely conscientious about their schoolwork. Reassure them that this schedule is only a first draft and that all first drafts can be changed. More important, explain to them that *this is a schedule of potential availability.* This is a crucial point, and will go far toward dispelling any stress they feel. The schedule signifies when they are (in theory) *available* to tutor, Not when they *must* tutor. Reinforce to them that *they never have to tutor if they are too busy* or if they need to study for a test. Their schoolwork must always come first, so they always have the option of saying "I can't tutor today." And here, I reassure them that it's okay and that I *want* them to tell me when they can't tutor. Their grades are always more important than their involvement in the writing center. Always, always.

So at this point, you have your schedule made (on paper) and most boxes filled in with at least one tutor's name. Now, this will be looked at by many pairs of eyes, so make it look professional, and make it look pretty. Go into your computer template and copy and paste the blank schedule. You now have in your software *two* blank copies of your schedule. One copy will remain forever blank, because that's the template you will be using year after year. So go into your other blank schedule and type in your tutors' names, box by box. When all your tutors are in your schedule, save the file, and then print out schedules for the next few months. Punch holes in it and then put it in your binder. And write the dates on this week's schedule, which will be kept on top. It should look very polished and professional.

Show your tutors the finished binder (colorful and shiny and pretty) and explain to them how it works. Explain everything to them in very simple terms. This is important. They need to be very fluent in using, reading, and modifying the schedule. *This is Week One. This is Week Two. Here are the days; here are the dates; here are the periods. The current week is always on top. When you set up a tutorial, write your student's name next to your name. When you finish a tutorial, set up the next appointment with your student. Write their names in the book, in pencil, and show it to them, so that they know it's "real."* Put the binder somewhere visible and accessible, and show your tutors where the binder is kept. It's the main prop in the play you're directing.

Tell them it's not for your eyes only; they have full access to the schedule anytime they want. They can look at it; they can write on it; they can put the new weeks out, they can write in the dates. The tutors are a crucial part of the writing center, and they can function with a certain amount of autonomy. And, if they're going to be absent on a school trip (etc.), they should come in and put a line through their names or tell you about the absence. Keep it simple. And, if they want to be *really* sharp, they can (if possible) send you an email when they're out sick. The schedule is fluid and changing, like the writing center itself, but it should be kept as up-to-date and accurate as possible. All of this (structure, autonomy, communication) will prevent problems and will help the writing center to run very smoothly.

And when put your schedule book out, now comes the fun part: setting up your first tutorial. It will happen soon, when you're not thinking about it. You'll be doing the things librarians do, and one day a student will walk into your library, come up to your main desk, and he'll say "Hi, I wanna sign up for . . . that writing thing."

"Okay," you say (stifling a laugh) and open the schedule book. "When are you free? It could be lunch, study hall . . . even after school."

"I'm free fourth period," he says.

"Great. Can you come in today? Or tomorrow? We have someone terrific for you."

"Tomorrow, I guess," he says.

"Good," you say. "I'll put you down for fourth period, tomorrow. What's your first name?"

"Steve."

And you say "Steve, you're gonna love this!" and you smile at your first customer. And you write his name in the schedule, big and bold, so he can see it, and you show it to him. He sees his name written in the box for tomorrow, fourth period.

"Okay Steve," you say. "You're all set. See you tomorrow, fourth period."

"Thanks," he says and walks away.

And *Bingo!* Your writing center is in motion. And now, we need to get a tutor for Steve.

This is one of your main directorial duties, so get ready to do this. A lot. When a student signs up, you need to pair him with a tutor. It's just common sense. I have learned from personal experience that you can never ever assume that a tutor will "know" when she has a student and simply show up. You can't count on her to come in the library and check the book. Your tutors are very busy and very young and are off doing the things kids do and creating a million student memories. You need to find them, tell them they have a tutorial scheduled, and ask them if they can make it. They usually can, but you need to make sure. And if they can't tutor, you need to find the next available tutor and ask him if he can make it. Here's how it goes.

You look on the schedule and see that there are three tutors available tomorrow, fourth period: Samantha, Ryan, and Katie. You need to reach out to them (one by one, if necessary) and ask very nicely if they can tutor tomorrow, fourth period. You decide to approach Samantha first, so you need to track her down and ask her if she can do this. In my first year of writing center operations, I did it the old-fashioned way. I looked up their schedules, walked to their classrooms, and then spoke with them as they left class. "Hey Josh, can you tutor sixth period today?" The building is big, so this was very time-consuming and very tiring, and I swear there were days when I walked five miles for my beloved writing center. *There has to be an easier way*, I thought. And then I went to a conference, and I found out that there was. And now, I'm no longer trekking all over the building. Which means that you don't have to, either.

At this conference, I encountered a technological marvel that was absolutely golden, and I knew immediately that it was perfect for the writing center. It's a text messaging service called *Celly*, and it's free (you can find it here: https://cel .ly/). When you create a Celly group, or "cell," you can use your phone to text the entire group, or you can send a text message to specific individuals. They receive it on their phones, and they can text you back. It's fantastic, and I'm sure you can see the benefits for the writing center.

There are certainly other texting programs out there, and many of them would work for this. However, I prefer Celly for a number of reasons. For one, it has been created specifically to assist with Education. As such, the designers anticipated the concerns of educators and brought in the stuff we like and got rid of the stuff we don't like. For example, Celly is completely private, so it's very safe. Although the messages bounce from phone to phone, there are no phone numbers exchanged, not a single one. Second, it can't be viewed by anyone who is not a member of the cell. It is 100 percent private. It's perfect for teachers and students to use, and it's not too complicated.

If you read their "Celly Privacy Policy," you'll see that "Children under 13 are not permitted to use Celly" (Celly: Privacy Policy). This concerned me, because some middle school tutors may be under 13 years old. I asked Celly about this, and they got back to me with great news: the *parents* of students under 13 can create accounts for their children, so their kids can use it. I was thrilled. This gives us the green light to use Celly, which means we no longer have to walk miles to track down our tutors. My feet applauded this miracle of technology.

At some point, you will have to create your "cell" with your tutors and train them in how to use Celly. A group meeting is the perfect time for this. Kids love texting and technology, so it makes for a great meeting. Send out a group email and tell them to "bring their phones." They'll find this exciting. *Wait, a teacher wants us to use our phones? What's going on?* And then meet with your tutors and have fun playing with Celly. But before the meeting, you need to do your homework and set things up. You'll need to spend some time on the Celly website, get a bit familiar with it, and create the cell for your writing center. It's not very complicated, and it's pretty easy to use. But it is new, and it does take practice. I won't go over every aspect of it here (that's up to you), but in brief, here are the steps:

1. You create a cell and give it a unique name (you will also create a new cell every year, because some of your tutors will graduate and others will take their places).
2. Your tutors request membership (you'll explain to them how to do this).
3. You accept them as members (individually, not as a group).
4. They choose unique usernames (these usernames must be completely unique to the Celly network. They must also be usernames that *you* will remember).

That's it, they're in, and you're ready to start exchanging text messages. It takes a little practice, but it's pretty simple, and it works beautifully. Once you get your tutors on Celly, spend the rest of the meeting practicing with them. Send practice messages about tutoring, and have them respond to you. I always start by sending group messages, such as "Hey Team, meeting tomorrow at 2:20. Hope to see you all there!" (and I really do send this message once a week). And I have them answer me back, with something like "I'll be there." I also send *individual* messages to every tutor in the room, such as "Hey Ryan, can you tutor tomorrow 7th period? Thanks!" (again, this is quite similar to the "real" messages I send). And I have students answer me back by accepting the tutorial with something like "I'll be there!" (positive thinking, right?).

During this meeting, I look for responses from every tutor, just to make sure everything is working and that they're doing it correctly. And I also discuss briefly what I call "Celly etiquette." I implore them to keep all conversations brief and focused exclusively on the writing center. This is not a social network; it's a professional one. And yes (I discovered), they can message each other via Celly. I ask them not to do this and to message me exclusively. Our Celly network is for the writing center, and for the writing center only. This is important (for obvious reasons), so please stress to your tutors the need to keep the Celly network 100 percent professional and related to the writing center. That is its sole purpose.

And now that you know a bit about Celly and how it works, let's revisit the above scenario for a moment. Remember Steve, your first customer? He's coming to the writing center tomorrow, fourth period, and you need to find him a tutor. At the end of the period, you send a text to Samantha, who is in her math class: "Hey Sam, can you tutor tomorrow 4th period? Thanks!" And the message goes to Sam. When the bell rings and she's packing up her books, she checks her phone and responds to you: "Yes, I'll be there!" And your first tutorial is ready to go.

As time passes, you will be scheduling more and more tutorials, and your binder will develop a well-worn look to it. It will contain lots of pages with lots of names scribbled on them, and this will be a wonderful development. It indicates that your writing center is being utilized often, and that you're helping lots of kids. But you may be wondering if this is the extent of records generated (and kept) by your writing center. *Is this it? Or should there be something else? Some other form of records?*

I have published numerous articles on school library writing centers, and I have presented at lots of conferences on this subject, and I am frequently asked (through email and in person) if we should generate any form of reports that are more detailed than paired names in a binder. After one of my presentations, one librarian put it this way: "What do you think about having the tutor fill out a report after every tutorial? He could give information about who he tutored, about the project, and about what he covered. This might be useful. What do you think?" It's a good question and it's certainly well-intentioned. However, my answer to this question is always a firm "No." And this is for a variety of reasons.

First, I'm always leery of mission creep and bureaucracy, and I'm always cautious of generating paperwork that doesn't serve a clear function. This, to me, smacks of bureaucracy and "paperwork for the sake of paperwork" (and one thing I'm not is a bureaucrat). But I'm most concerned for the tutors. Think of them. They're young and they're volunteers. Do we really want to have them fill out a report after every tutorial? No young person wants to do this. They would question its purpose and come to resent it and eventually come to resent the writing center. And we don't want this. As teachers, we live in a world of paperwork and data, so we have come to expect it, and we accept it as part of the occupational environment.

I view this as a leadership issue, one that takes insight and perspective. The writing center is immediate and action-oriented and is rooted in praxis and process and rough-and-tumble tutoring. I urge you vehemently to keep it streamlined and not bog it down in bureaucratic tasks like information-gathering and the production of paperwork. We must stick to our original mission to teach basic writing, and that's it. And we must do this no matter what happens and no matter what technological marvels the future holds. So I urge you: don't generate paperwork in your writing center. Generate *writers*.

Chapter 8

SHOUT IT FROM THE ROOFTOPS! AND FROM YOUR PA SYSTEM

Your writing center is like a small, delightful business. And for any business to succeed, it must advertise.

If you don't advertise and publicize, your writing center will remain underutilized, and your tutors will grow bored and drift away toward other more interesting endeavors.

In this chapter, I'm going to give you techniques for telling everyone in your district about the writing center: students, teachers, administrators, parents. And anyone else you can think of. Tell the secretaries, tell custodial, tell all your support personnel (many of these people will have kids in the district). Now that you've got this thing, everyone needs to know about it. And people talk. This will involve public relations, advertising, and marketing, and it will take time. Let it. As a matter of fact, it will take forever. You should never stop telling people about your writing center. Remember, you get a new crop of "customers" in your school every single year (in the form of incoming students), and they need to learn about it. And they need to believe in it.

So, in a sense, you need to run your writing center as if it's a business. You are the CEO, your store is located in the library, your tutors are your employees, your customers are the students who come to see you, and the product you're "selling" is writing instruction. Think about your favorite products and the most successful companies. Do they ever stop advertising? No, they advertise all the time, over and over. And that's one of the reasons they're so successful. And they get creative about it and try widely differing modes of advertising. And you should, too.

Your goal should be for your entire district community to know that you're there, just as they know of the Honor Society, the Drama Club, and the football team. As you do this, keep in mind that your goal is threefold: (1) your district needs to know what you are and what you do; (2) they need to know the logistics of access (where you're located, when you're open, and how to sign up), and (3) they need to believe in the quality of the "product" you're providing. And even when the word is "out" about the writing center, you'll still need to keep "pushing" your services. Public relations, communication, and advertising are continuous. This means that you'll need to become adept at marketing your new writing center. Everybody needs to know about it, so you must tell them about it—over, and over, and over, again. This is the only way to become part of people's consciousness. But how, exactly, do you do this?

When I first opened my writing center, I immediately told teachers and administrators about it. And my first avenue of communication was district email. Teachers especially need to know that the writing center exists and that it can help turn students into writers. I regard this as a new and different type of collaboration between the library and the classroom. Think about it: as a librarian, you don't know which students are struggling with writing, but classroom teachers do. And they can tell these students about the writing center and encourage them to go.

I wrote these initial emails very carefully. I know well that classroom teachers are extremely busy, and they get lots of emails, and long emails often get skimmed or skipped. Most emails probably get looked at for about three seconds. So, to make the message digestible, I made my emails short, simple, and repetitive and put "Writing Center" in the subject line. I wanted to give teachers a quick and basic knowledge of the writing center, and my goals were quite modest. I wanted them to know that we exist, what we do, and how students can sign up. So I sent out a short email (more like a sound bite) every day for two weeks, and I purposely made them a bit enigmatic. I hoped to build curiosity about the writing center, and, based on the feedback I received from teachers, I succeeded. Here are my emails from that first week:

DAY ONE: "We have a new writing center!"
DAY TWO: "The new writing center is located in the library."
DAY THREE: "The writing center teaches students how to write."
DAY FOUR: "The writing center is open during the day, and after school."
DAY FIVE: "Send your students to the writing center. We're located in the library, and we'll teach them how to write."
ETC.

This "sound bite" approach worked well, and teachers began asking me about "this new writing center." Sometimes, it's best to introduce new concepts slowly and gently. But I didn't stop there. To this day, I continue to send out emails periodically to the faculty, reminding them of the writing center and inviting them to send their students to us for writing instruction. I also "talk up" the writing center in person, whenever I chat with teachers. And I do this with teachers from *all* departments, not just the more "obvious" ones, such as English and social studies. I also touch base with department chairs, which is a very efficient way to disseminate information about the writing center. And I'm careful to approach every department, not just the usual writerly suspects. I describe how helpful we are, and I politely request that they mention the writing center during department meetings and encourage teachers to send their students to us. All of these interactions are tinged with tact and diplomacy. There's no need to seem pushy and desperate, because we're offering students something wonderful.

But your biggest moneymakers here are probably classroom teachers. During conversations, I am constantly inviting them to send their students to the writing center. I ask them about their upcoming projects and tell them that, no matter what the project is, we can definitely help. I describe the process and what we do, but I also make a rather bold suggestion that has increased traffic a good bit. I suggest to teachers that they might, if they want, offer their students extra credit for coming to the writing center.

But I do this very gently and very tactfully, because it is 100 percent the teachers' decision. I tell them that "Some teachers like to offer students a little extra credit for coming to the writing center. For example, one teacher told her students they could earn one extra point per visit, up to a total of five points. So some of her students came in for five visits, and they earned an extra five points on the project." This is true, and it worked very well. It got students into the writing center for five visits, which is optimal. But really, the purpose was threefold: students earned some extra credit (a tangible reward, which they love), they improved their projects, and, most important (and true to our mission statement), they gained valuable knowledge about writing.

When I offer this incentive to classroom teachers, I'm always very careful about how I present it. I always say "But this is just a suggestion; it's completely up to you." And I mean it. I don't like to seem pushy, and teachers don't like to feel pressured. But I find that, among teachers, there is very little middle ground here. Some teachers will gladly offer this bit of extra credit for the obvious payoffs it provides, while others are opposed vehemently to extra credit. And sometimes, their chairpersons have made extra credit anathema in their departments. But it never hurts to offer and to give people choices.

I also use pictures and posters to advertise the writing center. Who doesn't like to look at pictures? They're fun, they're pretty, they're eye-catching. They're also an effective mode of dispensing information. I made a big poster for the writing center, and I laminated it and put it up on a bulletin board in my library. For a visual focal point (an attention grabber), I used a stylized hand holding a pen and scribbling lines on a piece of paper (similar to the clipart on our schedule book). It's nice. On the poster, I provided (in large print, bullet point format) a brief overview of what we do. I kept the tone very friendly and fun and ended by inviting everyone to come to the writing center. But keep in mind that posters will get looked at for just a few seconds, so make yours eye-catching and make the information basic and highly accessible.

I also used a word processing program to make (and save) a rather snazzy looking single-page flyer. It's attractive, and it describes what we do in simple bullet points.

Need Help With a Paper?

Come to the

Writing Center!

Sign up in the library!

- **All tutorials are held in the LIBRARY**

- **All tutorials are ONE-ON-ONE peer instruction**

- **All of our tutors are STUDENTS in the High School**

- **We can help you with ANY paper or project in ANY subject**

- **We're OPEN during the school day (all periods)**

- **We're also open AFTER SCHOOL**

Sign up today!

Figure 8.1

This flyer has become a mainstay of marketing the writing center, and I have used it over and over. I post flyers strategically in my library—on bulletin boards, on walls, and on both sides of doors (always at eye level). I drop it on library tables and desks, where kids look at it just before they scribble on it. I hand it to kids coming into the library. And, during writing center meetings early in the year, I give each tutor ten copies, with the rather cryptic instructions to "put them where

DISTRICT LETTERHEAD HERE

30 September 20__

Greetings District Resident:

I am thrilled to tell you about the High School Library Writing Center!

We are located in the high school library, and we are open every day. Our purpose is not to "fix" papers, but to help Hauppauge students learn to *write*. We're in our fifth year of operation, and feedback (from staff and students) has been extremely positive.

Here is some more information about us and how we function:

- Students make appointments in the high school library. They can come as often as they want.
- We're open five days a week, during the school day and after school (until 3pm).
- We use peer-tutoring. All of our tutors are students at the High School.
- Students receive one-on-one assistance with their writing assignments.
- We can help students with any project in any subject.
- Tutorials last for a single period. Multiple tutorials (over consecutive days) work best.
- The writing center is open to *all* students, and it is *free*.
- Although specific assignments are usually the focus of a tutorial, we do not "edit" papers, and we certainly do not write papers for students. Our focus is not on "fixing" papers, but on transforming students into *writers*.

If you want some more information on what we do and how we do it, please feel free to contact me by phone or email. I hope to see lots of our students in the Writing Center!

Regards,

Dr. Timothy Horan
BA, MA, MSLIS, MS.Ed, AGC, DA
Library Media Specialist
Director of the Writing Center
Hauppauge High School
horant@hauppauge.k12.ny.us
(123) 456-7890

Figure 8.2

people will see them" (I can only imagine where they wind up). More important, every year I email a copy of this flyer to every teacher (and administrator) in the building, with the polite request that they print it out and post it prominently in their classrooms and offices (most of them do). And I also put it in the hands of parents.

A few years ago, right after I started the writing center, I was speaking with our wonderful teacher of German (now retired), when he gave me a brilliant suggestion in his beautiful German accent: "Tim," he said, "make sure parents know about the writing center. If you do this, I think you'll have more students than you can handle." I looked at him and thought *of course*. Of course! How did I overlook this?

Parents and guardians generally know how their kids are doing in school, and they know their academic weaknesses. And if a student needs help in writing, let's have the parents give them a nudge in our direction. Think about it: if we get parents on board, we have a community of friendly advocates "at home" urging their kids into the writing center. But how could I do this? I thought about it and came up with a good idea.

I decided to send a letter to every household in the district. But mailing out over a thousand letters is no small task (and it's pretty expensive), so I needed to get permission. After getting the nod from administration, I used district letterhead and composed a letter which introduced the writing center (and me) to parents and invited them to send their kids in for writing instruction. It was written with a professional (but friendly) tone and included an overview of writing center services, presented once again in bullet point format. And remember that snazzy flyer I mentioned above? I printed it on the other side of the letter. This provided a two-sided document with visual interest and repetition, which is good for learning. And besides, who can resist two for the price of one? (see figures 8.1 and 8.2, on pages 108–109)

When printed on district letterhead, the letter is exactly one page long, is upbeat in tone, and explains the writing center in clear and simple terms. Flip it over. On the other side is the flyer. It's visually attractive, highly readable, and contains much of the same information.

This felt great. Our mailing office had just sent out a two-sided document to every household in the district telling parents all about us. My writing center was gathering momentum, and people were learning about us. I was having fun, and I kept brainstorming and dreaming up additional ways to advertise the writing center.

A few years ago, I returned to school one evening for our "open house." And while I was preparing the library for inspection, I had a sudden flash of insight: I realized that a thousand pairs of parents were coming to the building. Of course, this represented a golden opportunity to advertise the writing center, and I wanted to take full advantage of it. But how could I communicate with all the parents in the building? I thought for a moment and came up with a simple plan. I quickly printed a thousand copies of the snazzy flyer and then walked down to the English wing. I approached the English teachers (I know most of them pretty well) and spoke with them individually and briefly. I explained what I wanted to do and asked them "Could you hand these out to parents?" I gave each teacher a generous stack of flyers and decided to press my luck. "And if you have time, could you mention the writing center to them? Thanks very much." And I walked away, feeling really good about this. It was a novel and creative approach, but also efficient and productive. And honestly, it was pretty darn easy too. I try never to miss an opportunity to advertise my beloved writing center.

Now, up to this point, I had been actively "recruiting" teachers, administrators, and parents. I still had to reach our target audience, the students. I thought about ways to reach them (beyond the flyers that were now hanging everywhere in the school) and came up with some methods that were fun and effective. I decided to have us mentioned in the morning and afternoon announcements (which are always done by students). This is a good idea, because kids listen to other kids. Kids trust their peers. So now, every day, the entire school hears about the writing center *twice*. The morning announcement I wrote goes like this: *Need help writing a paper? Come to the Writing Center! Sign up in the library and work with another student to become a better writer. Your writing skills will improve, and best of all, it's FREE! Sign up today, in the library.* It sounds terrific read by a young voice, and it's a great way to spread the word about us.

With the afternoon announcements, I let my tutors have fun and go a little crazy. At the end of a long day, a little humor can be a wonderful thing. To do this, I always look for a "theatrical" tutor (someone in the drama club or a natural "ham"), and I enlist her (or him) to make the afternoon announcements. I give these tutors license to say pretty much whatever they want, "as long as it's related to the writing center, and it's G-rated" (this always makes them giggle). They like the responsibility and the freedom. I started doing this in our second year of operations, and the first tutor I chose for this was "Krissy." Krissy was a drama student and had a wonderful personality. She was bristling with life and joy, and every time I saw her she looked as if she had just been given the gift of the entire universe and was getting ready to do kind deeds for everyone and everything, for all of eternity. She really did. That's exactly how she looked.

Anyway, I told Krissy what I wanted, and I let her design her own message. And every day, she announced her message with beautiful dramatic flair: "*A-a-a-a-attention students*! Do you have a *pesky* paper to write? Well, the writing center can help! We're in the library, and we're happening. . . .*r-r-r-right nowww*! So don't waste another minute. Come see us, and get that paper *done*! To *know* the writing center is to *love* the writing center!" Krissy's delivery was light and fun (perfect, really), and I smiled every time I heard it. And then something really wonderful happened.

That same year, I met a student named "Colin." He came into the library nearly every day, and I got to know him really well. He was creative and artistic, and I loved chatting with him. We got along great. It turned out that he was in the drama club and knew most of my tutors. It also turned out that he could imitate the voices of celebrities, and that he loved an audience. Although introverted, he entertained me with superb renditions of Bart Simpson, Bullwinkle (the cartoon moose), and actors such as Nicolas Cage. He was really amazing. And one day, I got an idea. A crazy, fun, terrific idea. What if Colin assisted with the afternoon announcements? And what if he imitated celebrities over the PA system? Would he go for this? I asked him, and he was thrilled by the thought of a large audience. He could do his imitations for the entire school! We were all very excited. I paired him with Krissy (they knew each other from the drama club), and I told them to simply "Make it good. And keep it G-rated." They both giggled and began collaborating for their first "celebrity" announcement.

And that afternoon, the announcement went like this:

Krissy:	*A-a-a-a-attention students*! This is Krissy from the writing center, and we have a special guest to tell us all about the writing center. *Bart Simpson*, what has the writing center done for you?
Colin/Bart:	I didn't do it! Well, uhh, yes I did. I took my skateboard to the writing center, and they were awesome, man. I used to hate writing, but now it's no problemo! Cowabunga dude, go to the writing center! It's better than a Krusty burger!
Krissy:	Thank you Bart Simpson! And he's right: the writing center *is* better than a Krusty burger. So come see us. We're in the library, and we're happening. . . .*r–r–r–right nowww*!

The kids loved it, and they thought it was hilarious. I was in the library when it came over the PA system, and I think I laughed for about five minutes straight. Bart Simpson advertising the writing center! What could be better than that? After that, Krissy and Colin settled on a routine. They explained to me they didn't want to overdo "the celebrity thing" and thought it would be more effective if done once a week. It was a great insight, and I agreed. So every Friday, we all looked forward to another celebrity raving about the wonders and beauties of the writing center. Bullwinkle assuring everyone that, thanks to the writing center, his grades were now "soaring higher than my friend Rocky, the Flying Squirrel!" Nicolas Cage came to the writing center because he "wanted the As! Not the Bs! *Not the Bs!*" (this last is a reference to one of Cage's sillier scenes, where his character is being tortured with bees. Don't ask). These announcements became very popular among the students, and I always appreciated the laugh they gave me on a Friday afternoon. And of course, they were very effective. There's nothing like having your product endorsed by a celebrity.

Word was now beginning to spread about the writing center, and one day I got an email from Mrs. "Brandt," the English teacher who runs the school newspaper. She had received several of my emails about the writing center, and she heard all the announcements, and she thought it would make a nice article in the newspaper, and could I get it to her before Friday? I was thrilled. What a fantastic idea and what a great way to let students know about us. I quickly sent her a response in which I thanked her, accepted the opportunity, and promised to get her the article before the deadline. I began writing it that day, and on Thursday afternoon, I sent her a terrific article that described the writing center in most appetizing terms. I made sure to address the *Who*, *What*, *When*, *Where*, and *Why* of the writing center, I described its wonders, and I invited every student in the building to come in, sign up, and learn how to write. And then I took a deep breath and waited. This was exciting.

A few weeks later, my article ran verbatim in the school newspaper, and it was wonderful to see. This was great press for the writing center, and I knew it would be read by many pairs of eyes: students, teachers, administrators, and parents (be assured, school newspapers always find their way home). Don't overlook this obvious medium; you should definitely write an article for your school newspaper. And this makes sense, because *you are a writer*. Remember that. And be sure to write a good article, because you will be judged on your writing (and this is not as ironic as it sounds). This is definitely one case in which form equals function, in which the medium is also the message. You're writing about writing. You've been "talking the talk," now start "walking the walk."

When you write your article, keep it simple and remember the basics, and be sure to address the journalistic pillars which describe the *Who, What, When, Where,* and *Why* of your writing center. Also, make sure to stress that it takes place during the school day and after school and that it happens in the library. Emphasize that students will be tutored by other students, because many of them will be drawn by the peer-tutoring aspect of the writing center. But mention that you're also a tutor, because some kids will prefer to work with you. And when you're finished writing a solid draft, do yourself a favor: *don't submit your article until you take it to the writing center.*

I'm very serious about this. Schedule an appointment with one of your tutors and have her go over it with you. I do this every time I generate a piece of writing, including when I'm writing for publication. I become the student sitting with a tutor, and this is a real writing center tutorial. I tell the tutors to "be merciless," and they are, and I always appreciate it. And I admit, I have included some of their suggestions in pieces that were published. I too am a student of the writing center I created.

And now that you have finished your article, see how much mileage you can get out of it. Where else can it be published? Your school probably has a few district periodicals and community newsletters, so try to run your article in all of those. Find out who edits or publishes them (this information is often included on the periodical itself), and then send these people a polite and brief email about the writing center. And *make sure you attach your completed article,* because there's nothing like a promise followed by an immediate delivery. Editors need to fill space in their publications, and they'll love getting a fully complete, high-quality article on a nifty new subject that's important to the district. It'll be like handing them a golden apple, and it's great exposure for the writing center. Give it a shot; you have nothing to lose. But there's one other thing to do with your article, and this one is a homerun.

Did you know that most school districts have a public relations department? Find out if your district does and then contact them with a friendly email. Try to find out who the "go to" person is for PR, and then make a friend of him or her. The public relations department has contacts in all the local media. If you send them your article, they can zap it out to local (or "town") newspapers. And for the next few weeks, be prepared to be treated like a celebrity: *Hey, I read about your writing center the other day!* It's a really cool experience. You'll enjoy seeing your name in print, and it will elevate your writerly credibility among tutors and teachers. And it will make you feel like a writer. And make no mistake: that's what you are. You're a writer. So stop doubting yourself.

Now, things were going very well, but there was one more thing I wanted to do. I wanted to tell every student in the school about the writing center. I wanted every student to learn where we are, what we do, and how much we can help them. And when doing this, I wanted to make sure that every student in the school got personally invited to the writing center, at least once. And I wanted this invitation to be "up close and personal" from another human being. But how could I do this? I thought about it, and I came up with a terrific idea. I would use my tutors to spread the word (remember, kids listen to kids). I decided that, every year, my tutors would tell the entire incoming class about the writing center (in my school, this is the ninth grade) and invite them in. (And now, I try to do this in the beginning of the year, so that these new students can start coming to us as soon as possible.) And, on our next Friday meeting, I explained my plan to them.

I put the chairs in a circle and told my tutors that I wanted them to go into classrooms and talk about the writing center and invite kids to come see us. Whenever their schedules permitted, they would go into ninth-grade English classes and introduce the writing center to our new freshmen. They would (I explained) do this in the first two minutes of class, before the teacher started her lesson. The message should only take about two minutes, and above all, they must not interrupt a teacher once she has started her class. I stopped and looked around. They looked a little nervous, but their eyes were bright, and I could see they were with me. I continued.

"I'm going to clear this with the teachers first, and set everything up. But please, understand this: there is a certain way to talk to teachers. Even though I will set this up with them, you first need to approach the teacher politely, and introduce yourself, like this: 'Hi Mrs. Smith. I'm Robert, and I'm from the writing center. Is it okay if I talk to your class today about the writing center? This should only take about two minutes.' If you do it like that, she'll probably say yes." I looked around. So far, so good. I kept going. "Now, you don't *have* to do this. So if there's some reason why you don't want to do this, please let me know after the meeting. Or on Monday. I can't read your mind, so you have to tell me. Okay? Please." I looked around the room; they nodded. I smiled. I passed around a paper that contained a short "speech" I had written. "Take a look at this," I said. "This is a quick overview of the writing center. You can read this out loud to the classes if you want, or you can just talk to them, if that works better for you. But this is the basic information I want you to give the ninth graders. Krissy, would you read this out loud for us?" She read aloud in her expressive actress voice:

> Hi everybody. My name is _____. I'm a tutor in the writing center, and I want to invite you all to come to the writing center. It's the greatest thing in the world, it's free, and you're going to love it. The writing center will help you with all your papers and writing projects, for the next four years. We're located in the library. Just walk in, and make an appointment. You'll sit with another student, who will help you with your writing. You can do this during the day, on your free period, study hall, or lunch period. Whatever works for you. And we're also open after school. So again, the writing center is located in the library, and we can definitely help you with all your papers. Any questions? (wait for five or ten seconds here). Thanks everybody! Thanks Mr(s). _____. So come to the school library writing center. It's really helpful, and you're going to love it!

Krissy stopped reading and looked up. "Thanks Krissy," I said, and looked around. "That's it. Easy, right? And when you do this, try not to be nervous about it. Smile. Be psyched. Show that the writing center is a happy place. And if students have questions, feel free to answer them, but please, *please* try to keep the whole thing to about two minutes. That teacher has a class to teach." This was new to all of us, and I let it all sink in, and I smiled at them again. I was excited about this new phase of our adventure. "Good?" I asked. "All set?" They read the speech over and nodded. I could tell they were jazzed about this new and important job, and a few told me they thought it was a "good idea." That's a pretty high compliment, coming from a high school student.

I spent the next few days using the writing center schedule to align tutors with ninth-grade English classes and getting permission from English teachers. Where there were gaps, I filled in and spoke to classes myself. It was a big logistical task, but it was fun, and in the end, we were able to speak with nearly all of the new freshmen in the school. This approach worked very well and was very effective, and traffic in the writing center increased almost immediately.

By doing this every year, I ensure that virtually every student in the school has been invited personally into the writing center, at least once. But my highest goal here is to give students a relationship with the writing center that will last for their entire time in the building. If we do this—if we can get students in the writing center for their entire school experience—we can transform them into highly skilled writers before they leave for their next destination, whether it's high school, college, or the workplace. And this is a tremendous gift to give students. I think we'll never truly know the good we do in students' lives, and in the world.

As word spread about the writing center, advertising opportunities began to increase. For example, I was in my library one Monday morning when a student named "Kathy" walked in and asked me an unexpected question. She said "Hey Dr. Horan, Eagle Watch wants to feature the writing center on its next broadcast. Interested?" She smiled at me hopefully. Now, let me give you some background information on this. Eagle Watch (named after our school mascot, the Eagles) is the school's television news program and airs on a cable channel. It is run by a highly accomplished teacher of broadcast and media, and the Eagle Watch team routinely puts together a program that is very polished and professional. It's viewed widely by students, parents, and faculty, and now my writing center was going to be featured on it.

I was thrilled.

"Yes!" I blurted out. "I'm definitely interested. How will this work? What do we do?"

"Great." Kathy said. "We'll work together on the segment. You'll provide lots of input on how this will go. But the thing is" (she looked a little nervous here), "we're on a strict deadline, and we need to film this coming Wednesday. That gives us two days. Can you be ready by then?"

"Yes!" I blurted again. "I'll definitely be ready." We chatted for a few minutes and worked up a basic outline of the segment. During fourth period on Wednesday, Kathy would come into the library with a microphone and a cameraman, and she would introduce the writing center and me. Then, she would film a tutorial in progress. Last, she would conduct interviews. She would interview the tutors, the students who use the writing center, and me. Wow. This was exciting.

I didn't have much time to prepare, so I began asking my tutors if they wanted to be on Eagle Watch. *And can you make it this Wednesday, period four? You can? Great! I'll see you then.* This was going well. Next, I had to find a few students who used the writing center on a regular basis. I tracked them down, assured them they weren't in trouble, and asked if they wanted to be TV stars. Thankfully, they were excited to help me out (and to be on TV), so I set up tutorials with them and a tutor. Yes! Everything was working out, so when Wednesday came, I wasn't too nervous. Kathy was wonderful and did everything she promised. No surprises. She filmed in the library for about a half hour, directing the action, and moving the camera like a professional. It was fun to watch. When she conducted interviews, I eavesdropped shamelessly, and I was thrilled and flattered by all the nice things the students and tutors were saying about the writing center. It was really gratifying to hear, and it confirmed for me that we really do make a difference in students' lives. And then it came time for my interview. I'm normally a bit camera shy, but Kathy was wonderful to work with, and I soon relaxed. And then it was over, and she and her microphone and her cameraman left the library, and things were quiet once again. It was a really cool experience.

A few weeks later, Kathy came back into the library and told me that Eagle Watch would be airing that night. But she had an advance copy on a flash drive, and would I like to watch it? "Yes!" I blurted for the third time, and we watched it together, on my computer, right there in the library. It was a wonderful three-minute segment on the writing center. Once again, I was thrilled and flattered by the nice things students were saying. It was nice to hear, and it was interesting to view the writing center through the perspective of a television camera.

When it ended, Kathy turned to me and said "Well, what did you think?"

"Wow," I said. "That was awesome! You're a pro at this. Thank you so much." Kathy smiled at me, nodded, and simply said "All in a day's work." And then she left the library, just like that.

Now, up to this point, I've been talking about lots of different ways to advertise the writing center: emails, PA announcements, personal presentations, posters, flyers, mailings home, newspaper articles, and a television program. But there is one other medium left to discuss, and that's *technology.* How might we use technology to advertise the writing center? And, in particular (you might be wondering), how might we use social media platforms (such as Facebook and Twitter) to enlighten our communities about the writing center?

I want to say that I have thought about this a great deal, and I must admit something: I remain skeptical about using Facebook and Twitter to advertise the writing center. I understand that these are certainly attractive venues. They're hip and happening and fun and can be a good way to reach and engage our students. I could easily create a Facebook page and Twitter account for the writing center and then post these links to the library website. And they would probably be viewed by some of our students and some of our parents. However (and although I love technology), I remain circumspect about the use of social media with regard to advertising the school library writing center. And this is for two primary reasons.

First, once we get past the knee-jerk groupthink impulse of "everybody's doing it," we must consider the logistics and ask ourselves "why?" Why should we use Facebook and Twitter to advertise the writing center? The writing center is an organization *internal to our school*, and our potential clientele is already under our roof. Facebook and Twitter are *external* to our school. Why go outside our school to reach people who are *inside* our school? Do you see my point? We're not advertising to anyone out there in the world; in fact, they are positively excluded. The people we want to reach are down the hallway and in the cafeteria. Why take the writing center outside the boundaries of the building? Why do we need that? I've thought about this quite a bit, and it really doesn't make sense to me. And this brings me to the next reason, which is more important.

Remember in Chapter Six, when I discussed how I keep the daily schedule in a binder? I do this for several reasons, one of which is *privacy*. I feel the same way with regard to showcasing the writing center through Facebook and Twitter. These social media platforms are not private. In fact, they are spectacularly public, and this brings with it a myriad of potential hazards and the possibility for unpleasant things to happen. There's no need to go into detail here, because you know what I mean. All of this can be bad for students and bad for the writing center. For all of these reasons, I have decided not to advertise my school library writing center through social media. In my opinion, the potential benefits are not worth the potential risks.

However, we should use other forms of technology to advertise the writing center. The most prominent electronic method I use is the web page I created for my writing center. A few years ago, my district moved to a new and interactive website which teachers can edit and customize. I immediately created an original web page for my writing center and put a link on my library's homepage. The link reads "THE WRITING CENTER (get help with your papers)." If you click on it, you'll be directed to the following information, which I crafted slowly and carefully:

WELCOME TO
THE HIGH SCHOOL LIBRARY
WRITING CENTER!

*

OUR HISTORY

Welcome to the High School Library Writing Center! The Writing Center was created in 2012 by Dr. Timothy Horan (Library Media Specialist, and Director of the Writing Center). Dr. Horan is a former teacher of high school English. Prior to that he was the Supervisor of the Writing Center at St. John's University, in Queens, NY (a writing center which he also helped establish).

*

WE ARE UNIQUE AND ORIGINAL

We are a "School Library Writing Center." This is an original concept created and developed by Dr. Horan, and there is no other writing center like us in the world. As the originator and expert on this new model, Dr. Horan has spoken on this topic at state and national levels, and has also been nationally published on it.

*

OUR MISSION STATEMENT

"The High School Writing Center does not 'fix' papers . . . we create writers."

*

LOCATION AND HOURS OF OPERATION

We are located in the Library Media Center. We are open during the school day, as well as after school. Students can sign up for appointments at the main desk in the library.

*

WHAT DO WE DO?

From thesis statements through final editing, we provide assistance with all phases of the writing process. Along the way, we'll help you with organization, development of ideas, research, and revising . . . and anything else you (and your writing) might require. Our ultimate goal is not to assist with individual papers, but to develop your skills as an independent writer.

*

WRITING CENTER TUTORS

All of our tutors are high-achieving students here at the High School. Carefully selected and then individually trained to conduct one-on-one writer's conferences, they are highly skilled in the writing process, and are available to help you with all of your academic projects. Dr. Horan is also a tutor, and you can work with him if you want.

*

HOW DOES IT WORK?

Your journey in the Writing Center begins by making an appointment (in the library). Next, students typically bring an assignment or project they're working on. All instruction is conducted by peers, in the format of the one-on-one writer's conference. This means that you (and your work) will have the focused attention of a highly competent tutor who has been trained in writing, as well as this type of instruction. Multiple sessions over a few days work best. Your tutor will guide you through successive drafts and revisions, and you'll be surprised at how quickly your writing skills will improve.

*

FREQUENTLY ASKED QUESTIONS:

- *Is this helpful?*
  YES! Your academic skills and knowledge of writing will definitely improve.

- *Is this Free?*
  YES!
- *Who can come to the Writing Center?*
  ANY student at the High School.
- *Who will be helping me?*
  Your tutor will be another student at the High School (or Dr. Horan, if you prefer).
- *Where do I sign up for an appointment?*
  In the Library.
- *Where do the sessions take place?*
  In the Library.
- *What subjects do you cover?*
  All of them.
- *When can I come to the Writing Center?*
  During the day on your free period, lunch period, and (with a pass) from Academic Resource Center. We're also open after school (until 3 p.m.).
- *Can you guarantee me a higher grade on my project?*
  NO. While visits to the Writing Center usually result in higher scores, your grade remains a transaction that is exclusively between you and your teacher.
- *Can I drop my paper off for final editing, and then pick it up later?*
  NO. While this may improve your paper, it will not help you to become a better writer.
- *Can I make an appointment for some final editing?*
  NO. While this may improve your paper, it will not help you to become a better writer.
- *But earlier you said you'd help with final editing, didn't you?*
  Yes. We'll assist with final editing when we assist with the paper from early stages through its evolution. Editing is not an end in itself; it's a part of an overall cycle. Remember, our goal is not to improve your paper, but to improve you as a writer.
- *I do my own creative writing. Can I have a tutor look at that, and critique it?*
  YES. Although we exist primarily to assist with your development as an academic writer, we can also assist with your own personal writing. Remember, our highest goal is to help you develop as an independent writer. Experience in multiple formats will certainly assist in this process.

*

WELL? WHAT ARE YOU WAITING FOR?
COME TO THE LIBRARY AND
SIGN UP FOR THE WRITING CENTER!
SIGN UP TODAY!

As I didn't have a guide to follow, this was challenging to write, so I took my time with it. My goal was to describe the writing center in fairly extensive detail, unlike the brief snapshots I provided in letters and flyers. I figured this would get read over and over, and I wanted viewers to gain a rather thorough understanding of who we are and what we do. As my writing center is permanent, this information is also permanent. It is staying on my website forever. If you want, you can use it as a guide as you design your own writing center web page.

When it comes to advertising and publicizing your new writing center, the most productive attitude is one of patience, conviction, and long-term thinking. Your writing center probably won't become widely known during its first year. I suggest that you discard ideas of quick success and think in terms of several years. There are no quick fixes here. At a minimum, allow an entire class to filter through your school, so that each student has multiple years to learn about (and visit) the writing center. Try to see your writing center as a reliable fixture in your school library; you're settling in and getting established for a productive and permanent future.

And if your tutors get impatient that things are a little slow in the writing center, assure them that they'll very likely be tutoring in the near future. And also remind them that they're pioneers in a new and unexplored land, and that they're the authors of a text that has not yet found its finish.

Chapter 9

I LOVE TECHNOLOGY! I REALLY DO. BUT . . .

I live in a snug little cabin on a beautiful lake, and I'm doing all the carpentry and decorating myself. And it's coming out great. Come on in, and take a peek. It looks like an Adirondack log cabin, circa 1950—knotty pine paneling, a river rock fireplace, and kitchen counters that I built myself with thick planks from an early American barn. It took me months, but they're rather magnificent, with a patina like polished bronze.

But if you open that wooden cabinet in the corner (I built it myself)—if you pull open those knotty pine doors—you'll find a large flat screen TV, a cable box, DVD player, and fancy stereo with CD player. The speakers are mounted up near the ceiling. It sounds great, and it's state-of-the-art electronics, but I can hide the fancy stuff when I want to and pretend it's not there—sort of like going back through time.

If you come into my home library (right this way, please), you'll see about 2,000 books. They're organized nicely, they're pretty, and they rest on floor-to-ceiling pine bookcases, designed and built and stained by me. It was hard work, but I enjoyed it. I always wanted a library in my house. But if you look at that desk I built—over there, below the window—you'll see a laptop and a modem sitting there and some wires like tangled yarn. That's where I wrote this book, or most of it. My four in one printer is hidden in the closet, behind big barn doors that I built from old wood my father gave me.

Do you see where I'm going with this?

My relationship with technology is a complex one. I love it (I really do), and I rely on it, but I also esteem the natural world and the old ways of doing things. Sometimes it's hard to improve on the old ways. And sometimes technology provides shortcuts around things that really matter. Now, I don't want this chapter to become a philosophical discussion of the merits and drawbacks of technology, because that's not what we're here for. But there are benefits and shortcomings to technology as it relates to teaching and education and (of course) to the writing center, so we must consider them. We must consider technology as it relates to our students, and, as teachers, we need to constantly ask ourselves what our students are actually learning. Sure, they can use technology to produce slick-looking products quickly and easily. But are they truly assimilating knowledge, or are they merely learning how to locate information and then use it in superficial applications to create a flashy end product?

As a teacher, librarian, and writing center director, I have noticed repeatedly that students (on all levels) are unwilling to generate original writing and knowledge. They don't trust their own judgments and conclusions as they read and think and study. This is an enormous omission in their educations and in their development into students, writers, and fully functioning adults. Fortunately, the writing center is the perfect environment in which to teach these skills. So let's address this consciously and strongly in the tutorials we hold. Let's try to fix this as much as we can.

When you're tutoring in your writing center, urge your students (whenever possible) to generate their own original writing and to create their own unique knowledge. Challenge them to think independently, to interpret texts and ideas, and to analyze closely the things they're studying. This method works especially well when students are studying primary sources (in any medium, in any discipline). Encourage them to extract knowledge from primary sources, to make observations, and to reach their own independent conclusions. This will help turn them into writers, rather than assemblers and regurgitators of others' knowledge. They will grow as students, as thinkers, and as human beings. And you never know when you'll change someone's life.

But it's a long and difficult process. When I became a teacher of high school English, and later a school library media specialist, I saw this struggle enacted over and over again. Students didn't trust themselves to generate original analyses, so they looked elsewhere for ideas, and the result was often plagiarism. Plagiarism has long been a problem for young students, but today it's different. The rise of the Internet has made plagiarizing tempting and easy like never before. It's now very common for students (even highly successful ones) to plagiarize (perhaps unwittingly) by performing Internet searches and then using the "copy and paste" function. Remember, these things weren't around when many of us were in high school and college, but consider this: *our students have never known a world without Google.*

When we consider their growth as scholars, thinkers, and writers, this puts them at a disadvantage, which is certainly ironic. The ease and simplicity of Google searches have made it extremely easy to plagiarize and have made it correspondingly unpalatable (and difficult) for young students to generate original analyses and writing. Why should they work hard when the "correct" answer is just a search term away? But if we allow this, we're doing them a disservice. As a writing center director, one of your jobs will therefore be to challenge your students to think creatively, to generate original writing and discourse, and to have them trust their own original judgments and conclusions. So get ready to teach independent analysis and original writing in an age of Google. It will be a challenge for you as well as for your students.

It's a complex thing, living in a juxtaposition. On the one hand, technology is wonderful and fun and makes our lives easier. I wouldn't want to live without it. On the other hand, it has stunted the intellectual growth of many students. And for a while now, I have been thinking about this issue. I have been pondering my own relationship with technology, especially the role it plays in my writing center. How do we approach technology and interweave it successfully into the pedagogy of the school library writing center?

My tutors and I use technology on a daily basis, and it is tremendously helpful. It improves productivity, it's fun to use, and I wouldn't want to run the writing center without it. But it begs questions. How do I use technology? And (more important) how are my students using it? These questions are important "real-world" concerns, but the most important questions for me (and the most difficult to answer) are these: what is the nature of the intersection between technology and the school library writing center? And what are the best uses of technology for the school library writing center? These are difficult questions, and they can't be answered quickly or easily. But I will offer this as a quick overview: when it comes to writing and the writing center, technology is a wonderful facilitator and helps tremendously with the logistics and mechanics of writing. However, the "soul" of the writing must remain human and must remain the original work of the student. Forever and ever.

Having been in the world of Education for some time now, I realize that technology is here to stay, and this is a good thing. It has increased my efficiency and productivity, it assists with research, and it can be lots of fun. However, I also feel that, to an extent, we educators have made technology itself the *goal*, rather than a means for attaining a goal. Many times I see projects that are based in technology, with little attention given to the original thought or creativity underlying the final product. The embedding of technology into education has created an academic culture in which we seem to be more concerned with the end product than with what students are actually learning. I think it should be reversed: academic projects should be (whenever possible) creative and original, and technology should be used in a supporting and presenting (or "packaging") role. Human beings will always need to know how to write and how to organize and present our thoughts. This is inescapable. To be truly successful navigators of the world and creators in it, we'll always need the abilities to think, discuss, evaluate, communicate, analyze, and say (and do) things that have never been said (or done) before. Technology, especially as employed in the writing center, should *assist* with teaching and writing; it should not become the goal itself. And it should certainly not substitute for an original and authentic human-produced artifact.

Despite our love affair with technology, humanity has had a long-standing fear of machines taking over. From Charlie Chaplin's *Modern Times* (1936) to a bunch of *Terminator* movies, we regard technology as a tiger in a paper cage, a powerful beauty waiting to devour us. Well, the takeover is happening right now, and it isn't as dramatic or interesting as armies of grinning cyborgs. The takeover is passive and pleasant (which is scarier), and if you want to see what it looks like, spend some time in your local fancy coffee shop and watch people on their laptops and cell phones. They're entranced, but there is little authentic human interaction taking place. Watch a group of young people hanging out together. Very often, they're not interacting with each other, but are texting and chatting with other friends at a distance. For some reason, the absent friends are somehow preferable.

But please don't misunderstand me; I'm not shunning or denigrating technology. I'm giving it great respect as a powerful resource to be harnessed and a tool to be skillfully used. And it definitely belongs in the modern writing center. It provides wonderful assistance for teaching (and producing) writing, and it should constitute a mainstay of your writing center. You and your tutors should be using technology in your tutorials on a regular basis. However, please keep this in mind: writing center tutorials, correctly performed, will stress authentic, original writing and will employ technology in a supportive and complementary role, rather than a primary one. Properly used, technology will increase a student's efficiency, productivity, and depth of research, while still allowing him to create an original and meaningful piece of discourse—which is extremely important to his development as a writer, thinker, student, and human being. It's a delicate dance, to be sure, but it can be learned and performed beautifully. Here are some of my favorite technological resources and techniques.

First, I urge you to explore the entire suite of Google goodies. As I discovered during a Google conference, Google isn't just a search engine. They do just about everything, so try to attend a Google conference if you can. But most germane to the writing center is Google Drive. I urge all students (and I urge you also) to do all your writing on Google Drive. I have recently made the switch myself, and I don't know how I survived (as a writer) without this resource. And what's so great about Google Drive? A few things, actually.

To start with, it's free. It's also simple to use. To get a Google Drive account, you simply create a Gmail account. This means that you may already have a Google Drive account, and many of your students will also. But oddly enough, even though most students are firmly plugged in, many of them don't know about Google Drive, or they simply don't use it. But it's a wonderful resource, and every student in the world should be using it. It's simple and it's highly effective. The interface is similar to Microsoft Word, so it will look familiar to students. They will be able to use it the first time they log on. Users also get 15 GB of free storage on Google Drive, which is a tremendous amount. More than you'll need in a single lifetime. You (and your students) will be able to write millions of pages on a Google Drive account.

Beyond these, there are two other enormous advantages. First, Google Drive saves *automatically* and often. Believe it or not, there is no "save" button. Think about that. This means that your students will *never lose their work*. Not a bit of it. Have you ever lost work? It's horrible. (I once lost a paper in graduate school [on an early word processor], and it was an awful experience.) All that work you put in has disappeared suddenly, and for all eternity. And you can't get it back. I once heard of an author who lost an entire book in a house fire, which was a tremendous tragedy. She actually wrote the book over, but was cognizant and sad that it wasn't the same book she had written earlier. I also heard of a grad student who lost an entire dissertation because his backpack was stolen (I don't know whether or not he resurrected his dissertation). These are true tragedies, and just the thought of them makes me shudder. When I finished writing my own dissertation (just as the Internet was percolating into our lives), I printed up three copies. I kept one copy in my apartment, one copy in my parent's house (in case I had a fire), and the third copy in my car, snuggled in with the spare tire (where it remains to this day). You just never know.

But now we have Google Drive. So let's say a student is working on a project (in your library or at home). She has written a beautiful 10-page paper. It's nearly finished and she's proud of her work and excited to hand it in. Alas, there is a sudden power outage, or perhaps the hard drive crashes. Or maybe Sparky (her dog) knocks the plug out of the wall and the screen goes terrifyingly blank. And the house is suddenly silent. And disturbingly dark. It's a scary moment, but there's a happy ending: she was writing her paper on Google Drive, so her work is saved. All of it. She won't lose a single letter or comma. All she has to do is wait for the power to come back on (or plug the computer back in) and log back into Google Drive. And there is her paper, pristine and perfect and pulsating with new knowledge. Crisis averted. It's beautiful. And Sparky is not in trouble.

But how does this miracle work? Simple: Google Drive saves to the "cloud." It resides on the Internet, so it's online storage. When I explain this to students, I say this: *Your flash drive is in your pocket. Your hard drive is in your computer. But Google Drive is in the sky!* (and here I wave my arms in a most dramatic fashion. Ah, the things I do for teaching). Flash drives can be lost, hard drives can crash, but Google Drive is forever. And this brings us to the other resounding advantage of Google Drive: besides never losing their work, *students can access it from anywhere.* And this is a marvelous innovation. When students work on a paper at school, they can come home and access it there, just by logging into their Google accounts. In fact, they can access Google Drive from anywhere in the world. I explain it to students like this: *Go to Disney World—it's there! Go to Australia—it's there! Go to the moon—it's there!*

When students write on Google Drive, all they need is a computer with Internet and they're good-to-go. No more emailing projects to themselves, no more flash drives, no more inaccessibility. However, if someone requires them to attach a Word document to an email (which is very common), it's not a problem. They can just copy the Google Doc and then paste it into a Word document and save it there. It transfers very easily. And there is one more resounding advantage to Google Drive, which I have learned through personal experience (and maybe you have too). Did you ever encounter a student who wrote his paper at home on a Mac, but he couldn't access it or print it in school, because your library is full of PCs? Well, Google Drive solves that problem also. As it's an external website, it behaves the same whether the student uses a PC or a Mac. Google Drive is terrific. It solves a million problems that young writers can experience. You should show it to all of your students and encourage them to use it for all their projects, from here to eternity.

As you tutor in the writing center, you might encounter some students who have a powerful block against writing. They can speak very well, but when it comes to writing on paper or tapping on a keyboard, they freeze. Other students may be unable to write for some other reason. They may simply be physically, intellectually, or emotionally unable (or unwilling) to engage in the act of writing. In your career, you may also encounter a student who doesn't have the use of hands. Or a student who is visually impaired and who can't see the screen of the keyboard. Let's use technology to help all of these students. At present, there are incredible resources available on the Internet—more than you know—and they are available for *free*. But they need to be found and learned, so you must approach this process with patience and perseverance.

When I encounter students who can't (or won't) physically write, I tell them they can write with their *voices* (which is a form of differentiation). And this gets their attention. They like it. I also tell them that writing is just the act of speaking, put down on paper. It's true. Think about it. Writing is simply human discourse frozen in time, unlike the ephemeral sentences we speak that disappear into the air. And, as we typically speak much more than we write, most of us are better speakers than we are writers. So if students seem unable (or unwilling) to write, you can suggest that they *record their voices* and then transcribe it later.

One of my tutors recently used this technique with a student, and it worked very well. This particular student preferred talking over writing, so she instructed him to dictate his essay into his *phone* (yes, there's an app for that). The student enjoyed using his phone's recording app, and he later played it back and typed it up. And is dictation a legitimate form of writing? You bet it is (and I regard this as an "accommodation"). It certainly worked for John Milton. Milton went completely blind in his early forties and dictated the entirety of *Paradise Lost* to family members and acquaintances, who wrote it down for him. And he had pretty good results with this method.

But where can students get recording equipment? On their phones, as I mentioned (this is a good choice, because most students are very attached to their phones). Also, most newish desktop computers have voice recorders already built into them. For example, I'm writing this book on a laptop that's running Windows 8.1. And built into this software suite is a program appropriately called "Sound Recorder." I like that name (it's clear and direct), and the program is easy to use. Students can speak into their computers (or headsets) and create (and save) voice files, much like creating files in Microsoft Word. And they can email the file to themselves for transcribing later. It's really easy to learn, and it's very effective.

But what if the student doesn't want to transcribe later? What if the student wants to speak directly into the computer and have his words appear on the screen, like magic? Well, we can do that also, and these programs are called "speech-to-text." This is another form of writing (and another accommodation), and it's a very effective time-saver: the student doesn't have to transcribe later. However, there are drawbacks: speech-to-text programs aren't perfect. The student must speak slowly and clearly, and the computer will definitely misunderstand some of the words spoken. For example, if the student says the word "grows," the computer may write "goes." The word "driving" may become "drive in." So sometimes words have to be respoken more clearly. It's like that. But overall, these programs work very well.

Now, you may not know this, but if you're using Microsoft Office, your computer already has a speech-to-text mode built into it. It's called "Windows Speech Recognition" (go to the Start menu; you'll need to search for it. It's not hard to find). In this program, everything a student speaks into a microphone shows up as text in a Word document. When Windows Speech Recognition is set up and the student practices on it, it's very effective and is about 90% accurate—perhaps even higher, with time and practice. And it's fun to use. It's really fascinating to watch your spoken words appear magically as text on a monitor.

Students can also write with their voices when using Google Drive. It's very easy to set up. After opening your Google Doc, click on the "Add-ons" tab and then select "Speech Recognition." From there, it's pretty intuitive and simple to use. And besides Word and Google Drive, there are lots of good (and free) speech-to-text programs on the Internet. One good one is called "Online Dictation" (https:// dictation.io/). I like this one because it's extremely simple and easy to use and it works well. I once used it with a student who couldn't write because of an injured hand, and he was able to complete his exam this way. When the student is finished, the text can be copied and pasted into a Word document or exported into Google Drive. And of course, as it's an external website, it works with a Mac. Speech-to-text programs represent an underutilized mode of voice-writing that many of your students will definitely appreciate.

However, please don't confuse "speech-to-text" with "text-to-speech." Text-to-speech programs are the reverse. They convert the printed word into the spoken word. This way, a student can have her work read back to her, so that she can hear what she wrote. Students can also hear websites read aloud to them if they want. These programs are highly effective when dealing with students who are visually impaired and with students who have trouble with reading comprehension (and you may encounter both in the writing center). If students are unable to *see* (or read) the words, they can use these programs to *hear* them, and they can get the education they deserve.

Microsoft Word has a text-to-speech application built into it. It's called "Speak," and it reads a student's writing aloud to him, so that he can hear what he wrote. This is effective, because our ears often pick up mistakes and awkwardness that our eyes miss. To access Speak, a student needs to locate it (in Microsoft Word) and then just turn it on. And it works well. To use it, you simply select text that you have written and then click on the (newly installed) "talking bubble" icon. You will be rewarded with a robotic voice that will read your work to you clearly and accurately.

Google Drive has something similar. This is free, but you'll need to install it. Just go to the Chrome Web Store and do a search for "Read&Write for Google Chrome." It's easy, it's free, and it takes under a minute to install. This extension will enable students to have their Google Drive text read back to them. The interface here is very interesting to use and to watch. The sentence being read is highlighted in yellow, but the word being read is highlighted in blue, which dances along, follow-the-bouncing-ball style. The aural components will be very helpful to visually impaired students, while the visual component will help students with reading disabilities. The Chrome Web Store also has a text-to-speech extension which can read *websites* aloud to students. It's called ReadIt!, and it's very effective and easy to use. After it's installed, the reader selects text in a web page, clicks on the (newly installed) sound icon, and a pleasant (and fairly human) voice reads the selected material aloud to the reader (or listener). And again, it's free.

Please understand that the above discussion is not meant to be exhaustive. My purpose is to suggest some good basic resources and to give you some ideas on how to use technology while tutoring students in the writing center. I have no doubt that, as you explore, you will discover your own additional resources that will enrich your writing center and help make tutorials more productive. And please forgive me for not providing exhaustive explanations on how to locate, install, and use these resources. I want to keep this book as human and readable as possible, and I don't want to clutter it with too many technical explanations. You can find everything you need to know on the Internet, often in the form of friendly You-Tube video tutorials made by people just like you and me. If you do some Internet searches, you'll find what you're looking for.

Now, at this point, we have covered some logistical applications of technology, especially as they relate to the mechanics of writing. I have discussed storing and accessing our own writing, and I went over different modes of writing and reading, via speech-to-text and text-to-speech programs. But remember, all of this is designed to assist contemporary students who stand at the edge of the Internet ocean. And they're anxious to explore.

But wait a moment; I want to change that metaphor. The Internet is growing so rapidly that students are no longer like sailors exploring a two-dimensional ocean. The Internet has become so vast that they are now like astronauts exploring the three dimensions of space. And they need our help with takeoff, navigation, and properly using the newfound knowledge they acquire during their journeys.

Many writing projects will require students to gather research that is reliable, accurate, and current. But the Internet is enormous and contains an incomprehensible amount of information. Some of this information is good, but much of it is bad. This means that students will need to locate information and then evaluate it thoroughly and efficiently. *Is the information accurate? Is it current? Does it fit with my project?* And here, I want to pose a scenario and a question to you. Let's say a student comes to the writing center and must write a research paper. But his research skills consist of doing Google searches and that's it. Needless to say, this isn't good enough. So here's my question: during a tutorial, would it be appropriate to help him find sources for his research project? When students come to the writing center, should we be teaching them the basics of performing academic research?

The answer to that question is a resounding *yes*. YES! Of course we should teach them how to perform good research. Teach it well and have fun doing it. Research is integral to the writing process, so the writing center is the perfect place to teach kids the entire cycle of locating, evaluating, and using information. I find that the one-on-one tutorial is perfect for this type of detailed instruction, but, as always, I like to keep things simple. So I want to point you toward a very good resource that can be an excellent guide for students, and this is called the "Big6" [*sic*].

You may have heard of this in library school or collegial circles; it purports to be "the most widely known and widely used approach to teaching information and technology skills in the world" ("Big6 Skills Overview," 2014). It is a model that breaks the research process into six major (and understandable) steps. And each step is broken into two smaller, successive steps. Here they are, taken verbatim from the Big6 website:

1. Task Definition

    1.1 Define the information problem
    1.2 Identify information needed

2. Information Seeking Strategies

    2.1 Determine all possible sources
    2.2 Select the best sources

3. Location and Access

    3.1 Locate sources (intellectually and physically)
    3.2 Find information within sources

4. Use of Information

    4.1 Engage (e.g., read, hear, view, touch)
    4.2 Extract relevant information

5. Synthesis

    5.1 Organize from multiple sources
    5.2 Present the information

6. Evaluation

    6.1 Judge the product (effectiveness)
    6.2 Judge the process (efficiency) ("Big6 Skills Overview," 2014)

If you look closely at the steps, you'll find that they're intuitive and that they follow a rather natural (and human) progression of investigation. In simplest terms, they are essentially telling us that we need to understand the task; we need to locate and read good information; and we need to organize and present it. I like this. It invites users to interact personally with the information gathered and with the entire writing process.

However, if you look a bit closer, you'll see that the Big6 is missing one crucial component, and it's one which I discussed earlier: *interacting with information (including primary source materials) independently for the purpose of creating new and original knowledge.* I hate to criticize the Big6 (because it's a wonderful system), but there is no step which clearly encourages students to think originally, to analyze, and to draw independent conclusions. And this is important stuff. If you follow the Big6 as it stands, your students will generate highly competent assemblages of information. However, the project won't be truly original, which means that it won't be terribly exciting for the reader, or for the writer.

I therefore suggest the creation of an additional (seventh) step, called "Analysis" (which means that the Big6 should evolve into the Big7). It should be placed at step five, and it should look like this:

5. Analysis
    5.1 Engage with resources (including, and especially, primary source documents)
    5.2 Analyze them independently and originally to create new knowledge

Challenging? Oh, yeah. But it will help turn students into thinkers and writers. And we need more of those.

Nevertheless, the Big6 remains an excellent tool to use during writing center tutorials. (And even if this seventh step isn't "officially" adopted by the Big6, you should still include the process of *analysis* in writing center tutorials. I will discuss analysis in greater detail in Chapter Ten.) I suggest showing the Big6 website to students and explaining the steps to them. It will be a good guide for them to use as they learn to write and after they leave the writing center and go on to college, workplace, and the rest of their lives. And I also suggest using the Big6 *yourself* as you tutor students and help them develop their projects. It's a logical progression and will help keep things organized.

The Big6 will certainly assist your students, but it will also benefit *you* as a tutor. As you master the art of tutoring writing, the Big6 will be a wonderful guide for you to use. So teach the steps to your tutors and encourage them to use it in their tutoring. And as *you* tutor, proceed methodically through the steps, always explaining to students what you're doing and why you're doing it. This will help to simplify and demystify the writing process. And the final step will allow both you and your student to reflect on the process and the product, considering what worked well and what could be improved. I really like the Big6; it feels very familiar and natural to me. It is an effective "common sense" approach to the writing and research process, and it's absolutely perfect for the librarian who runs a writing center. It makes sense, and it's simple, which I love.

But of course, our work doesn't stop with taking students through the steps of the Big6. Embedded within this cycle are complex tasks involving locating and evaluating information (especially on steps two and three). When students need to locate research for their papers, they almost invariably do a Google search. And this won't provide results that are consistently reliable. But it does provide a perfect opportunity to teach students the rudiments of performing high-quality academic research.

When locating research, I always start by taking students into our databases. My school district purchases a "package" of databases, and perhaps yours does also. Actually, most of the school libraries in my area purchase the same suite of databases through BOCES (Board of Cooperative Educational Services). These databases are amazing. Students access them through a link on our library homepage and then log into the databases with a district password. Once in, they have unlimited access to all of our databases (and we have over 60 of them). To assist students in choosing the best databases, they are organized into groups according to topic.

For example, some of the groups are labeled "Biography," "History/Geography," "Literature/Language," "Magazines/Newspapers," etc. This is a help, but there is so much information available that it can be overwhelming. And all the databases are a bit different from each other, so to be used well, they need to be learned. It's early-morning-cup-of-coffee stuff. But they're fun, and they provide excellent information that is current and reliable.

But if your district doesn't have any databases—and even if it does—tap into your local public library. Why overlook the obvious? It most likely has wonderful electronic resources available for the price of a library card. And what about you? You probably have a library card. Have you investigated the electronic holdings at your public library? Spend some time on this; I think you'll be surprised at what's available. It's free, and (with a current library card) it's perfectly legal. So build a relationship (even an electronic one) with your local public library. Learn how to access its electronic holdings, and pass this information along to students. I know that my own public library has databases that my school library doesn't. Together, we make a formidable team. And once you master these resources, encourage your students to get library cards (which is always a wonderful gift). And then they have access to two wonderful libraries: their school library and the local public library. And two libraries are better than one.

And now comes a wonderful (and highly productive) teachable moment: showing students how to *use* the databases properly. I find that most students—even advanced ones—don't truly understand how databases work, and the writing center tutorial is the perfect venue to teach them. So when I sit with a student, I make no assumptions about prior knowledge. I teach them how to use the databases, and I proceed slowly and methodically. My goal is to help them achieve an understanding of what databases are, how they work, and what they can provide. True teaching occurs during these tutorials, and engagement levels tend to be very high.

So why are databases a good choice when performing academic research? To put it simply, they provide high-quality academic articles—*articles*—written by scholars. And articles are a good choice for many students, because they provide reliable information in a brief format. And many of our students (especially our "nonreaders") will really like this. For the first time, these students will begin to think "Hey, I can do this." And then we have just made a difference in a student's life.

After showing students how to access the databases, I explain that there are two basic types of databases. There are online encyclopedias (and encyclopedia-*type* databases) which provide reliable, basic information. These databases tend to be well organized and user friendly and provide good, readable overviews of academic topics. The other type of databases provides students with articles from scholarly journals. In terms of scholarship, these latter databases provide access to the best and most academic sources of research. When teaching these searches, I always encourage students to choose the "full text" option, as this will provide students with the entire text of the article (as opposed to giving them just the bibliographic citation, which is not helpful to students). Additionally (I tell students), choosing the "peer-reviewed" option (whenever it's available) will usually provide the highest level and most scholarly results.

So, we have two different types of databases. However, the line between them is becoming increasingly blurred, as many of the "encyclopedia-type" databases are now providing links to screened sources on the open Internet, including (in many cases) direct paths to scholarly journal articles. This is a definite improvement, and many databases are striving to become "one-stop shopping" in the information supermall. This makes our job easier. As information specialists, we're living in a great time.

As I teach students to use the databases, I always try to make these lessons memorable and authentic. To do this, I use a mixture of modeling followed by scaffolding, and I use the student's project as the vehicle which drives instruction. As I teach the databases, I illustrate the steps (and principles) by helping the student find three or four articles *related to his paper*. This works much better than doing unrelated (and "fake") "dummy" searches. And is it "okay" to help students find articles that they can actually use? *Of course!* Why not? This is extremely helpful to students, makes them happy, and is a vital step on the journey of becoming a writer. And along the way (often in the same session), I also help the student begin the bibliography.

Most of our databases have a function that creates the bibliographic citation (it's usually indicated by a button that says "cite"). Through the miracle of "copy and paste," we're able to create a polished bibliography quickly and easily (and I usually paste this into a Google Doc, where it will remain until our next session). Then we print the articles out, and I hand them to students. I love putting printed articles into their hands, and students love getting them. They look sharp, they're still warm from the printer, and they're stapled in the upper left hand corner (by yours truly). And sometimes (time and resources permitting), I'll even give the student a folder, with the topic written on it, and the articles inside it. The writing center is certainly a place of many diverse gifts.

All of this may seem like "no-brainers" to you, but the process you're demonstrating (and the example you're setting) is indispensable for the student. And students love seeing tangible progress toward the completion of a paper. In their minds, this is a demonstration of the efficacy of the writing center and proof that the writing center is not a "waste of time." Remember, we're dealing with adolescents, many of whom have limited attention spans and a powerful desire to be doing other things. And if you place tidy-looking articles into their hands within 20 minutes of their arrival, it's a very powerful indicator that they're in a special place that can tangibly help them out in a very dramatic way. And at the end of the session, they leave quite happily, with new knowledge and new articles (and sometimes a new folder). There is simply no substitute for the one-on-one teaching that occurs in writing center tutorials.

The databases are wonderful, but sometimes students will need to search the open Internet for different types of resources. These searches will turn up a great variety of information, ranging from the good to the bad to the utterly bizarre, with everything in between thrown in for good measure. So we need to teach our kids how to evaluate the sources they find. Some sources will look quite good, but will be filled (sometimes intentionally) with errors. This means we need to teach our students the gentle art of website evaluation. When I do this, I try to make it interesting and fun (and tutorials should be fun—this is a very important ingredient to get repeat customers in the writing center). For example, when I tutor website evaluation, I show students several "hoax" websites. There are lots of these on the Internet; they look wonderful (and even professional), but the content is utterly ridiculous. Here are three good ones:

- "Whale Watching on Lake Superior" ("Freshwater Whale Watching Lake Superior," 2015)
- "Save the Pacific Northwest Tree Octopus" (Zapato)
- "Dog Island" ("Dog Island Free Forever," 2013)

Take a look at these websites. They look pretty convincing, and it's fun watching kids' reaction to these. And (with great satirical solemnity) I discuss the beauties of lake whales, the state of the arboreal octopus, and the merits of working on an island populated exclusively by dogs.

And then I break the bad news to them (I'm no good at fibbing, so most of them figure out that I'm kidding). *There aren't any whales in Lake Superior. Octopods don't live in trees. And there isn't an island where thousands of dogs live in freedom and harmony.* (And it's too bad, really. All these things would be so much fun.)

These spoof websites are entertaining to use during tutorials, and they work well. There is also another webpage called "11 Hilarious Hoax Sites to Test Website Evaluation" (Rao, 2012), which is fun and very helpful. Some of the links on the site no longer work, but it's a good place to view the landscape of hoax websites and to learn about such convenient products as "Dehydrated Water" (what exactly could that be? An empty water bottle?).

After showing students some hoax websites, I show them a terrific site on the evaluation of online resources. It's through the Cornell University Library and it's called "Evaluating Web Sites: Criteria and Tools" ("Olin & Uris Libraries," 2014). This site is remarkably thorough and detailed, and it covers all aspects of evaluating websites. It gives a great deal of excellent information on how to evaluate websites, but I really like this five-step summary, based on writings by Jim Kapoun:

1. **Accuracy**. If your page lists the author and institution that published the page and provides a way of contacting him/her and . . .

2. **Authority**. If your page lists the author credentials and its domain is preferred (.edu, .gov, .org, or .net), and, . . .

3. **Objectivity**. If your page provides accurate information with limited advertising, and it is objective in presenting the information, and . . .

4. **Currency**. If your page is current and updated regularly (as stated on the page) and the links (if any) are also up-to-date, and . . .

5. **Coverage**. If you can view the information properly—not limited to fees, browser technology, or special software requirements . . . then you may have a Web page that could be of value to your research!

("Evaluating Web Pages," 2015)

As you can see, the process is not terribly complicated and is rooted in common sense. When evaluating websites, the researcher must consider such factors as the accuracy of the material, the credentials of the author, and the age of the information. With regard to the age of information, I tell my students to look for information that is no older than "about five years." It's a good general guide, but I also tell them there is much "classic" information out there that has been around for decades and yet is still good.

I suggest showing this website to your students, explaining the steps to them, and then practicing the process. As always, it's best to keep this authentic and to evaluate websites related to the student's project. And when I teach this process, I employ modeling, followed by scaffolding. This works well and keeps the tutorial student centered. For a bit more information on these steps, and for a nifty printable chart (by the same author) that you can give to students, please see "Five Criteria for Evaluating Web Pages" (Kapoun).

And finally, there are the OWLs (Online Writing Labs). OWLs are websites devoted to teaching writing. These are intended mostly for academic writing, but many of them cover creative writing also. OWLs are a bit like writers' handbooks, and they attempt to explain all aspects of the writing process. They are usually well organized and user friendly, and many of them include brief multimedia presentations, which are fun and effective modes of learning.

OWLs are also a bit like electronic writing centers, but without the human element. The answers are there, but students have to work at locating and digesting the information. And for this reason they will never replace writing centers run by actual human beings. But they make wonderful support for writing centers, so you should make friends with several OWLs.

But which ones should you choose?

There are lots of OWLs on the Internet, and most of them spring from college and university writing centers. The best of these is the Purdue OWL. This OWL flies out of the Purdue University Writing Lab (their term for the writing center), located in Indiana, USA. I love the Purdue OWL, and I made it a permanent link on my library homepage. This site is huge and sprawling and is updated frequently. It's a virtual labyrinth that covers every imaginable aspect of writing, and if it doesn't answer your question, then you haven't looked hard enough.

It even has a page titled "Full OWL Resources for Grades 7–12 Students and Instructors" (Purdue Online Writing Lab, 2015) which suits our purposes perfectly. This page covers such topics as the writing process, thesis statements, and writing style (along with many others). The Purdue OWL is an amazingly complete writing resource that you, your tutors, and your students can use for every aspect of writing, and you'll never get to the bottom of it. It's an inexhaustible resource.

But also take a look at the Excelsior College OWL. This one is also fantastic. It's wonderfully organized and easy to navigate, and I especially love their use of brief video tutorials. It feels a bit less "monolithic" than the Purdue OWL (and perhaps more accessible), which many of your students will likely appreciate. But both OWLs are terrific and make a wonderful complement to writing center offerings. So use them both and show them to your students.

So there we are.

Properly used, technology can certainly be a wonderful and highly effective complement to your writing center.

But as we use technology and function under its magnetic spell, we must recognize it for what it is: it is an aid, it is an implement. And, amidst its seductive nature, we must remain careful to keep authentic and original writing at the center of our tutorials. Remember, for students to generate writing that has any true meaning, it must be an original product of their minds. It must be as individual and unique as they are. But don't get me wrong: I embrace technology with great enthusiasm; it is an indispensable component of the writing center. Properly used, technology can be the perfect device to help our students learn (and perform) the very human art of writing. Use it well.

Chapter 10

THIS CHAPTER IS ABOUT THE COMMON CORE, BUT YOU'LL LIKE IT, I PROMISE!

As the Director of your school library writing center, you need to be familiar with Common Core English Language Arts (ELA) Standards, especially as they pertain to writing. Like it or not, the Common Core has taken firm root in contemporary education and is probably impacting instruction in your school. But even if your state has not officially adopted the Common Core, this chapter will be very useful to you. I guarantee it. The techniques I discuss here are highly effective and will work for virtually any writing assignment. So read on.

Our journey to the Core starts at the beginning, which is the Common Core website (http://www.corestandards.org/). This website is well constructed and organized clearly and will answer most of your questions regarding the Standards. However, its best feature is that it does not bombard and overwhelm the new learner; it presents the Common Core clearly, efficiently, and simply. For an introduction to the Common Core, I suggest going to the site, having a look around, and doing some reading. I find the Standards to be informative and clearly written, and they're not terribly long. In fact, you'll be surprised at how brief they are.

On the Common Core website, near the top of the page, you'll see a link that reads "Standards in your State." If you click there, you'll see that most states (and many US territories) have adopted the Common Core. If you click on your own state, it will bring you to your state's Education page. There, you will find material on your state's particular adoption of the Common Core Standards (they may have been modified slightly), along with other material on it specific to your state. It's worthwhile to look at this and to learn exactly how your state is approaching the Common Core. After you view your state information, take a look at the baseline (national) Standards.

Go back to the homepage, click on "Read the Standards," then click on "English Language Arts Standards." If you click on "Download the Standards," you will be rewarded with the complete ELA Standards in a 66-page document. This will give you a good look at the totality of the Common Core Standards, and it's worthwhile to spend some time here and gain an overall view of the Standards. While you're there, you'll notice that the Writing standards are quite brief. The "Writing Standards K-5" are four pages long (18–21), while the "Writing Standards 6–12" are seven pages long (41–47). And that's it. I suggest reading carefully through all the Writing standards, so that you can gain a "global" understanding of Common Core Writing Standards. You'll find that they are not terribly overwhelming, and you'll see that they are quite applicable to your writing center.

If you want to look at the Writing Standards without scrolling through the entire document, simply click on "Writing." Easy. This will give you a drop-down menu listing grade levels from Kindergarten through twelfth grade. It's a really nifty and user-friendly system of navigation. Click on the grade(s) you want to explore (probably those grades served by your writing center) and then, *presto*, there they are, there are the Common Core Standards, pure and unadulterated. I think you'll be surprised at how brief and accessible they are. For example, if you click on "Grade 7," you'll see a title in bold that reads, "Text Types and Purposes" (in my opinion, a better and simpler title for this would be "Types of Assignments and Specific Requirements"). Under that, you'll see 10 different types of assignments, with requirements and goals for each type of assignment. Yes, we're in the inner sanctum of Common Core central and we're getting a look at the actual Common Core Standards up close and personal. For example, the first text listed there reads as follows:

> *CCSS.ELA-LITERACY.W.7.1* Write arguments to support claims with clear reasons and relevant evidence ("English Language Arts Standards, Writing, Grade 7").

That first line of code looks quite formidable, doesn't it? Very official and severe, like a new language for the privileged classes. So, let's decode it. Here's what it stands for: "Common Core State Standards, English Language Arts, Literacy, Writing, Grade 7, Standard 1." And that's it. Not so bad, right?

After that, the assignment itself requires some decoding, but it's pretty straightforward. I'll paraphrase what they're looking for: *students will write essays in which they argue a specific point of view, describe their assertions clearly and use textual evidence to back up their claims.* Again, it's pretty easy. The Standards are not as formidable as they're made out to be and, when you get past their veneer of academic jargon, you'll find simplicity and familiarity there. So you can take my passage above as a sort of keys-to-the-club snapshot of the Standards.

At this point, I encourage you to get a cup of coffee and read through the Writing standards. As you read, identify what they require of students and think about how your writing center can help. I also encourage you to read the "Key Shifts in English Language Arts" (available from the ELA Standards page). They're short, less than a page each. You've probably heard of the "Shifts"; you will find these extremely helpful. True to their name, the Shifts don't represent revolutionary changes; they describe a Shifting of existing boundaries, methods, and materials.

Here are the three Shifts, taken verbatim from the Common Core website (all emphases are theirs):

1. Regular practice with *complex texts* and their academic language
2. Reading, writing, and speaking *grounded in evidence from texts*, both literary and informational
3. *Building knowledge* through content-rich nonfiction ("Key Shifts in English Language Arts," 2015)

In terms of writing center instruction, we are most interested in the first two Shifts. And here, I want to explain something. Remember when I said earlier that this chapter will be useful even if your state didn't adopt the Standards? These Shifts are the main reason. They concern two indispensable skills: *reading comprehension* and working with *textual evidence*. These are integral pillars of learning and will help students blossom into writers and into fully developed and enlightened human beings. This is important stuff. So whether or not your state has officially adopted the Standards, you should teach both of these to your tutors, so that they can teach them to their students.

The first Shift concerns students' ability to read and understand complex texts, which is clearly a worthwhile endeavor. This Shift calls for a "staircase of increasing complexity," which means simply that the texts studied should get more challenging each year. And, according to this Shift, the purpose of having students read and digest complex texts is to prepare them for "the demands of college- and career-level reading no later than the end of high school." These are valuable goals, and the writing center can certainly assist with this.

But let's pause for a moment and think about how this relates to the writing center. The first Shift concerns students reading and understanding complex texts. Can—or *should*—the writing center help with reading? *Yes!* Why not? In Common Core methodology (and in contemporary middle and high schools), reading is often a prewriting activity, which means that a great deal of students' writing springs from what they read. And, as the writing center targets the entire writing process, we should teach our students to read carefully and well. But there is another fact which is not mentioned by the Common Core: *we learn to write through reading*. The more we read, the better we write. As we read, we unconsciously absorb the linguistic structures of written language. Personally, I was never taught to write. I learned to write by reading, and reading, and reading some more. And then I sat down at a toy typewriter and tried to emulate my favorite authors. In this way, my favorite authors became my first writing instructors. So yes, the writing center is the perfect place to teach reading. Teach it often and well. In fact, seize all teachable moments when they occur and teach everything you can. When you're in the writing center, you should reside in the land of "Yes." It's much more productive (and fun) than living in the land of "No."

But you may be thinking here that you're not a trained reading teacher, so how will you teach reading in the writing center and how will you train your tutors to teach it? Relax. You can do it. Sip your coffee and keep things simple. It's all rooted in common sense and in the basics. But you should start out knowing what to expect. When you tutor in the writing center, be prepared for many of your students to struggle with the act of *reading*. If they were highly skilled readers, they probably wouldn't be visiting the writing center.

I want to emphasize this point: as a writing center director (and tutor), you must be prepared to help students not just with writing, but also with *reading*. These students will have trouble with being motivated to read (and may even tell you they "hate" to read), and they will struggle with reading comprehension (which is the frustrated sibling of reading aversion). It's always shocking for a librarian to hear that someone "hates" to read, but (and I hate to say it) it's fairly common. So don't be surprised by it. And what do we do with these students? We teach them the best we can to read and understand texts. Stick with it, even when it's difficult and demoralizing. Make sure you train your staff to tutor reluctant or unskilled readers. Keep the methods simple; we don't want to overwhelm our tutors (or students) or cause them to shut down or avoid the writing center.

When tutoring students in the beautiful art of reading, you will begin by selecting a text for your students (and you) to read. And where will you find a text? There are lots of anthologies and websites to choose from, but a great place to find reading passages is the Common Core's "English Language Arts Appendix B" (available as a link from the ELA Standards page). This is a very large document with literally hundreds of texts on it to choose from. They are organized by grade level and are categorized by genre (stories, poetry, drama, informational texts, etc.). It's a remarkably deep collection of varied texts, and you will find lots to choose from. You'll also find other helpful materials there, so don't be afraid to spend some time with this document.

Another terrific site for choosing texts is ReadWorks.org. Honestly, I love this site. Its purpose is indicated clearly in its subtitle: "The Solution to Reading Comprehension." That's a catchy subtitle and sums it up pretty well. Definitely check this one out, because it's fantastic. And it is *free*. Just go there, make an account, and you're in the club. And if you're not too familiar with the landscape of scholastic texts, that's not a problem. It offers you a whole bunch of click-choices that will make your job easier and help you choose a great text for your student. And, according to the site, these texts are "aligned to the Common Core State Standards and the standards of all 50 states" ("ReadWorks.org: About Us," 2015), which suits our present purposes very well. It's a great time-saver for you and a wonderful learning tool for your student.

To find a passage for your student, click on "Reading Passages," then click "Get Reading Passages," and then provide input in the following parameters: Keyword; Grade (K–12); Lexile Level; Topic; Text Type; Skill/Strategy. When you hit "Apply," you'll be rewarded with a list of texts that will work well for your student. When you choose a text, you'll see a thumbnail of the passage, complete with nifty illustration. If you click on the tab that says "Standards," it gives you the Common Core Standards with which the passage is aligned. It's very cool. If you click "Download," you are given a printable text (quite nice looking), with ample margins for annotating. And even better, at the end there are reading comprehension questions to use with your student. You'll find multiple choice questions there, as well as narrative response questions (these require students to write full sentences and are great for writing practice). And yes, there is an answer key at the end. This is a fantastic resource. It's a wonderful tool for teaching reading comprehension and is a perfect complement to the Common Core Standards.

But when you print the text, make sure you print *two* copies of it. One for you and one for your student. This will allow both of you to look at the same text without physically "crowding" one another during the tutorial (which can be uncomfortable). And, when you have the geography and magic circle of the tutorial in place, let the fun begin. But it's a different sort of fun. Remember, this is a writing tutorial, but we're starting with a segment on reading comprehension. So what exactly do you do? How do we teach the art of reading deeply and well?

I start gently and ease her into it. I tell her to always read with a pencil in her hand. I'm already holding a pencil, so I hand her the other (the pencil is tactile, and students like that). I tell her that, before reading the piece, she should take a look at it and try to learn about it. What is the title? (This should give a good clue what the piece is about.) Who is the author? When was it written? How long is it? Where was it published? Etc. All of these things help give us a holistic idea of the piece and make it feel more familiar and less daunting. It's like a handshake with a new acquaintance.

I then talk to the student about how to read a difficult or academic text. I tell her that she needs to read *actively*, with a pencil in her hand, and scribble notes in the margin. Hold on; this is important, so I want to repeat it: students must learn to *read actively* and *take notes*. When she reads actively, she will engage with the material, ask questions, strive to understand it, and then generate notes of her observations. This note-taking (I explain to her) is called *annotating*, and it's an extremely important skill.

She must do these things (read actively and annotate), even if it means she reads slowly at first. So as you teach the skill of close reading, please be patient with your student. This is difficult, so reassure her that she's doing well and tell her that becoming a good reader takes time and practice. It's a skill like anything else, and she will get better at it. In fact, if she does it enough, it will become a habit for her. Personally, when I read anything, from a novel to a newspaper, I read with a pencil in my hand. It's become a habit, but a good one, I think.

During this instruction, I always stress that the skill of annotating is extremely important when reading academic literature. As your student reads, she should constantly mark up the text with notes and underlining. If the book is not her own property, give her a stack of Post-It notes (sometimes called "sticky notes"), because they're the most useful thing in the world. But show your student how to use them. You can write on them, stick them in the book (they stay in place thanks to a glue strip), and they don't damage the book when they're removed. You can leave them sticking out, where they become bookmarks which indicate important passages (with headings written on the visible tabs). And if you want to get *really* fancy, you can develop a color-coded system, keyed to your outline. Post-It notes are so cool.

And students love nifty props like this; it makes them feel organized and in control of their work.

But amidst the props of pencils and Post-It notes, make sure you explain how to annotate efficiently and well, because it's very important to their development as readers. And this brings us to the skill of reading actively. As students read, they should jot down main ideas, summarize paragraphs, agree or disagree with the author, flag items that pertain to a specific assignment, etc. They should also get used to underlining unfamiliar vocabulary words, looking them up, and writing brief definitions next to them. This is a valuable part of annotating and is extremely important for reading comprehension (and vocabulary development is also heavily stressed by the Common Core).

As the session continues, I tell the student that *every text is about something* (remember that one?), so she should always ask herself "What is this text about?" As she reads, she should also ask herself "Do I understand what I'm reading?" If the answer is "no," then she needs to go back and reread the material. If she doesn't understand what she's reading, she's wasting her time. If her mind wanders as she's reading (very common for all of us), she needs to stop, go back, refocus, and reread. Information doesn't get into our brains by reading; it gets in there by *understanding*. One good technique for reading comprehension is scribbling a short summary of each paragraph in the margin next to the paragraph. When doing this, she should try to isolate the main idea(s) of the paragraph and then jot it (or them) down. This "summary" is just to capture the main idea of the paragraph and (optimally) can often be done in a *single word*. It's sort of like creating an outline in reverse.

As she reads, she should also constantly ask herself questions and jot notes in the margins. Here are some good questions to ask:

- What is this paragraph about?
- What did I just read?
- What are the main ideas here?
- What is the author's point of view?
- What are some themes here?
- What is the main message of this piece?
- What does the author want me to learn from this?
- How does this text relate to my assignment?
- What are my own personal observations about this piece?

These are all good questions and will help assist the student in developing the ability to read and understand complex texts.

And that's the first Shift. It's all about reading comprehension. This is important material and dovetails perfectly with the subject of the second Shift: teaching students to write from *textual evidence*. This is crucial, not just because it's Common Core, but because it's an essential part of any meaningful writing (as well as interacting with the world). Think about it: when we write, we are always creating knowledge from some sort of "evidence." In personal essays, the "evidence" might be drawn from memory, feelings, experiences, events in our lives, people we know, etc. In text-based essays, the evidence is drawn from outside sources called "texts."

But what exactly is a text? I'm going to engage in a bit of theory here, but I find it deeply constructive and eminently related to our purposes. And I explain this to students also, because it's helpful, but I keep it simple. I start this conversation by asking students "What is a text?" They usually tell me it's something they can read. "Yes," I say. "That's correct." But then I tell them that there are other types of texts in the world. And I ask them *How do we define a "text?" What exactly is a text?* This puzzles students, so I tell them that a text is *a body of ideas that can be interpreted* (and this is my own definition). It's a pretty broad definition, but I think it's a good one. So according to that definition, is a *car* a text? Yes, it is. Is your school building a text? Yes indeed. Is an ancient Greek vase a text? Definitely (John Keats certainly thought so). And what about *you*? Are *you* a text also? Yes, you are (and probably a rather interesting one).

In fact, just to illustrate the main principle here, I give students (and I'm going to give you) a short list of different types of texts in the world: a comic book, an interview, a movie, a painting, a radio show, an Egyptian pyramid, a person, an ancient coin, a fossilized Tyrannosaurus rex, the sky, a forest, a mountain, a dog, a lake, a fish, a song, a dance, a sunset, an album of music, and let's make it the Beatles, because they're my favorite. These are all texts. Do you see? Nearly everything in the world can be considered a text and can be "read" and studied and interpreted. It's great for kids to know this, because it helps them understand that a written text is just one type of medium that contains ideas and can be interpreted. And there are also many other types of texts.

However, there is a pragmatic, educational benefit for helping students to understand this. In middle and high school, the texts studied are often written texts. Books, essays, stories, plays, poems, etc. However, students are being increasingly asked to look at, analyze, and write about texts of widely differing media. These are sometimes categorized and referred to as primary and secondary sources, but they're all still texts. (Just to clarify these terms a bit, Picasso's painting *Guernica* is a primary source, while a *biography* of Picasso is a secondary source.) These prewriting sources may be written texts, but they may also be *artifacts* (such as political cartoons, historical photographs, or cave paintings), films, sculptures, natural wonders, inventions, etc. Students are increasingly being asked to study these things, to formulate original theses, and to write original narratives about them, synthesizing the texts and using them as "evidence." Many teachers (and some standardized tests) require students to perform these tasks and often refer to them as "document-based questions" or "DBQs." Thus, teaching students to work with "nontraditional" and panmedia texts [my term] is a very productive and beneficial thing to do.

As you can see, the ability to write from evidence is not relegated to the second Shift in the Common Core, but is an increasingly utilized skill for students to learn and master. (And, as it requires students to analyze and to think creatively and originally, it's also very handy in the real world.) And the writing center is the perfect place to teach it. But it's a complex and difficult skill, because it often requires students to look at texts and *infer* meaning from them. In other words, students must be able to "read into" texts and to analyze them carefully and perceptively in order to arrive at independent conclusions in order to create original knowledge.

And this is explicitly called for in the second Shift, which states that "Students should be able to answer a range of *text-dependent* questions, whose answers require inferences based on careful attention to the text" ("Key Shifts in English Language Arts," 2015). Students must be able to not only read and understand complex texts (the focus of the first Shift), they must also be able to analyze the text, interpret it, and make inferences based on it. This is a tricky and difficult skill to teach (especially to young students), so you and your tutors will have to proceed slowly, methodically, and patiently.

When tutoring this skill in the writing center, I begin by stressing that *every text contains information*. However, some of this information is literal (stated clearly, on the surface), and some of it is hidden. It may be suggested by the text or it may be hinted at by the author. The surface information is usually easy to understand, but the "hidden" information needs to be interpreted or puzzled out and (in a sense) "decoded." In other words, to "infer" something means to arrive at a conclusion that was not explicitly stated in the text. It's tricky.

I begin teaching this to students by giving them the following simple example: "It is raining out. My shirt is wet." Here's my question: based on the information provided, how did my shirt get wet? Here's an answer: *We can conclude reasonably that I have most likely been out in the rain without a raincoat, and the rain has made my shirt wet.* However, I didn't explicitly state that the rain has made my shirt wet, and it is possible that my shirt might be wet for other reasons. But still, the above conclusion is the best one, given the information provided. That's an inference.

This is a difficult concept, so I go slowly. I tell my students that every text contains hidden meanings and, sometimes, skillful authors give their readers hints or clues that must be interpreted. This means that readers must sometimes interpret (or "infer") the meaning of a passage. *What is the author suggesting in that passage? What can you infer from that statement?* It's hard to teach inference, and it's a difficult skill for young students to learn, so I do this through examples, modeling, leading questions, and lots of patience.

When I teach this to kids, I like to keep things very simple and concrete. I have had great results with a very basic model for analysis that is essentially a variation of the "summary and commentary" paradigm. I explain this to students and then write a peculiar-looking sentence in the notes I generate for them: "When _____ happens, it means _____." This simple model is the basis for all analysis, in every discipline. Think about it. We might be studying *Hamlet*, the Amazon River, a moon rock, an Egyptian pyramid, or Van Gogh's *Starry Night*, but it's always the same pattern: we move from a description of the thing being studied to the meaning extracted from it. It's really very simple: summary and commentary; description and analysis; fact and conclusion; text and interpretation. It's a simple, repetitive pattern, but it's extremely effective. I always explain this to students (and you should too), because they have never been taught this. Not in these simple terms. When they understand this basic pattern, I follow it up with a clear demonstration of how to use this model in written, academic form. This is a crucial component to helping them learn how to employ textual evidence correctly, so I'm going to show you how I teach it to students.

Using a chunk of written text is essentially a five-step process. After choosing a quote (or paraphrase, or summary) to include in your paper as a piece of textual evidence, the student should do the following:

1. Introduce the quote.
2. Provide the quote.
3. Provide a citation.
4. Explain the quote.
5. Interpret or analyze the quote, or make an inference.

I will now explain what each step means. Let's say a student named Ken comes into the writing center. He must write a paper in which he analyzes the character and motivations of Jay Gatsby, and he must use the text of *The Great Gatsby* as his "evidence." He has located a quote he wants to use. Shortly before the story's conclusion (on page 189 of my copy), Nick Carraway (the narrator) states that "Gatsby believed in the green light." Ken likes this quote, but he's not sure what to do with it. Here's what I tell him:

"Okay Ken, it's a good quote. Let's start by introducing the quote." Introducing the quote means just what it says. You don't start the sentence with the quote, you say something about it first. *Your* words come before the quote. And it might be quite simple, like this:

> Towards the end of the novel, Nick Carraway states that "Gatsby believed in the green light."

Now, as this is a quote from a source, you must include the citation. Here, you should explain to the student that the structure of the citation will differ according to the teacher's preferred document style. If the paper is written in (for example) Chicago style, it will include the last name of the author, the year the text was published, and the page number. I explain to Ken (briefly and simply) that there are different document styles in the world and that he should ask his teacher which one to use (but for our purposes here, let's say the teacher prefers Chicago style). Now, with the citation tacked on, the introduced quote looks like this:

> Towards the end of the novel, Nick Carraway tells us that "Gatsby believed in the green light" (Fitzgerald, 1995, 189).

At this point, we have an introduction, a quote, and a citation. We need two more things.

Next (I explain to Ken), he must *explain what the quote means*. We discuss the quote, and after a few minutes, I ask Ken to write down his explanation. He writes:

"Here, Nick is describing Gatsby's personality. He is telling us that Gatsby was an optimist, and felt hopeful about the future." Now, Ken's passage looks like this:

> Towards the end of the novel, Nick Carraway tells us that "Gatsby believed in the green light" (Fitzgerald, 1995, p. 189). Here, Nick is describing Gatsby's personality. He is telling us that Gatsby was an optimist, and felt hopeful about the future.

I tell Ken that he's doing well, and that he needs one more piece of the puzzle, and it is perhaps the most challenging one. He must *interpret the quote* and find the meaning that is suggested by it. He must infer meaning from this strange, short statement. I work with Ken. I ask him leading questions and model the process of interpretation. Finally, I tease an original interpretation out of Ken, and he jots it down, and it reads like this: "In this quote, Fitzgerald is suggesting that chasing our dreams is a good thing. We need to stay hopeful about the future, even if it's possible that bad things might happen." *Nice work Ken. You're doing very well, and I think that's a terrific interpretation.* And now, Ken' completed passage looks like this:

> Towards the end of the novel, Nick Carraway tells us that "Gatsby believed in the green light" (Fitzgerald, 1995, p. 189). Here, Nick is describing Gatsby's personality. He is telling us that Gatsby was an optimist, and felt hopeful about the future. In this quote, Fitzgerald is suggesting that chasing our dreams is a good thing. We need to stay hopeful about the future, even if it's possible that bad things might happen.

Do you see how that goes? It's a very simple example, but I think it's a good one. And our friend Ken, he's sitting there, blinking at what he just accomplished, and I can read his mind. He's thinking, "Wow, so that's how it's done? I never knew that. It looks pretty good!"

Please understand this eminently: *students don't know how to do this*, and the writing center is the perfect place to teach them. They have never before been shown this sort of simplified step-by-step process of textual analysis. And they will thrive on having it explained in numerical, step-by-step fashion, as I did above. These five steps, even though rigid, constitute a ladder into understanding and learning. And, if students go through this process a few times, they won't need to look at a list of five steps anymore. They'll remember the steps, know them intuitively, and begin to understand the process of analysis and interpretation.

That last step, however—the step involving original analysis—is the most difficult, so we need to help students with that. To assist with this, I do exercises with students, and I use several high-interest, real-world examples. Here, I usually start with *visual* texts, because (to put it simply) kids like to look at pictures and then talk about them. For instance, I often ask students what they're interested in. If it's *cars*, I might show them a photo of a new Corvette and explain that *this is a text* and it needs to be interpreted, just like a book. I start by asking them to describe the 'Vette by using meaningful details. "Look closely at the car. Can you describe it to me? What do you see on the car?" I then move on to more "interpretive" questions, such as

- What do you like about this car?
- What might have been some goals of the designers?
- Why do you think the tires are so wide?
- What kind of person might buy this car?

It's a good exercise and gets the kids looking past the surface of the car and (more important) the surface of a text.

I also show a photo of a young couple eating in a restaurant. I ask students to describe the scene, noticing (and using) as many significant details as possible. "Look closely at the picture. What's happening here? Can you spot about five significant details that tell the story in the photo?" When they understand the photo and give me accurate feedback, I move on to more challenging (and inferential) questions, such as:

- Tell me something about their personalities. What are they like?
- Notice their body language. How do they feel about each other?
- How long have they been together?
- Are they married?
- If not, do you think they'll get married?
- What kind of jobs do you think they have?
- And so on.

These exercises are designed to get the student thinking beyond description and drawing original conclusions and making suppositions. This works very well and makes a nice introduction to analyzing text.

But I leave the best one for last. One of my favorite paintings in the world is *Breaking Home Ties* by a genius named Norman Rockwell. Have you seen it? It's marvelous, and (like all great art) filled with sadness and wisdom. There's also a terrific backstory to the painting that I share with kids (and I'll share with you now). In 1960, Rockwell sold the original painting to a neighbor for $900. The neighbor (an artist) then painted a passable copy of the painting. Over the years, the original disappeared (!). The neighbor's copy was believed to be the original and was celebrated and displayed in museums. When the owner passed away in 2005, his sons discovered the original painting hidden behind a false wall in their father's house. In 2006, it sold at auction for $15.4 million ("Rockwell Found Behind Fake Wall," 2006). Not bad, huh? It's a great story. Kids love it, and it increases their engagement with the subject.

The *Breaking Home Ties* painting shows a young man in a train station sitting with his father and their beautiful family dog. The young man is getting ready to head off to college and (judging by his body language and facial expression) is thrilled about it. But his father and the dog are absolutely heartbroken. It's a masterpiece, filled with telling details that give us an intimate glimpse into this fine American family and into the sorrowful workings of the human heart. And, of course, students can identify with (and perhaps envy) a young person who is about to leave for the adventure of college life. But you're older and wiser, so I want to caution you: if you study this painting for long enough—and if you're a bit sensitive (like yours truly)—make sure you have some tissues handy.

I always show my students a high-quality copy of this painting (the details are very important), and I ask them to look at it carefully (if your library doesn't have a copy, the Internet certainly will). I tell my students that the painting is a text, and they need to "read" it. What's going on there? What do you see? And I grow quiet as they look. They love it. Many of them can identify with the elements of family, dogs, college, and sadness, so they're fascinated by it. I start by saying "Look closely at this painting. Notice the details, because they're all important. *What's it really about?*"

They offer explanations. I listen, I agree, I compliment. When they stall, I point out details and ask leading questions:

- What's on the boy's lap? [it's his lunch]. Look carefully at his lunch. What do you notice about it? What does it tell us?
- What's happening with the dog? Why did Rockwell include the dog in the painting?
- In what direction is the boy looking? Where is his father looking? Why?
- Look at the boy's suit. Tell me about it. Does he wear suits often? How can you tell?
- Look at the boy's books. What do you notice about them? [They have bookmarks. They're not packed.] Why? What does this tell us about him?
- What is the father holding? Why is he holding both hats?
- Tell me about the boy's personality.
- Tell me about the father's personality.
- Tell me about their relationship.
- Let's say that the boy has a mother. Where might she be? Why isn't she there? Tell me about her personality.
- What are the major themes of the painting?
- Is the painting happy, or sad? Pick one and explain your point of view by using details from the painting.

Give your students *Breaking Home Ties*, and see where they go with it. It's lots of fun and a great exercise for helping kids interpret, make inferences, and support points of view with textual evidence. I love this exercise.

After working with several visual texts, I move on to written texts. Here, I start with small chunks of text, usually a sentence or a paragraph. For example, I give students a beautiful sentence from E.B. White's marvelous essay "Once More to the Lake." This essay is about White taking his young son to a lake that he (White) used to visit when he was a young boy. He writes: "I took along my son, who had never had any fresh water up his nose and who had seen lily pads only from train windows" (McCuen, 1989, 395). See the simple beauties of that sentence and the way it hints at deeper truths? We're in the presence of a master. (And it's certainly no accident that the central metaphor of the piece is a lake, with its beautiful surface and mysterious, hidden depths.) When I do this exercise with a student, I ask her "So, what is happening on the surface of that sentence?" And she reads it, over and over, and then tentatively whispers "He's taking his son somewhere? And maybe his son doesn't like to swim? Or maybe his son has never been swimming in a lake?"

"Yes," I say, "Good work. You're off to a great start." Smiles and compliments go a long way. I continue to ask leading questions, until she thoroughly understands what the sentence is about. And now comes the hard part.

I explain to her that the sentence is also hinting at certain things. I ask "What's it hinting at? The author is giving us clues about other things. Look closely at the sentence. What can you see there?" And I give her time. She reads it over and over, her lips move silently, and her eyes narrow in concentration. It's a difficult task, and if she's stumped, I offer some leading questions: "We know the boy has never been swimming in a lake, right? And we know they take train rides. What could that possibly mean? Think about it." And after some modeling, prodding, and more leading questions, she arrives at the following inferences: "They travel together through the countryside on a train, so maybe they live in a city. He's a writer, and he travels a lot by train, because he's so busy. But he takes his son along, because he loves his son. He seems like a very good father. He wants to take his son to the lake, because he wants to get them both back in nature." And I smile and compliment her again, and she feels good about her wonderful achievement.

See how it goes? These are all inferences growing out of an isolated sentence. I find that exercises like this are very helpful to students. They may not become "pros" at inferential thinking immediately, but it's extremely helpful for them to understand that the skill of reading involves interpretation, inferences, and decoding clues left there by writers. And if a frustrated student asks me "Why do writers do this? Why don't they just say what they think!" I tell them this: "It's because life doesn't tell you what it thinks, and sometimes you have to figure things out for yourself." A sad bit of business, but alas, an eternal truth.

When I feel the student is ready, we do something a bit more challenging. I give her Robert Frost's wonderful poem "The Road Not Taken" and ask her to read it, annotate it, and tell me what it's about. This is much trickier than it appears. Most people have read this poem at one time or another, and nearly everyone thinks it's about how we must make our own choices in life, stay true to ourselves, and resist stampeding with the herd. That's cozy, simple, and saccharine sweet, but it's also quite wrong. And I can just see Robert Frost grinning at how he fooled us. He was extremely brilliant and loved to embed his poems with layers and deep meanings and would never offer the world such a trite little cupcake.

Encourage your students to read this poem carefully, to notice what's in the text, and what's *not* there. As she reads it, ask her to underline significant words and passages. Ask her "What's the poem about? Are the roads really different? Is one road really less traveled than the other?" (hint: if you read closely, you'll see that they're described *three times* as being the same!). Then, ask your student about Frost's enigmatic last two lines: "I took the one less traveled by, / And that has made all the difference" (Baym, 1995, 1771). If the roads are indeed "equal" (and they are described as such), what does the narrator mean? Can we believe the narrator? Also ask your student to consider the ending. Is it a happy ending? Is it sad? Or is it something else? And, as she's puzzling this out, make sure she uses the text as evidence to support her analyses and conclusions.

When your student has gone as far as she can go, employ leading questions and modeling and guide her toward the truth (because the narrator of this poem is definitely lying to us). This poem is told by an "unreliable narrator" and (to sum it up quickly) it's ultimately about the very human predilection to lie to ourselves (and others) that we did the "right" thing, that we made the right choices, that the life we're leading is the best possible life for us. It's a convenient, comforting notion, but it's not necessarily the truth.

The fact is, we can never know for sure what's behind a door we never opened. We simply don't *know* how our lives would have turned out had we gone to a different college, moved to a different town, or pursued a different career. But we tell ourselves that our colleges and our locations and our jobs are all "meant to be," and it's a cozy thing called *rationalization*. We all do it, from time to time. It helps us get through difficult days and difficult times in our lives, and it's a harmless bit of mental self-preservation. This poem is a really nifty peek inside the human mind and human heart and how we lie to ourselves to make ourselves feel better and to look better to others. In this poem, Frost has given us a fantastic and perceptive short masterpiece of psychology.

The exercises I described above may take several sessions. That's okay. Remember, your goal is not to "cover" material, but to teach your students, and long-term learning is always better than short-term "cramming." Not long ago, I got a phone call from a nervous parent whose daughter "Jayne" (in the ninth grade) was having trouble with reading comprehension. She was taking honors and AP classes and was a very intelligent and hard-working student. However, she found some of the readings to be quite challenging, especially when they contained subtle passages that required inference and interpretation. After some small talk, Mom got around to the subject of her phone call. She told me that Jayne enjoyed working with me in the writing center, but that she's struggling with reading comprehension, and would I work with her on this? And could I meet with her in the mornings, before school? I shut my eyes and rubbed my temples at this unexpected bit of work coming my way, because my mornings before school were reserved for writing the book you're reading right now.

It was a tall order, but yes, I would be happy to help out. And here's what I told Mom, right there on the phone: "Sure, I'll be happy to work with Jayne. But we need to look at this in the long term. We can't expect any quick fixes here. She'll most likely develop slowly over the next few years. This will be a long process, and she'll improve slowly." And Mom understood that and thanked me. So I worked with Jayne for the next few months, doing the above exercises in reading comprehension and textual analysis and, in general, having a good time with it. And Jayne did well with the material and seemed to pick up these skills quickly. And in June of that year, Jayne sent me an email, thanking me and telling me that she scored a 98 percent on her final exam in English. There was lots of reading comprehension on the exam, but she nailed it, and she gave much of the credit to our early morning sessions. It's always nice getting an email like that, and I was quite proud of her. These techniques definitely work.

But besides these practice texts, you will also (of course) help the student with her actual assignment. She most likely has an assignment which grows out of reading and understanding a particular text, such as an article, essay, or poem. Think about the things we discussed in the early parts of this book. Make sure you know the assignment and the central question(s) that she is responsible for. What is the project? How does the text relate to the project? What, exactly, must she do with the text? When you know exactly how the text relates to the assignment, start reading the text with your student. If it's short enough, you might skim the entire thing (through the lens of the task) and get a sense of what the text is about and how it relates to the assignment.

Here, I suggest reading the text out loud, while the student follows along on her copy. I find this works well, because the student is *reading* and *hearing* the text at the same time, which can boost comprehension. As you do this, both of you should read with pencils in your hands, so that you can make notes on the text. As you annotate your copy, take your student through the process of annotating, and begin this by telling her what to write down. This is an excellent form of modeling and keeps her involved in the lesson. Plus, these notes will be a useful resource when she goes home later and reads the text over.

When it comes to reading the text, I know that some tutors ask their *students* to read it aloud, but it's not a good idea, so don't do it. It makes students feel uncomfortable and self-conscious, especially if they're not good readers. But when you're working on a specific portion of text, I recommend reading it aloud so that you're both on the same page (literally). This is excellent modeling for the student, and it's a great learning tool. She is seeing and hearing the text and learning that reading aloud can be helpful when trying to understand a difficult passage. (Honestly, I still do this when reading something difficult—I read it aloud to see how it "sounds.") When I'm reading aloud to a student, I'm conscious of *how* I'm reading: I read clearly and at a slow conversational speed and use inflection appropriately, to bring meaning out of the piece. All of this transmits a message to the student that a text is not just boring, meaningless ink on a page. It's human experience translated into words on paper.

Students need to know that there is an actual person behind every written text. And the ideas contained in the text are common to all of us. This is very valuable knowledge for students.

As I read the text aloud to the student, I notice things, annotate, and discuss my observations with her. As you do this, make sure the student is annotating. She should be underlining and scribbling notes in the margins. Don't be afraid to be directive here and suggest annotations to her. She is still learning this skill and she'll need these notes when she goes home later. As I read aloud with her, I ask leading questions and discuss significant points, always keeping in mind the assignment. I encourage students to ask questions if they have them (and they should!), and I'm not afraid to say "I don't know." Your job is not to have all the answers. In fact, I don't know anyone who does. As a writing center director, your job is to help students become independent writers. And along the way, do your best to help them become independent readers and thinkers.

Bear in mind that you probably won't read the entire piece with the student. This is ok; in fact, it's very common. End the session when it's supposed to end; and do it with a blissfully clear conscience. However, encourage the student to read the rest of the text *tonight* (while the lessons are still fresh in her mind) and urge her to annotate on her own. Also, tell her that most texts (especially difficult texts) need to be read, over and over, to fully understand them. And this is the absolute truth. If she asks you "How many times should I read it?" tell her "About five times is a good number," even though there is no "right" answer to this question. Students thrive on structure like this. And tell her to bring her annotated copy to the next session (perhaps it will be tomorrow, or the day after?). And before she leaves your library, do your best to schedule her next session (write it in the snazzy schedule book and show it to her), smile at her, and tell her she's doing great.

And now comes *your* homework, valiant director: do your darnedest to read the rest of the piece and annotate it. Get a good sense of what it's about and how it relates to her task. Be prepared with chunky bits of knowledge to discuss. And write your notes right on your text. That's the right place for them. This will get you prepared and motivated to deliver an excellent tutorial the next time she comes to the writing center. You will also be setting a good example and showing the student that you care about teaching her. There's nothing like showing up to a session fully prepared and with a smile on your face.

Well, that concludes our chapter on the Common Core. Was the material here a surprise? Perhaps you thought it would be dry and clinical, whereas it turned out to be quite human and accessible, and maybe even fun. Aligning your writing center with Common Core Writing Standards is easier than it sounds. As you can see, I suggest focusing your tutorials on the central skills of reading comprehension and using textual evidence. The one-on-one tutorial is excellent for that kind of instruction. I urge you to teach all these skills to your tutors, but, as always, keep your instruction "human" and pleasant. And urge them to do the same.

Chapter 11

A CLEAR AND ENJOYABLE WRITER'S GUIDE

Well, we're getting close to the end of this book. I decided to wrap things up by giving you a clearly written and reader-friendly writer's guide. I think this will answer a great many of your questions about writing, so you can pass this information along to the students you tutor.

In this guide, I provide tips and pointers that will teach you some basics about academic writing. I labeled each section, because I thought this would help make this information more organized and readable. I also kept the second person, for the sake of consistency and readability. I'm writing to you, your students, and anyone who wants to learn the lifelong art of writing.

In choosing which topics to discuss, I relied on my experience as a teacher of writing and literature and as a writing center director and tutor. As I wrote this chapter, I tried to target some of the errors made most often by students, and I tried at all times to be as clear as possible. As you read this material, you'll find that I covered some of these topics earlier in this book. That's okay. Repetition creates deep and long-term learning, and that's the important thing here.

But I want to mention that some of this information is *subjective*, which means that much of it is my deeply held belief (drawn from my extensive experience and education), rather than established "fact." That's okay. This is the nature of *writing*—it's more of an *art* than a science. Nevertheless, I stand by all of the information contained in this chapter, and I believe that learning these techniques and practicing them can help you become a better writing center director, tutor, and writer. And, if anything in this guide is not clear, or if you want a little more information on the writing process, feel free to reach out to me on the "School Library Writing Centers" forum which I created. I'll definitely get back to you, and we'll have a nice chat. I promise.

WHAT'S A THESIS STATEMENT?

To put it very simply, a thesis statement is a sentence (or two) that says what the paper is about. Crafting a clear, specific, and focused thesis statement is one of the most crucial steps in writing an academic paper. Indeed, its importance cannot be overemphasized. And *when* should a thesis statement be created? That's impossible to say. Sometimes the student will be given a topic. Sometimes he will know exactly what he wants to write about. Sometimes he will need to research a topic in order to gain information and develop a thesis as he learns. Sometimes he will begin research and writing and alter his thesis as the paper progresses.

But no matter how or when a thesis is created, a composition should begin with an original, meaningful, and academically viable thesis statement. Without a solid academic thesis, you're (metaphorically speaking) beginning a long journey without a map; you're building a house on quicksand. In other words, the thesis statement should act as a guide as you develop a paper. If it's not guiding you, then either the thesis must be changed or the paper must be changed. If the paper and you are not being guided by a clear thesis statement, the paper will suffer from a lack of focus and substantive meaning. When formulating a thesis, you should ask yourself some questions:

- Does this thesis have some relevance to important, contemporary, real-world issues?

- Am I somehow belaboring the obvious?

- As far as I know, has this question or topic been covered before in a similar manner?

- Can I sum up my thesis in a single, clear, understandable sentence? (This is important; the best ideas are very often the clearest and simplest. You should be able to "speak" your thesis in one clear and tidy sentence.)

Remember, every paper should be *an original contribution to knowledge*. Think of it as a brick in the edifice of human understanding. If an academic paper is done thoughtfully and well, you will become an "expert" on the topic. For all of these reasons, it is imperative to spend time and energy on the construction of a highly specific thesis statement. Regarding the scope of a thesis, you should keep in mind the length of the project. As most school projects are relatively brief, you should strive for a thesis that is *narrower* rather than broader in scope. Consider the following examples of titles/topics/theses:

- *Shakespeare*: Is this about the man, or his work, or both? It's much too broad a topic to cover in (for example) a five-page paper, or even a 5,000-page paper. Literally millions of pages have been written on this subject, and they're still being written today. No good. Needs to be more specific.

- *Shakespeare's Comedies*: still much too broad. What do you want to say about his comedies?

- *Shakespeare's Play* The Tempest: Getting better, but still too broad. What do you want to say about *The Tempest*? What's the paper about?

- *The Character Prospero in Shakespeare's* Tempest: We're getting warmer. What do you want to say about Prospero? What's the paper about?

- *The Character Prospero in Shakespeare's* Tempest *as a Stand-in for Shakespeare Himself*: Bingo. This is a very well-crafted and highly specific thesis (although not an original one; scholars and theater-goers have been saying this for the last four centuries). But for a middle or high school student, this is a good thesis statement that would probably yield a very good paper. I would look forward to reading a paper like this. I would also look forward to writing a paper like this, but hey, that's me.

TYPES OF THESIS STATEMENTS

Think of the thesis as answering an important question. I covered this in some detail in Chapter Four, but I want to talk about it some more, because it's so important. The type of thesis statement you write will depend largely on the type of paper you're writing. There are really only four kinds of thesis statements, keyed to four kinds of papers:

1. You will "teach" your readers information on a specific important subject (this goes with the informative essay).
2. You will analyze a complex issue or text (this goes with the analytical essay).
3. You will take a firm stand on an important controversial subject and "argue" your point (this goes with the argumentative or persuasive essay).
4. You will tell the reader about an important event in your life (this goes with the personal narrative).

If the student is allowed choice, help him choose his topic wisely. For example, an informative essay on the "Life of George Washington" will be meaningless and dull (and the student certainly won't enjoy writing it). It's been done ad infinitum, and if I want to know about Washington's life, I'll look under "W" in an encyclopedia. When the student is allowed choice of topics, encourage him to choose a topic that is academically viable and that he (and the reader) will find interesting.

When writing an informative essay, the thesis should indicate two things: the thing being analyzed and how (or why) it's being analyzed. Or, to phrase it differently, the thesis indicates the *thing you're writing about* and *what you're saying about it*. This type of thesis can be used with papers that require research ("There were many causes of World War Two"), with papers that analyze a literary text ("The Symbolism in Edgar Allan Poe's short story 'The Cask of Amontillado'"), or with narrative essays based on the student's original thoughts and knowledge ("Bullying in Schools Needs to be Stopped").

Regarding the argumentative essay, you will take a firm stance on an important topic, and you will argue your beliefs clearly and logically. In this type of essay, you *mustn't play "both sides of the fence"*; doing so will make your paper lifeless and dull, like eating sand-flavored jello. Here are some topics with good arguments on both sides:

- Technology is good.
- Technology is bad.

- Violence in the media has negative effects on consumers.
- Violence in the media has no effect on consumers.
- Internet content needs to be censored and regulated.
- Internet content must remain uncensored and unregulated.

If choosing to write an argumentative essay, you should (whenever possible) make sure that *you actually believe in what you're saying*. Readers are smart and can detect notes of sycophantic phoniness (trust me). For example, if a student is interested in Global Warming, but is still largely undecided about it, she may wish to do some reading and research on the topic first. This will help clarify her thinking on the subject until she has firmly made up her mind. However, *you should never choose a side based on "popularity" or what you think your teacher (or reader) "wants" to hear.* The job of a teacher is to *judge the merits of a paper*, not whether or not he agrees with you. Therefore, argue your beliefs honestly and logically, and don't be afraid to "offend" readers who might disagree with you. Take a firm stance on an issue and argue your thesis with confidence.

Be aware, however, that in your research you will encounter very good arguments on both sides. Keep in mind that the word "essay" comes from the French verb *essayer* (pronounced ESS-ay-ay), which means "to try." In an essay you are *trying* to say something important, and this often involves *trying* to persuade readers to agree with you. Let me repeat this: in an argumentative essay, *you're trying to convince your readers that your point is the right one*, and those who disagree with you are wrong (or somewhat misguided). You should therefore always attempt to bring in *counterarguments*. These are passages in which you briefly discuss opposing viewpoints and then show why they're wrong, or why your opinions are stronger and more valid. Counterarguments will, of course, require research, and they often come toward the end of a paper. Fledgling students frequently have a tough time dealing with counterarguments, but if they're handled well, they can contribute substantially to the power of the central argument.

For more information on counterarguments, see Marius' *Writer's Companion* (especially pages 53 and 54). I used this book when learning the academic argument, and Marius' ideas have helped shape my thinking on the subject.

THE TITLE AND THE THESIS

When I'm writing my own papers, I often consider the *title* and *thesis* as being nearly interchangeable (at least in terms of ideas). This is something you should strive for. The title should say very clearly what the paper is about. Likewise, the thesis statement should say very clearly what the paper is about. However, you should vary the language between these two so as to avoid redundancy. Also, do not attempt to pique the readers' interest by providing "teasers" or using purposely obtuse, nebulous, or obfuscatory language. See what I mean? Writing prose that no one can understand is easy; *it's much more difficult to write clearly and simply.*

Therefore, in your writing, strive always for clarity and present your information as clearly as you can. Use a thesaurus sparingly, don't overcomplicate in an effort to sound academic or pedantic. No one likes to read "academese"; you will make your reader struggle and you will lose him or her (in more ways than one). Further, you will lose your own unique voice (even *you* won't like the sound of it), and your reader will be well aware that you're writing to *impress* rather than to convey knowledge. When in doubt, *write the way you speak*; you can always go back later and edit. Know what you want to say and say it clearly.

Now, you may be wondering "where in the paper should I place my thesis statement?" I discussed this in Chapter Four, but I want to mention it again. The thesis statement goes in the introduction and (in many cases) can be the very first sentence in the piece. However, it can also be the last sentence (or two) of the introduction. When deciding where a student's thesis should go, here's a great tip: *ask the teacher*. Direct your student to ask his teacher where she wants the thesis placed. And then follow the teacher's directions. This is an easy solution, so don't overlook the obvious.

But if the teacher says it can go either place, I favor placing it *first*. First sentence in the introduction, first sentence the reader reads. This is clear, direct, and efficient. I like to *immediately tell the reader what the paper is about*; I don't like to keep him guessing or waiting. There's no reason for it. Also, most fledgling writers are not going to build a sense of suspense in their readers; only the finest professional writers can be confident of doing this.

However, there may be times when it's appropriate to push the thesis statement to the latter end of the introduction. Perhaps you want to start off with an interesting anecdote. For example, let's say you're writing an informative paper about animals indigenous to Africa, and you went on a safari this past summer. That's too good to miss, so your paper should start off like this: "This past summer, I spent two weeks on safari in Africa." How's that for an opening? I would be hooked and would gobble up the rest of the paper ravenously. And I'd probably seek you out, tell you "you're not in trouble," and ask you about your trip.

DEFINE YOUR TERMS

As you write your paper, you will most likely need to define some terms. By "definition of terms," I am referring to a part of your project in which you clarify and explain words or concepts that might be unfamiliar to your readers. Note: *I just defined the term "definition of terms."* Now that you know what it means, I can proceed with confidence that you'll understand the following detailed discussion of this topic.

Does that make sense?

Here's what I mean: in your central thesis, there will most likely be abstract concepts or specialized terms that your reader needs to know in order to truly understand your overall argument. *Never assume that your reader knows exactly what you're talking about*; give him or her enough information to understand your argument. For example, if you're writing a paper on *Chaturanga*, you need to tell your reader the meaning of this strange word. It might go like this: "Chaturanga is an ancient game that comes from India. The game of chess was taken from Chaturanga." And how did I learn that delightful tidbit? I once tutored a freshman as she composed a paper on Chaturanga. And I told her (a bit quizzically, I admit) that she needed to define her term. She did, her paper became much clearer, and I learned about Chaturanga.

Do you see the purpose of defining your terms? It's very important. You can't assume that your readers will be experts on your topic; after all, how many people know (or would agree on) precise definitions of "theatre of the absurd," syzygy, or diaspora? Explain clearly what terms such as these mean; don't keep your readers guessing; that's a sure way to lose them.

And there is another reason to define your terms. Many words and concepts resist strict definition, and therefore you must *define them as you're using them in your project*. Please make sure you understand this concept. Precisely what do we mean by the following terms: *politics, feminism, justice, adolescence, political correctness, literature, art?* When precisely does a *short story* become a *novelette* become a *novella* become a *novel?* As there is a great deal of disagreement and "wiggle room" on terms such as these, you must *define them as you use them in your project*. Check out the following examples:

- For purposes of this paper, I am defining "adolescence" as being between 14 and 18 years of age.
- The term "feminism," as it is used here, refers specifically to the pursuance of social and occupational equality regardless of gender.
- The reader may take the term "literature" as referring specifically to substantial works of *fiction* that are concerned primarily with examining, exploring, and explaining the human condition (by "substantial," I am referring to literary works of approximately 300 pages or longer).

Do you see? In the examples I provided, you'll notice that I was simple and direct; you'll also notice that I avoided dictionary definitions. This is a good idea; dictionary definitions tend to be dryly written, and they probably won't contain the shades of meaning you wish to convey. In terms of *placement*, it's usually best to define your terms early in your paper, either in the introduction or shortly after. After all, your goal is to ensure your readers' understanding from the very beginning of your project.

THE *ORDER* IN WHICH YOU SHOULD WRITE YOUR PAPER

Here, I am going to talk about the *order* in which you should write your paper, and I'm going to ask you to trust me on a few things. First (and I said this earlier), write your introduction *last*. If you write it first, you will most likely discard the introduction later. Begin instead with the middle section (or body) of the paper, which usually means begin with the second paragraph. Here's the reason: as you write your paper, you will learn, you will create and uncover new knowledge, you will discover how you *really* feel about things, and the research you perform will add new and unexpected dimensions to your thinking and your writing. If you write your introduction first, one of two things will almost certainly happen:

- You will suddenly become aware that your introduction no longer fits the body of the paper, you will throw it out, and you will not be a happy camper.
- You will become "indebted" to your introduction, and you will feel the need to make the body of the paper fit the introduction. This will crush fortuitous discoveries, dowse sparks of joyous creativity, and destroy the organic manner in which a good paper grows. Again, not a happy camper.

Yes, every paper worth its academic salt has a *growing* and *developing* period in which you make discoveries and realize that you know things you didn't know you knew (strange, but true). Trust me; this will most likely happen as you write your paper. Writing expert Peter Elbow in his excellent work *Writing Without Teachers* uses the metaphors of "growing" and "cooking" to describe the slow genesis of a good paper (see chapters Two and Three, respectively). Like a good meal, it requires careful preparation and a combination of ingredients, followed by a time of slow mental and lexical simmering. And before I digress any further, let me sum up the major point I'm trying to make: *don't start by writing the introduction, skip it till later, and start with the second paragraph.* And be prepared to discard *that* once you catch some momentum.

Now, here's a rule about writing that may take some time to sink in: *you don't know what you're going to say until you say it.* If you're painting a picture, you don't really know what it's going to look like until it's finished. If you plant a rosebush, you don't know what it's going to look like until it grows. Here's the deal: let's say you've written the body of the paper, you've done the research, and you feel pretty good about it. Now you can stand back and say out loud (or to yourself) *Aha! So that's what my paper's really about!* Only when you have written the bulk of your paper will you know what your paper is really about, and this is *because it's finished* (tautological, but true).

But don't break out the happy-camping tools yet, now comes time to write the *conclusion.* A conclusion is similar to an introduction; both give encapsulated statements as to the paper's central meaning. In a sense, a well-written essay or paper has a "circular" structure: the end returns to the beginning. So, when you're happy with the middle section of your paper, you can go ahead and write the conclusion. In it you will repeat your central point or points, and you will discuss (or repeat, or clarify, or emphasize) any conclusions you've reached. Think of it as a type of summary. And if it somehow does not echo your central thesis, it *should,* so you need to work on it until it does. And remember, your conclusion will play the last notes that reverberate in the mind of your reader, so make them memorable ones; this is the place for lasting last impressions.

Once you're happy with the body, the conclusion, and the introduction, go ahead and write a title. Yes, *choosing a title should be the very last thing you do.* As the paper is now complete, this is the best time to choose a "name" that truly fits your paper. But choose carefully; titles are very important and often set the tone for what follows. It should be catchy and specific, not too long and not too short; above all, *it should say exactly what your paper is about.* Don't try to "lure" readers with fuzzy titles which suggest that mysterious intellectual goodies await; only P.T. Barnum could get away with that. Your title should clearly describe your subject and topic as well as the angle you're pursuing; it should therefore reflect and anticipate your thesis statement. Think of your title as a "miniature portrait" of your paper.

PLAGIARISM

When you write an academic paper, you are joining an intellectual discussion that has been taking place for several thousand years, so you need to speak the language correctly. First of all, providing quotes, paraphrases, and references (along with the accompanying citations) is *not* an acknowledgement of intellectual inferiority; it makes you look scholarly and *sharp*. The finest scholars do this, and *this is how it's done*. When I see properly formatted citations in a scholarly work, my opinion and trust of the writer are raised immediately. I think *here is someone who has done his homework. He has taken the time not only to read what others have been saying, he has given them credit. Further, I am confident that anything not cited in this work must therefore be original to the writer.*

Plagiarism (intentional or unintentional) is a destroyer. It destroys scholarship and reputations. At its worst it is dishonest; at its best it indicates shoddiness and laziness. This is not a matter of "getting caught." The writer probably will, but that's not the point (believe me, it's quite easy for a professional teacher to spot plagiarism). Help your students produce intellectually honest documents that they can truly be *proud* of. Scholars work hard to get published; students (and other writers) *must* take great pains to give them the credit they deserve. Additionally, referring in papers to "heavy hitters" gives scholarly work tremendous credibility. The logic goes something like this: "A noted scholar agrees with my ideas, so I am probably right."

Nevertheless, there is some gray area here. Often when I tutor, the question comes up: *What exactly do we have to cite?* The answer is this: *anything and everything that is not absolutely your own original thoughts or ideas* and that's not "common knowledge." If you're reading the work of a scholar, *and* you have a sudden flash of insight as a result of your reading, *and* that insight becomes part of your paper, *you must give that scholar credit.* Commence such discussions by stating something like "I owe this discussion to Harold Bloom's chapter on *Hamlet* in his book *Shakespeare: The Invention of the Human.*" A sentence like that exudes honesty and high-level scholarship, and if you do this in your writing, you're golden. The fact that "no one will know" where your thoughts came from *doesn't matter;* make it your goal to produce a document that radiates honesty and intelligence; your readers will easily sense this, and their *trust* in you will rise (this is a good thing).

Now, what exactly do I mean by "common knowledge?" It's pretty simple: common knowledge is something that basically everyone knows and very few would dispute. *The grass is green. The sky is blue. The Beatles are from England. Many people keep dogs as pets.* These are all examples of common knowledge. However, the following two statements are not: *The Beatles are the greatest musical group ever. Dogs are the most beautiful animals in the world.* Although we all know that these two statements are true (just kidding), these are actually matters of *opinion,* and they would therefore require citations. *If you're not sure whether or not something is common knowledge, give it a citation.* You can never be accused of plagiarism if you provide citations, and I have never heard of a student getting into trouble for having too many citations.

ORIGINAL WRITING AND THE PURPOSE OF RESEARCH (PROBABLY THE MOST DIFFICULT ASPECT OF A RESEARCH PROJECT)

Nevertheless, there is one way in which you *can* have "too many citations" (hang on, don't get confused). This is really a matter of having *too much of other scholars' work and not enough of your own.* Yes, you *can* have too much research in your paper and not enough of your own original writing. This is a very important point, because it's a common (and crucial) mistake that many students make, so read this carefully and make sure you understand what I'm saying. *The purpose of research is to support and develop the writer's own original points, findings, conclusions, and ideas.* Many times (most, in fact) when I read students' research projects, I find that they are conglomerations of others' thoughts, with students simply supplying connective tissue and transitions between blocks of text that other people have written. This is not a truly *original* research project, it's an assemblage of things that others have said and is uninspired and unoriginal, and therefore unexciting.

Nevertheless, with research projects, the student *must* include research, and so this is a delicate balance, an invisible ratio that is hard to quantify. In any research project, *there is a target ratio between original writing and incorporated research.* I can't give you exact specifications here (they don't exist), but let me try to explain. When you're undertaking an original research project, your writing will blend *your own original ideas with the research of others.* Merging your ideas with the ideas of others ensures that you are in effect not "talking to yourself" and that you have joined the scholarly "conversation." Your own writing represents *originality* (truly the most exciting and important part of any research project), while research gives your ideas context (in relation to the thoughts of others) and academic *credibility.*

Think of it like this: adding research to your own writing is like adding sugar to coffee. You want some sugar, but not too much. You want to enhance the flavor, not overwhelm it. Of course, this is not an exact science (no aspect of writing or coffee is); it involves judgment calls, and it relates to a whole bunch of criteria specific to your particular subject, thesis, and personality. Therefore, *I can't say precisely how much research you should put into your project.* However, let me offer these as general guidelines: in my own research papers, I strive for about 90% my own original words, thoughts, and ideas, with the remaining 10% of the paper derived from research sources. I want my own voice to carry the predominance of the paper, because then the paper is truly *mine,* and I can feel truly proud of it.

In terms of our middle and high school students, I can offer this: they are fledgling writers and developing scholars, so I would encourage them to have every paper they write *at least* 50% their own original words, thoughts, and ideas, and the remaining 50% drawn from their research. If less than 50% of the paper is original, then it's not truly theirs. It belongs to the writers whom they have referenced and cited. When this happens, they can't feel a true sense of pride or ownership for their work (and we want them to feel that their work is truly theirs). As a writer and researcher, you want to include enough research to substantiate and support your main points and conclusions, but not so much that it becomes "someone else's paper." Try to avoid pasting large chunks of text into your project; a cogent paraphrasing is nearly always preferable (and must be cited).

For students, trusting themselves to generate original writing and ideas is probably the most difficult and scariest part of academic writing. It may cause a sense of panic, as they think *I can't possibly carry the bulk of a research project! I'm just a middle school (or high school) student; what do I know?! No one will care about my opinions! Isn't it good enough to find, assemble, and report what the "experts" have said?* To answer this last question, *no*, it's *not* good enough, and a paper that simply regurgitates what others have said is boring and meaningless. Think about it: nothing original has taken place; you've simply repeated what others have already said. Do your best to be original; strive to somehow break new ground.

As you write, strive to make the bulk of your project absolutely original. To do this, I always tell students to write as much of the paper as they can *before consulting the research of others*. I stumbled upon this method as an undergrad, and it is extremely effective. As a student of literature, I frequently had to write original analyses of literary works. To avoid the dreaded act (and charge) of plagiarism, here's what I did: I first read the work of literature (a primary source) and developed an original thesis. Next, I would analyze the literature in terms of my thesis, and I would write an original essay. *Only when my essay was complete would I consult research* (in the form of literary critics). I used their ideas to supplement, elucidate, and buttress my main points, occasionally "disproving" their views through counterarguments. This may sound like eating dessert before dinner, but it's a solid method that accomplished two worthwhile goals: first, it forced me to be original. Had I looked at the critics first, I would have subconsciously adopted their ideas as my own, and my creativity and analytical skills would have shut down. Second, as my essay was entirely original, plagiarism became an impossibility.

Let me explain this in slightly different terms. If you begin by reading the professionals, this will almost certainly shut down authentic creativity because there's a certain psychology in place: *they're* the published professionals, and you will begin to doubt your own views. Don't do this; you're a real writer, your views have validity, and they *matter* (for a further discussion on the subject of original writing, see William Zinsser's chapter on "Style" in his terrific book *On Writing Well*. I have read and taught this book, and many of Zinsser's ideas have inspired much of my thinking about writing). Therefore, when you have decided upon a solid thesis (which may involve some prior research; I will address this apparent contradiction shortly), go and *generate as much original prose on your topic as you can*. This will become the framework for a truly original piece of scholarship.

For example, let's say a student is writing a paper in which he analyzes the theme of *fate* in *Oedipus Rex* by Sophocles. He will read the original text, mark it up, look for pertinent passages, and write an original essay based on his own close reading of the text. After that is completed, he will look at the findings of others. He will head to the library (or the Internet), locate the research, and see how it fits in with his work. Wherever a scholar makes a similar point on a similar subject, he will insert the quote and then (ideally) provide additional commentary based on the quote. And he might be surprised to discover just how many authors agree with his findings.

Nevertheless, there are times in which you will need to perform research *before* you start writing. Different types of research projects require different methods of investigation. If you're composing an *informational* project and using your paper as a vehicle to "teach" readers about a specific subject, you will most likely begin with a "survey" of existing literature regarding your topic. This means, of course, that you'll begin your project by doing a fair amount of research on it.

As a graduate student I once wrote a paper analyzing storytelling techniques in different cultures around the world. Now, this was not a "literature" paper; it was anthropological in nature. So this was one time in which I had to do a great deal of research (prior to writing) in order to "survey the landscape," and this is because I knew absolutely nothing about the subject. *After doing the research*, I constructed an original thesis statement and then created original analyses of several anthropological studies in terms of my thesis. The result? An original piece of scholarship that my professor (Dr. Ahrens) and I were both proud of. In looking back, I see that this method does not differ greatly from my methods of performing literary analysis: I got to know my subject (through research), I developed an original thesis, I analyzed my subject through the lens of my thesis, and I used research to support my conclusions.

As there's no way I can address all possible contingencies, let me offer some simple guidance before I conclude this long section: *every good research paper requires a substantial original component*. And remember, don't lean too heavily on your sources; they're there to support *you*. Trust your abilities as an independent writer and original thinker; you'll be surprised at what you can accomplish.

HOW MUCH RESEARCH SHOULD I INCLUDE?

At this point you may be wondering "how many works should I cite or consult during the composition of my project?" Well, there is no definite answer for this; it depends on such factors as your topic, the availability of research, and the time you devote to this project. However, I can offer a basic guideline. When I was in graduate school, I developed a rule for myself (more of an "equation"), and it worked very well for me. Here it is: let's say I'm writing a 20-page paper. We now have the number *20*. Half of 20 is *10*. We now have the numbers 20 and 10. For a 20-page paper, *20 is the maximum number of sources to include, and 10 is the minimum number of sources to include*. And in the middle of the numbers 10 and 20 is the number *15*. This is your target: *for a 20-page paper, you want about 15 sources*. It's a good basic rule for academic writing, but I think it works well. Now, let's apply this rule realistically to middle and high school students. If a student is writing (for example) a five page paper, I would encourage him to include about three or four sources. This would work well, giving the paper a nice balance of original writing and scholarly substance.

Regarding the *age* of your sources, it's a common belief among scholars (and I agree) that recent, up-to-date research is usually better than older research. When I write papers, I try to include research no older than *five years*. Nevertheless, there is a great deal of older research that has stood the "test of time," so use your own best judgment here. To sum it up, recent scholarship (of up to five years old) often displaces earlier scholarship and therefore is usually preferable.

INSERTING RESEARCH

Be attentive when inserting research into your paper; done well, it can add tremendous scholarly weight to your writing. When performing research, get used to skimming lots of information (books, articles, websites, etc.). When you find a passage you want to include in your paper, make sure you mark it (with pencil or "sticky notes") so that you can find it later. This will save you the trouble of reading everything twice.

Now, let's say you've come across a particular sentence or passage that you want to include in your paper because it somehow strengthens your argument (perhaps by echoing or expanding a point you made). You can bring it into your paper in one of three ways: *direct quote, paraphrase*, or *summary* (and remember, *all* of these must be cited). A direct quote is just as it sounds: a word-for-word transcription of an original source, encapsulated in quotation marks. A paraphrase is a "translation" of the original source into your own (simplified) words. Let me give you a good tip here: a paraphrase is usually about the same *length* as the original and works well when the original is wordy or hard to understand. A summary is a *shortened* version of the original. Here's another good tip: a summary is usually much *shorter* than the original text from which it is drawn. Perhaps you love the ideas contained on a single page, but you can summarize them in two or three sentences.

When inserting research, think of it as having five layers, sort of like a big sandwich (I covered this earlier, in my chapter on the Common Core). When using a quote, for example, you should *introduce* your quote (in your own words), then *give the exact quote* (word for word, enclosed in quotation marks), provide an in-text *citation* (this often includes the author, year of publication, and page number), *explain* the quote (literally, what is the quote describing?), and then *comment* on the quote, or interpret its meaning (ideally in terms aligned with your thesis). The "comment" portion allows you to deepen and enrich the overall academic flavor of your project, also allowing you to increase its *originality*. Think of included research not just as a way to "verify" your points, but as a springboard for creating new knowledge and developing original writing. The "comment" portion is a place where you elaborate on the quote, describing how it contributes to your argument or advances your thesis. An incorporated quote (with all of its components) might look something like this:

> Good writing does not have to sound complicated; indeed the best writing is often the simplest. Therefore, remember that "the secret of good writing is to strip every sentence to its cleanest components" (Zinsser 2006, 6). Here, Zinsser alludes to a rule

discussed earlier in this study: good writing is simple and direct. In this, he privileges the audience above the writer, suggesting (subtly) that authors should write for their readers, not for themselves.

And I want to mention something one more time, because it's so important: when quoting, paraphrasing, or summarizing, you must always, *always* include a citation. This will prevent the dreaded charge of plagiarism. To sum it up, each inclusion of research will usually have five parts:

1. Introduction (in your own original words): Good writing does not have to sound complicated; indeed the best writing is often the simplest.

2. Quote, paraphrase, or summary: Therefore, remember that "the secret of good writing is to strip every sentence to its cleanest components."

3. Citation (where did this information come from?): (Zinsser, 2006, 6). (Please note that this is a Chicago style in-text parenthetical citation; other systems do this differently.)

4. Explain the quote (in your own original words): Here, Zinsser alludes to a rule discussed earlier in this study: good writing is simple and direct.

5. Commentary or analysis (again, your own original words and insights): Zinsser seems to privilege the audience above the writer, suggesting that authors should write for their readers, not for themselves.

CAN I SAY "I" AND "ME"?

Undoubtedly you've noticed that I've been using "I" and "me" in this book; you'll also notice that the world hasn't ended as a result of this. Philosophically speaking, *I see no problem with students using 'I' and 'me' when writing.* After all, you haven't lost your identity just because you've written something. In his discussion on this topic, Zinsser states, "I urge people to write in the first person: to use 'I' and 'me' and 'we' and 'us'" (2006, 20). I agree with him completely.

However (you knew there was a "however" coming, didn't you?), *it's usually best to avoid these personal pronouns in formal academic writing.* Leaving yourself out of the mix gives your project an appearance of formality and *objectivity* which is often desirable in writing of this nature. Let me say then for the record: *it's probably best to avoid using the pronouns "I" and "me" when composing formal academic projects.* If the student wants to use the first person in his formal writing, he should first *ask his teacher if he can do this.* If you ask *me,* I'm going to say use "I" and "me" when you are referring to "you" and "yourself."

Many writing teachers suggest using the term "this writer" as a formal alternative for "I," but *this writer* considers this a ghastly bit of unpleasantness to bring into an otherwise innocent research paper. This writer also feels that the term "this writer" is sufficiently unusual and stodgy sounding as to cause the unsuspecting reader to halt and wonder for a moment what the heck the writer is talking about. In short, if you want to refer to yourself or your views in your paper, ask your teacher first. I would if it were me.

EDDITT . . . EDDIT . . . EDIT

Earlier in this book, I talked a bit about editing. I said that *we don't edit papers in the writing center.* And it's true; we don't. Doing a pass-through edit on a student's paper would probably improve the paper, but it wouldn't help the student learn to write. But when you work with a student from the conception of a paper through its end, editing becomes a legitimate part of the writing cycle and should be taught to your students.

So teach your students how to edit. It's one of the most important parts of learning to write. In fact, I can't stress enough the importance of good editing. Editing involves removing errors, revising content, and in general "polishing" your paper until it looks as professional as possible. It usually involves steps such as the following:

- Revising the *content*, so that the basic underlying ideas of the paper adhere to the given assignment. They should also be sound, focused, and organized (remember the Big Three).
- Improving paragraph length and structure.
- Improving individual sentences. Do they read clearly? Are your sentences appropriate (and varying) lengths? Your sentences should not be too long or too short. However, *their lengths should vary.* Sentences of varying lengths add interest to papers, while sentences of similar lengths are predictable, hypnotic, and sleep-inducing.
- Polishing language so that it sounds academic, professional, and suited to the task.
- Using appropriate vocabulary (but not necessarily "exotic" words).
- Eliminating contradictions of meaning, if any exist.
- In general, making the paper read smoothly and logically.
- Eliminating mistakes of all kinds (grammar, punctuation, spelling, etc.; make it your goal to turn in a paper without a single error. Remember, this "mechanical" editing usually comes toward the end of the writing process).
- Etc.

Now, I want to ask an important question: *should you edit as you write, or save the editing until you finish a draft of the paper?* There's no harm in limited editing as you compose. If you misspell a word, or you don't like something you wrote, and it's bothering you, go back and fix it. However, I strongly recommend that you *leave the heaviest editing for last.* Try to write a full draft of your paper from start to finish. *Capture the ideas first* and establish the flow of your entire paper first, because *editing can wait.* Honestly, it can. Your paper's not going anywhere. You can't know truly what you want to include or delete until the paper is nearing completion (as I said earlier, you won't know what your paper is really about until it's just about finished).

Further, excessive editing "as you go" will interrupt the flow of your thoughts and will shut down any momentum you might be developing. You should therefore *capture your ideas first* on paper or monitor; you can always go back later and edit heavily (and you should). And (I'll say it again) please use Google Drive. If you're not using Google Drive, *make sure you save your work in at least two different places* (three is better). Hard drives have been known to crash; flash drives have been known to get lost.

When you finish a full draft of your paper, now is the time for some serious editing. Turn in a paper only after you have "rewritten" it at least 10 times. Don't worry; this is quite easy on a computer. Editing like this works best when it is spread out over several days. So please encourage your students to start writing their papers *early*. It will improve their writing dramatically. As you edit, make it a habit to go repeatedly through a three-step process: *Read, edit, save*, etc. (Of course, if you use Google Drive, which I recommend, your work saves automatically.) Do this over and over; when you can find nothing to change or improve, your paper is nearly finished.

Nevertheless, I strongly believe that the most important and effective editing (and perhaps the most difficult) is associated with the "Delete" button. (Please note that parts of the following discussion were inspired and informed by William Zinsser's excellent chapter on "Clutter," in his book *On Writing Well*. This book has become part of my writer's consciousness.) Don't fall in love with your own writing; no one loves the sound of your voice as much as you do, so please don't make your readers work harder than they have to. In the world of writers, there's an old saying (and I have no idea who said it first; if I did, I'd give him or her credit): "don't be afraid to kill your darlings." It's not an elegant or graceful statement, but it gets its point across: clear, direct, and economical writing (and here I'm talking mostly about academic writing) is always preferable to writing that is long-winded for the sake of being long-winded.

So do your best to always keep your writing short, clear, and direct. If you write something five pages long and you can make your main points in three pages, then *cut it down to three*; there's no reason to make your reader work harder than she has to. Think about it: if you send your friend out to get a pizza, suggest the most direct route. If you send him on a longer "scenic" route, you need a very compelling reason for doing so. In the meantime, you're getting hungrier and your pizza is getting cold.

As you edit your writing, please understand that the best editing involves making your work shorter. This point is so important that I'm going to say it again: whatever and whenever you write, *go back and find places where you can make it shorter and more concise*. Chances are that you can chop out 25 percent of it, and if you're careful, you'll retain all (or more) of the meaning. Zinsser is a big fan of aggressive editing, believing that most first drafts could be reduced by *half* (2006, 16). And this is a great mercy for the reader.

Always look closely and carefully at your work and ask yourself what you're trying to say. Then, see if you can say the same thing in fewer words. Almost always you can.

Nevertheless, as with nearly everything in writing, this involves judgment calls, and you *can* overedit, losing information vital to your argument and crushing the life (and character) out of your paper. As you edit, therefore, be like a miner looking for gold nuggets. These are places where your writing somehow "comes alive," where you raise questions that deserve an answer, or where you have "glossed over" points that require greater detail, explanation, or analysis. When expanding your writing, make sure it somehow *advances your thesis*; if you don't, you risk losing the focus you've worked so hard to attain. When you find gold nuggets in your writing, mine them accordingly. Recognizing and expanding the gold you've discovered (in accordance with your thesis) will make your paper stronger and more substantial, while contributing to its focus. As you write (and edit), keep asking yourself the following questions:

- Have I unintentionally raised any questions that are asking to be answered?
- Have I left out any information or points vital to my thesis?
- Will this essay somehow leave my readers puzzled or dissatisfied?

If the answer to any of these questions is *yes*, let the Delete button take a breather for a while and use the *Insert* button instead.

When you're just about finished editing, there are a few final steps that can help give your project a truly professional feel. Print out a paper copy (we call this a "hard copy") and then *read it over with a pencil in your hand*. This is very important. Your eye will detect errors on paper that it missed on the monitor. Also, don't be afraid to read your paper *out loud*, either to yourself or to a friend or family member (or have this person read the paper to you). Our *ears* frequently detect errors and clumsiness that our eyes have missed. If you spot an error, or something doesn't look or feel right to you, pencil in a correction or improvement. When you have read and marked up the entire paper, head for the computer and fix it there. When there's nothing left to fix, print it out and hand it in. And then go and feel great about yourself.

CONCLUSION

In this writer's guide, I have provided practical, real-world guidelines regarding the composition of academic papers. If you understand and follow the suggestions contained here, I think you (and the students you tutor) will emerge better writers. At the very least, I hope that this chapter has helped to clarify in your mind some of the mysteries of academic writing (in terms of purpose, process, and product). If so, I have accomplished my major goals.

Remember, however, that writing is an immensely complex and individual task, and that you (and your students) will likely spend a lifetime developing and refining your individual writer's voice. This is a slow process, but not a painful one; it usually involves lots of reading and lots of writing. Be patient with yourself (and your students) and keep teaching them the glorious, magical art of writing. And, if you have any questions (which you should), don't be afraid to ask them on the "School Library Writing Centers" forum. I hope to see you there! And I hope you enjoy your wonderful new writing center.

YOU'VE REACHED THE CONCLUSION!

We're just about at the end, and I have to admit something. Well, a few things, actually.

I'm a little sad that our time together is over. But there's always the online forum I created. Remember that? I mentioned it in the Introduction. Have you joined it yet? I hope so. If not, go ahead and join it now (http://slwc.freeforums.net/). I want to mention again that it's free, fun, collegial, and educational. And if you join, our time together can continue. That would be nice. So go and join and tell me about how your school library writing center is shaping up. And tell me (I hope) how much you enjoyed this book. I would like that.

And I want to admit something else. Writing this book was a big job. It took over my life for a good long while, filling my time, my thoughts, and sometimes even my dreams. But that's okay. I worked hard and enjoyed every bit of it. It was a daunting task, and from time to time I would stop typing and sit and think about school library writing centers. Their purpose. Their rollicking nature. Their open-ended intensity, like a high-stakes sports game. I'm very excited about them, and I'm enthusiastic about my own writing center and about having them spring up all over America and eventually (I hope) all over the world. Our students need them—and us—so, so much.

Before I go, I want to tell you a few more stories. First, I want to tell you about a certain student I worked with over the past few years. I'll call her "Veronika." We got along very well. Turns out she was a champion horseback rider and a very interesting kid. It was fun working with her, and she came to the writing center and worked with me, over and over. It was nice getting to know her and watching her writing skills grow and develop. And when I helped her with her final high school paper (just before she left for college), I said this to her: "Veronika, now that you're about to graduate, you won't be able to work with me anymore." She was a little sad about this, and so was I. (I don't handle "good byes" very well at all.) But I continued. "So when you get to college, I want you to find the writing center, and bring all your writing projects there. Pick the best tutor you can find, and then keep working with him or her. Your college will definitely have a writing center, so promise me you'll do this." She promised me, thanked me for the advice, and thanked me for helping her over the past few years, and, just like that, she was gone. Out to the real world, to college, and then (I'm sure) to do something wonderful. I really enjoyed working with her and hearing about her horses and all the trophies she won.

A few weeks ago, I got an email from Veronika. *Wow. This is a surprise.* She told me that she went to her college writing center, but that she wasn't happy with the tutoring there, and would I help her with her paper? I wrote her back, and said of course I'd be happy to help her out. I asked her to "share" it with me on Google Drive, and then (this is very subtle) I began the "interview" phase of the tutorial, right there on email. I wanted to really understand the situation, so I asked her this: "I'm curious about your college's writing center. It sounds like they didn't provide the help you need. What happened over there?" She emailed me back, thanked me for helping her, and said that they helped her "a little with grammar, but at the end of my paper the tutor [a professor!] really did not help." And then she said "I like your style better, you let me put most of my ideas into my papers."

Ah, my heart, my heart.

Compliments—genuine compliments—are one of my weaknesses, and I was extremely thrilled and flattered by what Veronika wrote. Flattered by her kind words and her gratitude and thrilled that my writing center was impacting students beyond the boundaries of high school. I think I'll be savoring Veronika's compliments for the rest of my life. How could I possibly resist helping her? Also, it was clear that she understood (perhaps unwittingly) what writing centers are and what they do. They're not grammar factories; they help students infuse their writing with their souls and with their being. Does this make sense? All genuine writing is a slice of the writer's soul, put under a magnifying glass.

But I was also alarmed slightly by what Veronika said. What, exactly, was happening in this particular college writing center? Obviously, I can't "fix" whatever problems they (or other writing centers) are having. Also, this was an isolated incident, so I don't want to presume too much. But it was confirmation that what we're doing (the way I describe things in this book) is wonderful for our students and is helping them grow as writers and as people. This book that you have in your hands right now—*this* is the way to go. I say that with the utmost confidence. These methods will work for middle school, high school, and even (as you can see) the college environment.

I asked Veronika to call me in my office, and she shared her document with me on Google Drive and, together on the phone, we discussed the assignment. I gave her suggestions, listened to her responses, and worked with her, and I watched her assignment blossom right there into something really special. It was open on my computer monitor, and I watched the cursor move like magic in "real time" right in front of me, as Veronika made changes and brought out the hidden beauty in her essay. Her piece was about her magnificent horses and about growing up and becoming an adult. It was beautiful, and Veronika appreciated all the help I gave her. And then, for the second time, we said goodbye, and I wished her well.

And now I want to tell you about another student who came to the writing center over and over. I'll call her "Jessica Ashton" (this is not her real name). Jess and I got along very well, and she is probably the sweetest person I have ever met. She wanted to be a teacher, she loved school, and she even got me a Christmas present. She knew I love my coffee, so she got me a gift card from a fancy coffee shop. And she wrapped it in pretty paper and presented it to me with a smile.

Ah, my heart, once again. The absolute beauty in small gestures like these. I'll never forget it.

Well, this morning—*this very morning* as I write these words—and I'm not kidding—a student came up to me and said "Jess says 'hi.'"

I looked at her. "What?"

She smiled. "You remember Jess Ashton? You used to help her with writing? She says 'hi.'"

"Oh, *that* Jess!" I said. "Sure, I remember her. Tell her I said 'hi.' She's in college, right? How's she doing?"

"She's doing good. Oh, and she wrote her first essay about you."

I blinked at her. "About *me*?" I processed this information. "She wrote an essay about me," I repeated, idiotically. I looked away for a moment, in shock, and then asked a silly question: "What was it about?"

She thought a moment. "It was about, like, the person who had the biggest impact on your life."

I stood there with my mouth open a little. I couldn't believe it. This time, I was well past flattered and thrilled, and I didn't quite know what to say. This had never happened to me before. So I just said "Wow. Tell Jess I said 'thanks.'"

"Okay," she said and smiled and walked away.

Yes, that happened just a few hours ago. I'll never forget this day. How can I tell you what this means to me? These things—the stories of Veronika and Jess—they're indicators of something huge. Something very special is happening. Yes, school library writing centers are *special*. We're doing special work, and I believe we'll never truly know the impact we're having on students.

We're at the beginning of something wonderful, you and I, there's no doubt about that. We're breaking new ground, and this is tremendously exciting. We're pioneers, slashing new trails, braving unknown territory, and making new discoveries. Let's be bold together; let's keep pushing forward no matter what. Let's expand together the boundaries of the comfortable and the known, and let's experiment and celebrate our spectacular triumphs, and learn from and laugh at our magnificent mistakes. And let's keep going, no matter what, and let's have fun along the way. In case you haven't noticed, having fun is very important to me. I usually don't do things unless they're fun. Or unless I have to do them.

And now, I want to tell you something else. Please listen carefully. I believe—*I firmly believe*—that *the school library writing center is the next step in the evolution of school libraries*. It is *this* and nothing else. But this requires a visionary mindset. As school librarians, we need to take this next step in our libraries and with our students. We need to expand our offerings and our pedagogical versatility and become a more necessary part of students' educations and a more prominent part of the scholastic landscape.

And this is for two enormous reasons. First, the efficacy (and necessity) of school libraries is being increasingly questioned amidst the revolution in the information environment and the exponential advances occurring in technology (seemingly on a daily basis). I hate to say it, but in a sense, we have to "prove" our worth. Not to ourselves, of course (we know we rock), but to those who don't truly understand school libraries and what we do. If we don't exist, we can't help students. It's that simple. And they *need* us. And this brings me to the second reason: *we need to exist so that we can help our students.* In fact, they're the only reason we exist. So we need to help them. And help them. And help them. And help them.

Right now, there are various movements happening in school libraries and changes to our infrastructure and in the way we teach and do business. Yes, in the educational environment, change is the only constant. However, *nothing can replace writing.* Nothing *will* replace writing. New technologies will emerge, media will evolve, teaching methods will change, but students will always need to know how to read and research and think and organize their thoughts and talk about what they know and how they feel. *They will always need to know how to write.* There are some things in human nature and human civilization that don't change, and the need to express ourselves well is one of them. And school library writing centers provide something indispensable that students can't get anywhere else. Not anywhere else in the world.

Properly established and maintained, school library writing centers can (and must) become central to the pedagogical offerings not just of the school library, but of the school and the school district. In this way, they can save us from the groundless charge of being "obsolete" (and don't think it can't happen). School library writing centers can save us from extinction. It's a powerful statement, I know, but I believe it to be true, and I believe it will become truer and more evident with the passage of time. Our schools and our students need school library writing centers. They need them badly. And right now, they need them more than ever. So before I go, I want to tell you a few more stories (by now, you know I love telling stories). I'm telling these stories to show you how necessary school library writing centers are in the world. As much as you think they're needed, they're needed more than you think.

Just a few years ago, I was completing my fifth degree—a master's in Education—when something very interesting happened. I was taking a course called "Literacy in the Academic Subjects, Grades 7–12," and, true to its name, it was all about increasing students' literacy skills across the disciplines. It was a fun course with a fun professor, so I decided that, at some point, I would get to know her a little. I'll call her "Dr. Mason." Now remember, this was an Education class, and most of the students in the class were in their early- to mid-twenties, or thereabouts. Some were a bit older. They had recently completed their bachelor's degrees, and they all wanted to be teachers. (Keep this in mind: they were going to be *teachers.*) They were young, and bright and excited about the world and about their upcoming professions.

I was one of the "older" students in the class. I was in the middle of my teaching career, I already held four degrees (including a doctorate), and I regarded the professor more as a peer than a dispenser of wisdom. She held a PhD, she was respectably published, and she was very intelligent and very sweet. I knew we'd get along, so, after a few weeks, I introduced myself and told her a little about my background. She was a professor of Education, so I thought she'd be interested that a genuine full-time educator was taking her class. During our conversation, I mentioned (quite humbly) that I'm an "expert" in writing, that I run a writing center, and that I'm very passionate about this field. She was interested in this, and when I got to know her a little better (over the next few weeks), Dr. Mason asked me for a favor. "Could you come to class a little early next week?"

"Sure," I said.

I met her in her office a week later, and we started talking about education, and teaching, and writing, and stuff like that. At some point she grew quiet and leaned toward me as if about to confess a terrible crime. She looked a little nervous and cleared her throat and said "I'm writing an article with Dr. Perkins, and it's just not working. Would you take a look at it, and tell me what you think?"

I was surprised, and very flattered, of course, and I think I laughed a little. Here I was, a humble school librarian. Imagine a university professor coming to *me* for writing advice! I took it as a great compliment.

"I would love to," I said.

Well, she brought the article up on her computer, and I read the first few paragraphs, and I immediately saw the problem. I didn't need to read any further. There were three major topics introduced on the first page, and there should have only been *one*. And I tried to point this out as tactfully as I could.

"I see the problem," I told her.

"You do?" She looked at the screen. I nodded.

"See how you introduce this major point here?" I said, pointing to a passage on the screen. "And you've got this other big topic here." My finger circled a different group of words. "And then you introduce another topic down here." I tapped my finger down low on the monitor. "See? You introduce three major topics on the first page, which means the article is lacking focus."

"Oh," she nodded.

"The article should really be about one thing," I continued. "The thing to do is decide what the article is really about. Which of these three topics do you want to focus on?" And then I said (a bit more abstractly) "You have to decide: what does this article 'want' to be about?" I let that sink in.

She thought a moment and nodded. "I see what you mean," she said. "I'll talk to Dr. Perkins. Thanks."

"My pleasure," I said, and meant it.

It was such an elementary mistake, but there it was. The article wasn't working because *the article didn't know what it was about*. And this was because the *writers* didn't know what it was about. For me, this was slightly astonishing. *Wow*, I thought, *sometimes even published university professors need the writing center*. Yes,

I was in Dr. Mason's office, but this really was a writing center moment. Remember, the writing center is not a place, it's a process.

And then we packed up and went to class. I went to my small desk, and she went to her big desk. And I sat and listened and thought about what just happened. It made me feel pretty good about myself, but it was also an interesting glimpse into the soul of writing. I suppose it takes a lifetime to learn to write, but perhaps we are never truly its masters. And, later in the semester, I got further confirmation just how necessary writing centers really are—on all academic levels.

It was about a week after we handed in our first major writing assignments. I got to class a little early, and, as usual, I chatted with Dr. Mason. She was a little upset. She had graded our assignments, and there they were, stacked neatly on her desk, graded and ready to be handed back.

"I graded the papers," she said.

"Okay," I said, and nodded.

"No," she said. "Not okay." She slapped her palm on them and shook her head in frustration and whispered to me. "The *writing* on these!" she said. "You wouldn't be*lieve* it." She flipped through them, looked at her comments, and shook her head again. "The mistakes. The poor construction. No development of ideas." She pulled out a paper and looked at it. "No sense of grammar . . . poor punctuation . . . bad spelling, even with spell check." She shook her head again and waved her hands in the air and whispered fiercely. "These are *graduate* students! They're going to be *teachers*! I don't know what to do. I want to fix everybody's writing, but it just seems impossible."

What could I say? I nodded my head. "I know," I said. "It's very common. People just don't know how to write."

That night, before she handed back the papers, she gave the class a rather serious "talking to" about writing.

"People," she began (and she was very sweet about it), "I have to say, I'm very disappointed at the writing on most of these papers. Please pay careful attention to your writing, and work at it. Make sure you proofread all your papers carefully before you hand them in. Try to have zero errors in grammar, punctuation, and spelling. Pay attention to simple mechanical errors. Please learn the differences among the words *to, too*, and *two*," she said, writing them on the board, and explaining them, pointing to each one. "And please learn how to correctly use the words *there, their*, and *they're*. They're very different." Again, she wrote them on the board and explained them and pointed to each one. She continued for a few minutes, delivering rudimentary lessons to graduate students who would be teachers in just a few years.

I sat there and watched them. They looked a bit uncomfortable and a little embarrassed, as if caught doing something wrong, and the room was very quiet. But honestly, I was a little shocked by the whole thing. I agreed completely with Dr. Mason. They all had earned bachelor's degrees. They were all graduate students. And in a short while, they would all be teachers. Teachers! Teachers who couldn't write. They still needed *there, their*, and *they're* explained to them. To, *too*, and *two* didn't add up. How is this possible?

But I also felt bad for them. Not because they were being reprimanded, but because they never learned to write. Whose fault was it? The culture? The school system? Their own? Cell phones, video games, too much television, not enough reading. All of the above? In terms of our purposes here, it doesn't really matter. I'm not interested in finger-pointing. I'm interested in teaching people how to write.

And so Dr. Mason concluded her gentle reprimand, and the class continued as usual, working hard, with perhaps a bit of humility thrown in. The course was a nice experience, and I was always happy to come to class a little early and chat with Dr. Mason and to stay after and chat with her again. We got along really well, and sometimes we would talk about writing, and sometimes she would give the class pointers on how to write. I know she was deeply and genuinely concerned about her students' lack of writing abilities. It was very obvious. And one night after class, after the other students left, she confided something interesting to me.

As a university professor, part of her job involves mentoring doctoral students as they work on their dissertations. She told me about this process, and once again, she shook her head, and said something that surprised me (and by this point, I thought I was beyond surprises). She threw her hands up in the air and let them drop by her sides. "Most of my doctoral students can't write," she said. "These are *doctoral candidates.* They're getting doctorates in Education, and they can't write! I'm giving them lessons in grammar and punctuation. You wouldn't believe it!"

I shook my head. "Wow," I said, and I meant it.

"I don't know what to do," she said. "I can't submit a dissertation that's poorly written. So I'm teaching them how to write, and how to edit their projects." She shook her head again.

I was genuinely surprised, but I believe it. It's hard to imagine. People who are going to hold doctorates in Education are not able to write well. Are you starting to see how pervasive this problem is? *People can't write.* I mention these anecdotes to help *you* believe it and to help you understand the depth of this educational muddle. This is a problem. If professors and graduate students need help with writing, then your own students certainly do and to a much greater extent. This provides an obvious rationale for school library writing centers, but also raises a looming question: if older students can't write, how should we rectify this problem? Here's what I say: let's start teaching them to write when they're very young and then bring them along slowly, year after year, creating deep, long-term learning. And a writing center is the perfect place for this to happen. So create a writing center, and then stick with it, year after year.

And that brings us to the end of my book! I hope you enjoyed it, and I hope you now feel prepared to create and run your very own school library writing center. And if you still don't feel ready, return to my book, and flip through the pages once again. Do that as often as necessary. Do that until the book is worn out. But if you're stuck, or if you have a question, or if you just want to chat, join my forum (http://slwc.freeforums.net/) and send me a note. I'll definitely get back to you. But please understand, the forum is partly social, but it's much more than that: it's very important to the success of this initiative. It's a way to get us all together, to chat, to get to know one another, to learn from one another, and maybe even swap war stories. Remember, we're at the beginning of a new (ad)venture, so we're like lone pioneers creating new trails in an untrodden wilderness. And that can be an awful lonely place to be. There is no centralized location for us to meet and chat; there is no echo chamber where all our voices can be heard. So let's get together on the forum, where we can support each other, encourage each other, and realize that we're not alone in this wonderful business.

You're going to love creating and directing your school library writing center and tutoring students in the very human art of writing. You'll find it deeply rewarding, and you'll be helping kids more than you can imagine. And there are other perks as well: you'll elevate the status of your library, and you'll highlight your skills as a wonderfully versatile and indispensable educator. These will benefit you and your library and school librarians everywhere.

So start your school library writing center and watch the ripples spread through your district, and outward, like a golden coin thrown into a magical fountain. And, when enough school library writing centers are created, the ripples will begin to intersect, and we can begin to effect profound change on the educational landscape. But along the way, make sure you enjoy the process. In fact, make it a goal to enjoy every second of directing your writing center. You'll be happier, and you'll do a better job. So remember what I said earlier in this book: if you're not having fun, you're doing something wrong.

Thank you for spending this time with me. Now go and create your school library writing center!

BIBLIOGRAPHY

Baym, Nina (et al.), ed. *The Norton Anthology of American Literature*. 4th ed. New York: Norton, 1995.

"Big6 Skills Overview." The Big6. January 1, 2014. http://big6.com/pages/about/big6-skills-overview.php (accessed August 7, 2015).

Celly: Create Your Own Social Networks. https://cel.ly/ (accessed September 5, 2015).

Celly: Privacy Policy. https://cel.ly/privacy (accessed September 5, 2015).

Chrome Web Store. https://chrome.google.com/webstore/category/apps (accessed September 26, 2015).

Common Core State Standards Initiative: Preparing America's Students for College and Career. 2015. http://www.corestandards.org/ (accessed September 5, 2015).

Dinesen, Isak. *Out of Africa: And, Shadows on the Grass*. International Vintage ed. New York: Vintage Books, 1989.

"Dog Island Free Forever." Dog Island Free Forever. 2013. http://www.thedogisland.com/ (accessed September 28, 2015).

Elbow, Peter. *Writing Without Teachers*. London: Oxford University Press, 1973.

"English Language Arts Appendix B." Common Core State Standards Initiative. http://www.corestandards.org/assets/Appendix_B.pdf (accessed September 5, 2015).

"English Language Arts Standards, Writing, Grade 7." Common Core State Standards Initiative. 2015. http://www.corestandards.org/ELA-Literacy/W/7/ (accessed September 5, 2015).

"Evaluating Web Pages: Questions to Consider: Putting It All Together." Cornell University Library. September 22, 2015. http://guides.library.cornell.edu/c.php?g=32334&p=203773&preview=ad0bac0490cf7ab0653096fe3b4a0fee (accessed September 26, 2015).

Excelsior Online Writing Lab (OWL). "Welcome to the Online Writing Lab!" http://owl.excelsior.edu/ (accessed September 7, 2015).

Fitzgerald, F. Scott. *The Great Gatsby.* New York: Scribner Paperback Fiction, 1995.

"Freshwater Whale Watching Lake Superior." North Shore Visitor. 2015. http://www .northshorevisitor.com/activities/whale-watching/ (accessed September 14, 2015).

Hemingway, Ernest. *A Farewell to Arms.* New York: Scribner, 2003.

Horan, Timothy. "The Common Core and Your School Library Writing Center." *School Library Monthly* 31, no. 7 (May–June 2015): 5–7.

Horan, Timothy. "Daily Operations of Your School Library Writing Center." *School Library Monthly* 31, no. 4 (February 2015): 5–7.

Horan, Timothy. "How to Start Your School Library Writing Center." *School Library Monthly* 31, no. 1 (September–October 2014): 8–10.

Horan, Timothy. "Publicizing Your School Library Writing Center." *School Library Monthly* 31, no. 5 (March 2015): 5–7.

Horan, Timothy. "The School Library Writing Center: Advanced Techniques for Tutors." *School Library Monthly* 31, no. 3 (December–January 2015): 5–7.

Horan, Timothy. "The School Library Writing Center: Training Tutors." *School Library Monthly* 31, no. 2 (November 2014): 5–7.

Horan, Timothy. "Technology and Your School Library Writing Center." *School Library Monthly* 31, no. 6 (April 2015): 5–7.

Horan, Timothy. "Your School Library: The Perfect Place for a Writing Center." *School Library Monthly* 30, no. 8 (May–June 2014): 5–7.

Joyce, James. *Dubliners.* New York: Bantam Books, 1990.

Kapoun, Jim. "Five Criteria for Evaluating Web Pages." http://ux.brookdalecc.edu/library/ 5criteria.pdf (accessed September 2, 2015).

"Key Shifts in English Language Arts." Common Core State Standards Initiative. 2015. http://www.corestandards.org/other-resources/key-shifts-in-english-language-arts/ (accessed September 28, 2015).

Marius, Richard. *A Writer's Companion.* 3rd ed. New York: McGraw-Hill, Inc., 1995.

McCarthy, Cormac. *The Road.* New York: Alfred A. Knopf, 2006.

McCuen, Jo Ray. *Readings for Writers.* 6th ed. San Diego: Harcourt Brace Jovanovich, 1989.

"Olin & Uris Libraries." "Evaluating Web Sites: Criteria and Tools." February 13, 2014. https://olinuris.library.cornell.edu/ref/research/webeval.html (accessed August 14, 2014).

Online Dictation. https://dictation.io/ (accessed June 18, 2015).

The Purdue Online Writing Lab (OWL). "Full OWL Resources for Grades 7–12 Students and Instructors." 2015. https://owl.english.purdue.edu/owl/resource/677/01/ (accessed August 6, 2015).

The Purdue Online Writing Lab (OWL). "Welcome to the Purdue OWL." 2015. https:// owl. english.purdue.edu/owl/ (accessed August 6, 2015).

Rao, Aditi. "11 Hilarious Hoax Sites to Test Website Evaluation." TeachBytes. November 1, 2012. http://teachbytes.com/2012/11/01/test-website-evaluation-with-10-hilarious- hoax-sites/ (accessed August 7, 2015).

"ReadWorks.org: About Us." ReadWorks.org. 2015. http://www.readworks.org/rw/about (accessed September 28, 2015).

"ReadWorks.org: The Solution to Reading Comprehension." ReadWorks.org. 2015. http:// www.readworks.org/ (accessed September 28, 2015).

"Rockwell Found Behind Fake Wall." Norman Rockwell Museum of Vermont. 2006. http://www.normanrockwellvt.com/fake_wall_story.htm (accessed June 3, 2015).

Zapato, Lyle. Pacific Northwest Tree Octopus. "Help Save the Endangered Pacific Northwest Tree Octopus from Extinction!" http://zapatopi.net/treeoctopus/ (accessed September 28, 2015).

Zinsser, William. *On Writing Well: The Classic Guide to Writing Nonfiction.* 30th Anniversary Ed., 7th ed. New York: HarperCollins, 2006.

INDEX

About the Author

Dr. Timothy Horan (BA, MA, MSLIS, MSEd, AGC, DA) is a Library Media Specialist and Director of the Writing Center at Hauppauge High School, New York. As the inventor of the School Library Writing Center, he has presented on this at state and national conferences, and authored a series of articles on it (which became the basis for this book). Look for his other volume on this subject, *Create Your School Library Writing Center, Grades K-6* (available from Libraries Unlimited). In 2013, the Suffolk School Library Media Association recognized him as "School Librarian of the Year." Email: School.Library.Writing.Center@gmail.com. Follow him on Twitter: @SL_Writing_Ctr.